KNITTING

with

WIRE

A

<u>VERY</u>

practical

guide for the

HOME

WORKSHOP

DEDICATED to all those who had to study

The Classics and Languages when they

Really wanted to be in a Workshop.

ISBN 978-0-473-26156-6

Knitting with Wire

has nothing to do with knitting, and very little to do with wire. The aim of the book is to share information and ideas that I have gathered over 40 years, making furniture, joinery, and then kaleidoscopes, with anyone that has an interest in working with their hands in a wood or metal workshop. For me, the joy of working in the workshop is twofold. I am principally driven by the result. If I want to make something, I am prepared to bend the rules as far as 'correct 'workshop practices are concerned, except in regard to safety. So, I will make my own tools, alter tools to suit the situation and try above all to get the required result, with the best possible quality for the lowest possible outlay!! Secondly, I love to have the machines and tools working beautifully.

The title, **KNITTING with WIRE** comes from my upbringing in New Zealand. 'Kiwis' are renown throughout the world for their innovation and creative approaches to problems. During the period of European settlement there, beginning around the early 1800's, the settlers were, of course, extremely isolated from their homelands of Europe and beyond. So they became incredibly resourceful. Replacement parts for machines and farm implements were months if not years away, thus they had to rely on their own creative ingenuity to get by.

As forests were cleared farming began. The fences at that time were made from wooden posts strung with Number 8 (a reference to the diameter) wire. This large diameter, soft wire was therefore very common, and quickly became a ready resource to use when the 'correct' items weren't available. Vehicles, boats, farm implements, and household goods were often repaired with or fashioned from Number 8 Wire. The phrase "you can fix (repair) it with a piece of Number 8 wire" become a national philosophy.

Knitting is a relatively simple task, but it is one which belies its incredible technological and imaginative heritage and its ancient history.

Consider: to knit, you first need to realise that you can actually make a thread from a fibre, and that the thread itself might be useful. The world is full of fibres, so you need to recognise that a particular fibre can be made into a thread. Then you need to think of how make that fibre into a thread. Even a very simple Spinning Jenny, really just a weight on the end of the thread, takes a good deal of thought both to make and use.

And think of the imagination that it took to go from there to a spinning wheel!!!

Next you must realise that the thread you have made can be formed into sheets and those into clothing.

Then you must think of a way to tie knots with only one thread, unlike tying shoes, which takes two. Add to that the making of the knitting needles and there you have it. What stunning foresight and creativity!!

KNITTING with WIRE encourages all those thoughts: the idea of building on the work and inventions of thousands of clever people over many thousands of years (the Knitting), and to think outside of the square and tackle tasks creatively (the good old Number 8 wire).

This would have been impossible to write without huge input from Robyn, who corrected all my grammar and spelling mistakes. Eternal thanks.

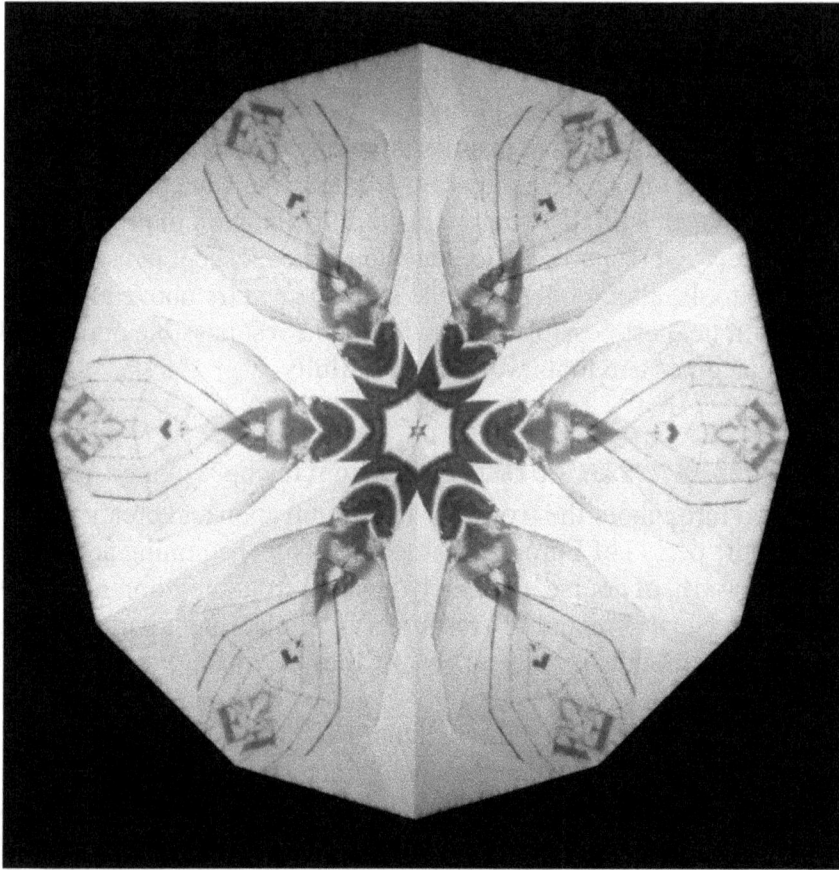

Creativity is a lot like looking at the world through a kaleidoscope. You look at a set of elements, the same ones everyone else sees, but then reassemble those floating bits and pieces into an enticing new possibility.

Rosabeth Moss Kanter

CONTENTS

My Workshop.

OVERVIEW

KNITTING with Wire

is intended to give some really useful and practical hints, ideas and workshop practices, aimed at making your workshop time more enjoyable, productive and, of course, **SAFE !!**

It is not a particularly technical journal, but rather focuses on the more practical side of working in a workshop. The various chapters are arranged, as you might imagine, into subjects. While some are specific to a particular activity, say the wood lathe, the majority of them are common to almost any workshop discipline. For example, a drill press can be used with a host of different media, electric motors can turn wood lathes, grinders or compressors, and careful measuring is as important when you are making a china cabinet as it is when you are building a Potter's Wheel.
I have used a combination of photographs and diagrams to illustrate the various points.

Hugely important within the workshop is the never to be forgotten area of **SAFETY**.

Safety is important, primarily for yourself, but of course, for any other person in and around the workshop area (a table saw or lathe can throw a piece of wood or steel a surprisingly long way, and with a huge amount of force) and the machine itself. The use of Safety equipment such as Eye, Ear and Dust Protection should become a habit. It should be so ingrained that it feels wrong to start a machine without them on!! Accidents always happen at breathtaking pace, so a shard of wood will leave the saw blade at a horrific speed (the peripheral speed of a 12 inch saw blade is over 200kms per hour) and there is no time to dodge. The use of Safety Equipment must happen **before** the accident might. Be sure to clamp firmly, start at low RPM, use slow cutting speeds, and small cuts first before increasing any of the above. Ensure all machines are correctly wired and have sound earthing **before** turning them on.

As there are two main systems of measuring in use throughout the world, imperial inches and the metric millimetre, I have shown no allegiance to either, and have used both.

Disclaimer:

Please take the ideas here and use and develop them as you can, but the responsibility for general safety and successful completion of the tasks remains at all times with you.

I accept no responsibility in any regard what so ever.

MEASURING and MARKING

Measure Twice, Cut Once!!

Measuring would seem to be a very simple operation, but it can be surprisingly tricky. There are a host of different measuring devices; rulers, tape measures, verniers, micrometers and protractors and more, and these can then be in metric or imperial measurements, or both.

Rulers and tape measures give the least accurate results, but are quite adequate for most joinery work and for resizing material for further use. Rulers tend to be more accurate for their length because they don't suffer from the very inaccurate end piece that plagues the poor old tape measure.

But of course, a 10 meter ruler would be a nightmare!!

Workshop rulers (unlike school rulers), have the advantage of being able to be read right to the end, useful if you need to measure the depth of a hole, or if you want to butt the ruler right up against something. A tape measure won't do this accurately because of the error inherent in the little end piece. This end piece gets looser and looser as the tape is used; when the tape retracts into the body, the little end piece gets another jolt. This error becomes less of an issue when measuring long distances, but over the kinds of distances commonly found within the workshop, it can be a problem.

When accuracy is an issue with the tape measure, start the measurement at a place other than the end, say at the 100mm mark to keep it simple. Just don't forget that your measurement is always going to be 100mm too long. It's not as convenient as using the end piece of course, but you can lock the tape so it will stay in place and put a heavy weight on it to hold it steady, or have someone hold it for you.

You can test the tape accuracy with a simple test.

Measure, say, a metre on a piece of wood using the standard end piece, and then compare the result by starting with the 100mm mark, which will give the more accurate reading.

You can, of course, allow for that amount of error, usually plus rather than minus (because the error of a tape increases with use).

A Scribe

A scribe is a very sharp tool, like, for instance a steel pencil or knife, which is used to leave a mark or sharp line, to show a measure of length.

You can make a really good one from an old round file, like this chainsaw sharpening file. Snap the file off some way down the length, to make sure you're into the hardened section, (the ends are soft) and carefully, so as not to overheat and so lose the temper (if you do, see the section on tempering), grind a very sharp point on it, at least as sharp as a sewing needle.

The scribed line will be a small fraction of 1mm in width, so a sharp pencil is less accurate than the scribe, a blunt pencil worse, and chalk is really only fit for driveways and cricket pitches !! But with any of them, because there is an inevitable error, you need to develop a system that works for you.

Say you want to cut some wood for a table leg, or steel for a car trailer, with a tape. An accuracy of .5mm is adequate. Start from the 100mm mark (unless you know the inaccuracy of your tape measure) and mark with your scribe at the required length. The trick is to then carefully observe, without moving the measure, exactly

WHERE YOUR MARK REALLY IS!!

The tape's mark itself has a width, and therefore an error, (but a very small one), so does the scribe or pencil. When you've made your mark, look very carefully and see how accurate it is. Is the ruler's (or tape's) mark **on** your line, or **before** or **after** your line? Don't go changing the mark if it's off the line, just remember where it is. So say to yourself, leave the line visible (if you're short) when you make your cut, take the line (if you're long), or split the line if you're correct. With practice you will become surprisingly accurate.

Here's a good example of 'leaving the line'. The waste wood is to the left hand side of the line, where the blade is cutting.

Vernier Callipers

(invented by Pierre Vernier in the early 1600s) are a much more accurate way of measuring. They will measure inside, outside and depth. They are available from 100mm long up, depending on your needs and budget. They are also available with a digital readout, which is great for those of us who need glasses!! Choose the best quality tool you can afford, preferably one with an auto shut down if it is a digital, I hate finding that I've left it on all night wasting the battery .....

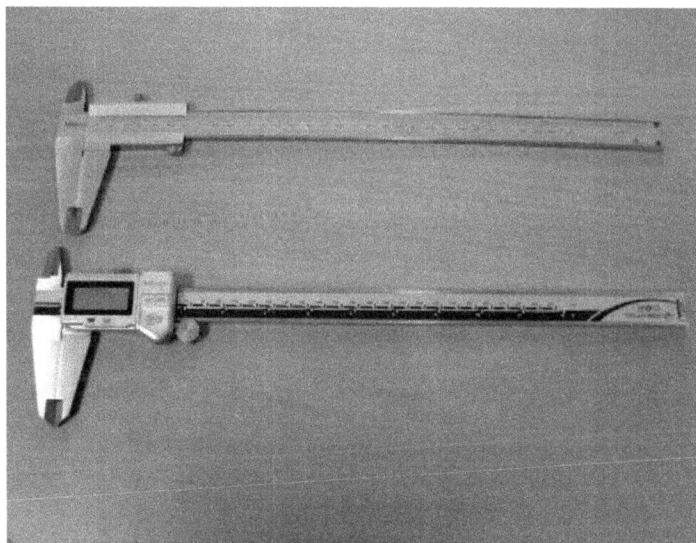

Analogue and Digital Vernier Calipers.

A vernier calliper is quite adequate for most woodworking tasks, and any engineering work, with a margin of around .02mm. Always stop the lathe to use a vernier (or micrometer for that matter) so it is not damaged, or even thrown across the room. Make sure the vernier's jaws are clean, and with digitals, often close the vernier to check and reset the zero if required.

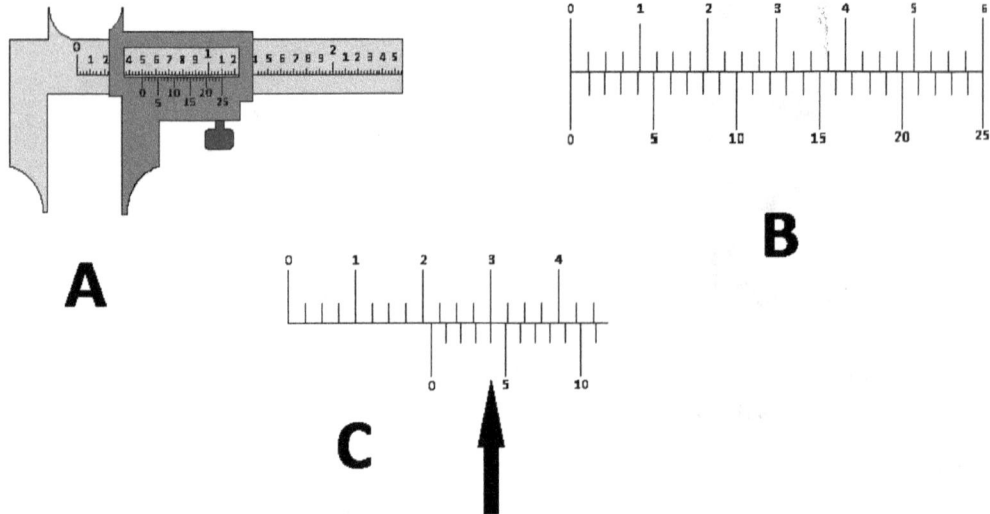

This diagram of an **analogue** Vernier, 'A ' shows the basic instrument. ' B' shows the slide closed, with both scales reading 0. The slide works by having 25 divisions in the same space as the main body which is divided into 24, and are 40ths of an inch. Thus the difference between the divisions is 1/40 x 1/25 = 1/1000, or 0.001 inch.

' C ' shows the slide reading 2 full tenths (8 x 1/40), no 1/40s (the vernier scale 0 has not reached the first 1/40th after the 2) and 4 x 1/1000, because the 4th division on the vernier is the one that lines up with a line on the main scale (and it doesn't matter which main scale line it is, you just need to know which of the 25 **vernier divisions** is the one that lines up).

So it reads .2 + 0 + .004 = 0.204 inch.

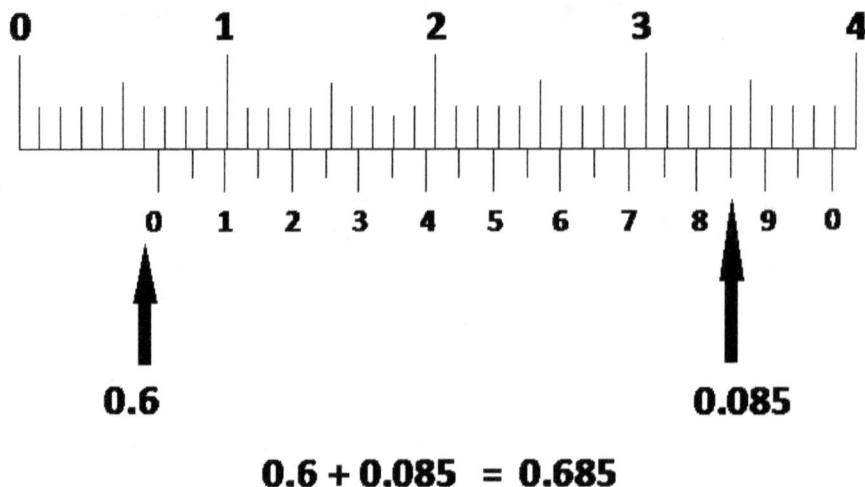

0.6 + 0.085 = 0.685

A reading from a **metric** Vernier.

For really accurate measurements, use a **Micrometer**, shown below. These are the tools for highly critical measurements, engine parts and the like, with very low tolerances. They are very specialised tools, and don't have the same range of abilities that verniers have, so they won't measure inside, outside and depth, all in the same tool. They are, of course, indispensible for many kinds of exacting work, but come with the extra price that you'd expect!!

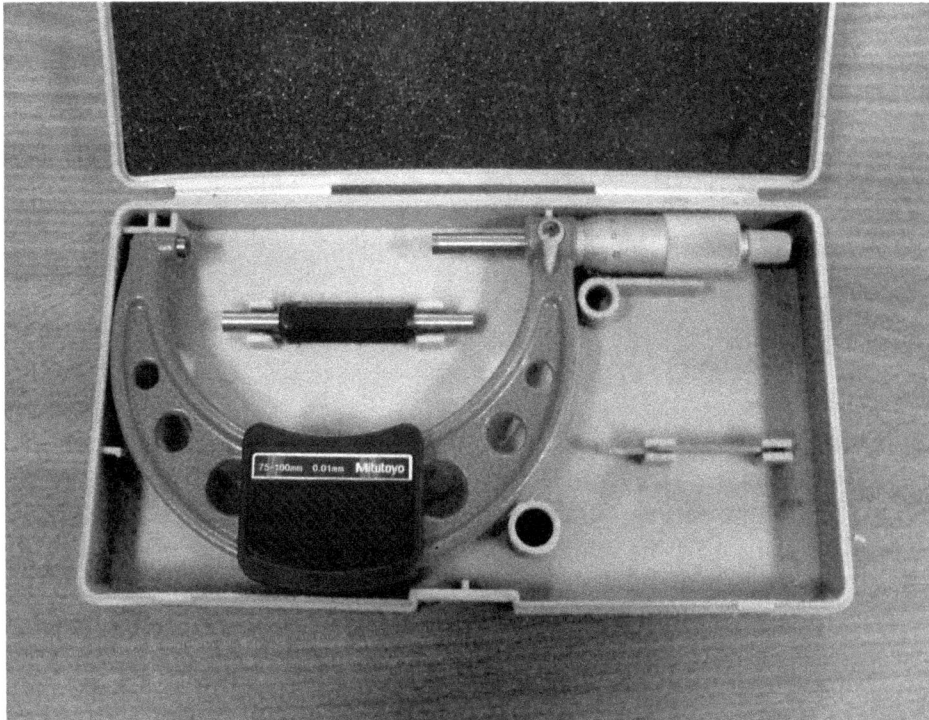

A Micrometer.

The micrometer is a precisely made instrument.
The item to be measured is placed between the Anvil and the adjustable Spindle, which slides in and out of the Sleeve, on a Thread, when the Graduated Spindle is turned.
The Thread has 40 threads to the inch, so one complete turn of the Thimble moves the Spindle 1/40th (0.025) of an inch.
The graduations on the Sleeve are in fortieths of an inch = 0.025 inch. The Sleeve is divided into groups numbered 0, 1, 2, 3 etc, each group having 4 divisions of one fortieth of an inch, so 4 x 1/40 = 4 x .025 = 0.10 inch between each number, all the way up to the full inch.
The Thimble is divided into 25 divisions, each represents one twenty-fifth of a full turn, (the full turn being one fortieth of an inch), so 1/25 x 1/40 = 1/1000 = 0.04 x 0.025 = 0.001 inch, measured from the top line on the Graduated Sleeve.

In other words, if we turn the Thimble 1/25th of a turn, one division, then the Spindle will move 1/40 x 1/25 = 1/1000 = 0.001 of an inch.

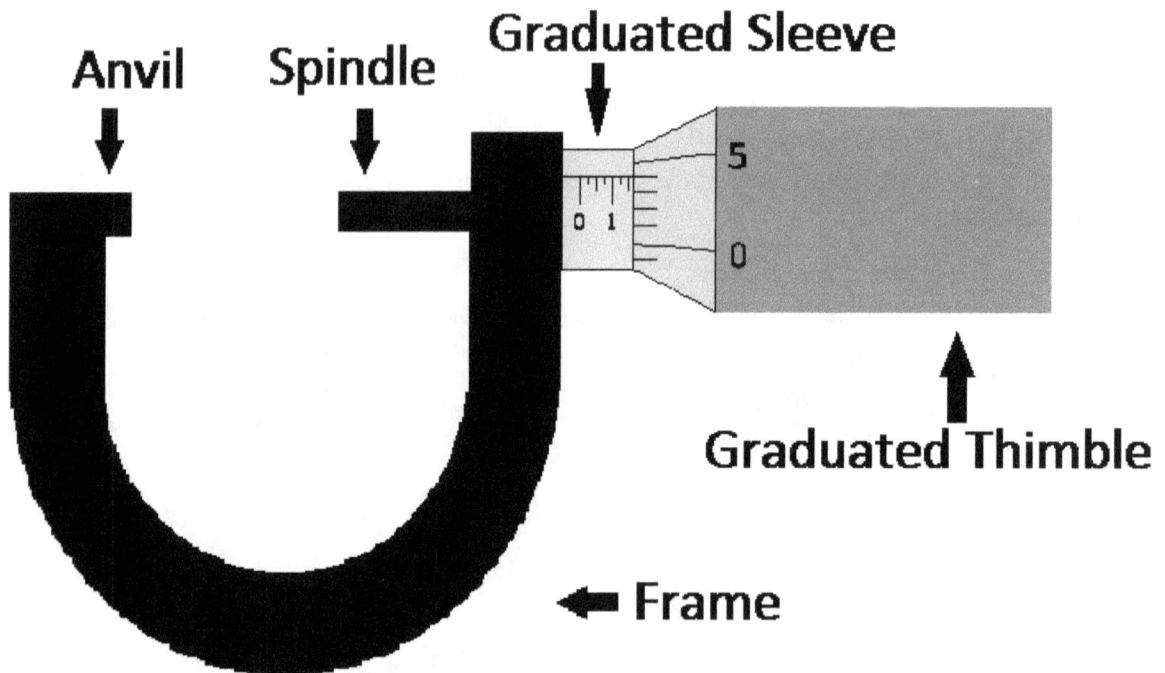

Anvil   **Spindle**   **Graduated Sleeve**

0 1   5   0

Graduated Thimble

← **Frame**

In the diagram above, the Thimble has uncovered the ' 1 ' on the sleeve, (but not the ' 2') and then 2 divisions on the Sleeve after the ' 1 '. The Thimble has the forth division aligned on the line of the Sleeve. So the reading is 0.1 (the number 1 on the Sleeve) + 2 x .025 (the two divisions after the number 1) + 0.004 (the four divisions on the Thimble). So it's 0.1 + 0.05 + .004 = 0.154 inch.

The Metric version is shown in the other diagram, below, of the Thimble, and it works in a similar way. Here, the extra row of lines above the numbered scale reads in 0.5 millimetres. The Thimble shows 0.0 X, where X is the unknown.

This diagram has the Sleeve showing 6 full millimetres. The Thimble has exposed a 0.5 line after the 6th full millimetre and the graduation on the Thimble shows 2. So the reading is 6 + 0.5 +.02 = 6.52 mm.

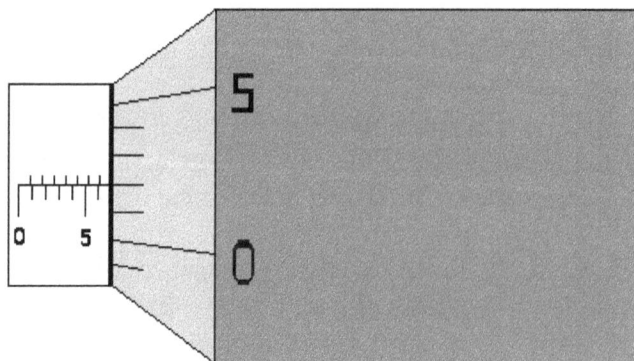

0   5   5   0

If you are using an engineer's lathe, you measure the diameter, using a vernier or micrometer, of the last cut, and subtract from it the size you need. If the piece measures 25mm, and you want 24.5, you need to lose .5mm diameter. Set for .4, and then measure. If it's important, don't go for the final size until you are VERY close, and just taking off a whisker. Always work the cut in, towards your work.

A wood lathe will typically be turning much larger diameters. It doesn't matter if a bowl or table top is plus or minus quite a considerable amount, so accurate diametric measurements are largely meaningless. Generally with a wood lathe the **length** is more crucial than diameter, chair legs need to be the same **length** more than they do the same **diameter**. Not the case with making a friction chuck or spigots, but more about that later.

A **Dial Gauge** is used for accurately measuring linear distances. The dial amplifies any small differences in the length of the plunger. Digital ones are available too.

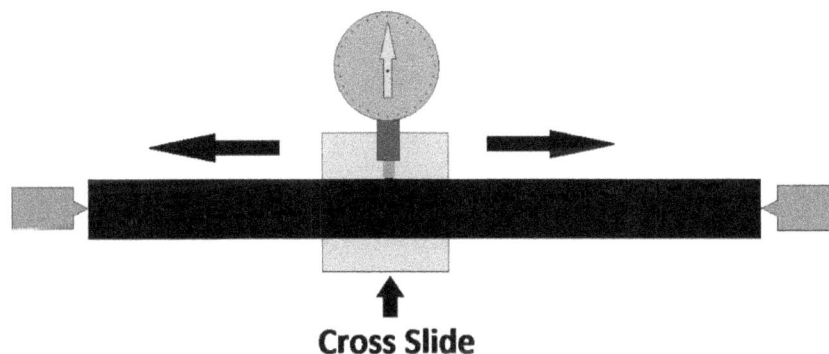

Cross Slide

This diagram shows how a Dial Gauge, mounted on the cross slide of the lathe, can measure the difference in the height, and therefore the diameter of the work piece. As the cross slide carriage is moved sideways to and fro across the work, here being held 'between the lathe centres (points)', the small variations in the height are amplified and shown by the needle moving around the dial.

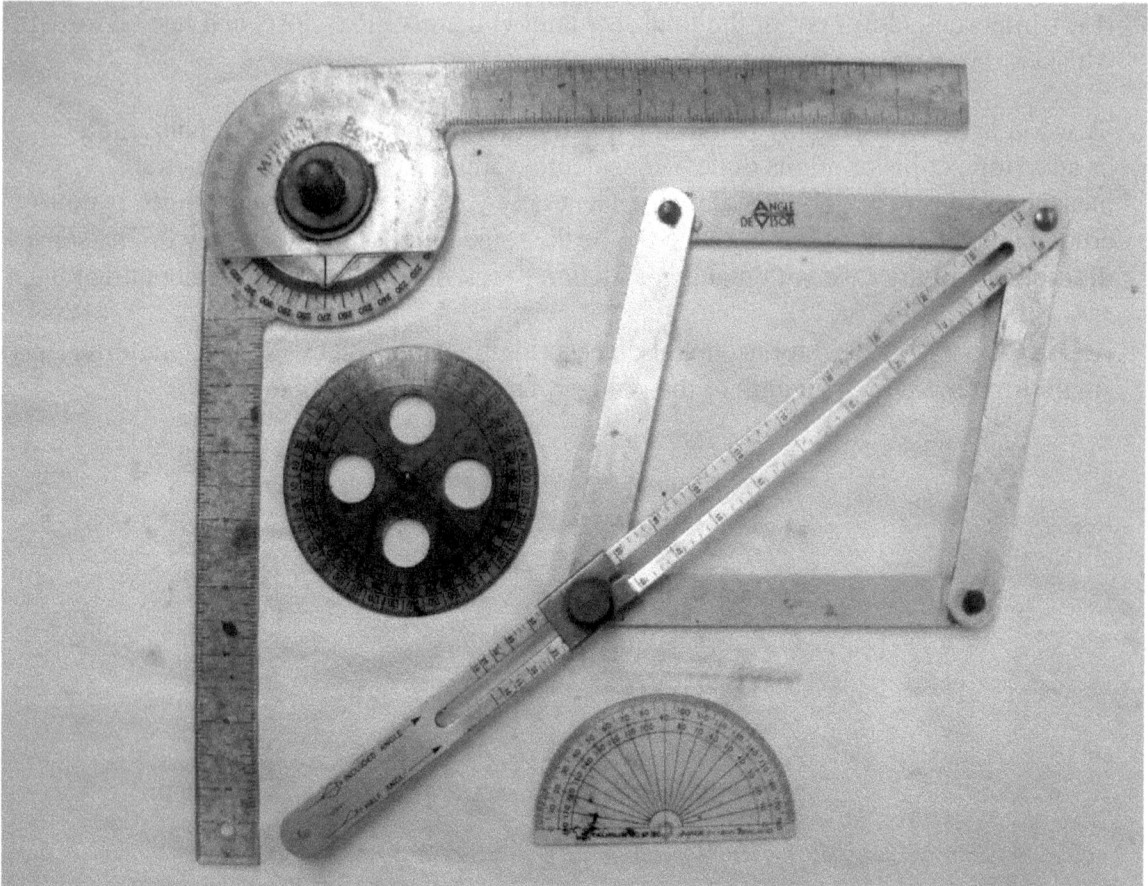

Some different kinds of Protractors.

There are many different kinds of protractors and ways of measuring angles.

The classic school protractor will give a fair reading for a quick estimation, but a protractor with a central fulcrum and long arms is a much better way of getting a good result.

Centre Finding

Before turning, you first need to find and mark the centre of your piece, particularly with a wood lathe. On a square or rectangular piece mark two diagonal lines (from corner to corner) and where they intersect is the centre.

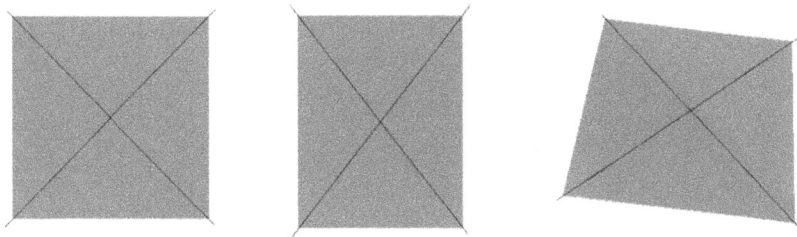

Finding the centres of various shapes of 'wood' with diagonal lines.

The 'centre' of the odd shaped piece on the right hand shape will be in the centre enough to mount in the lathe. Use a moderate RPM to start with, in case the piece is out of balance, until it is roughed out.

To find the centre of a round piece, a rough centre can be found using a tape, ruler or vernier calliper, by measuring the diameter, halving it, and marking this amount from the edge of the piece. Repeat at 90 degrees. If you repeat at 180 and 270 degrees as well it will be more accurate, especially if the piece is not exactly round, like a tree branch. The centre is in the middle of the marks.

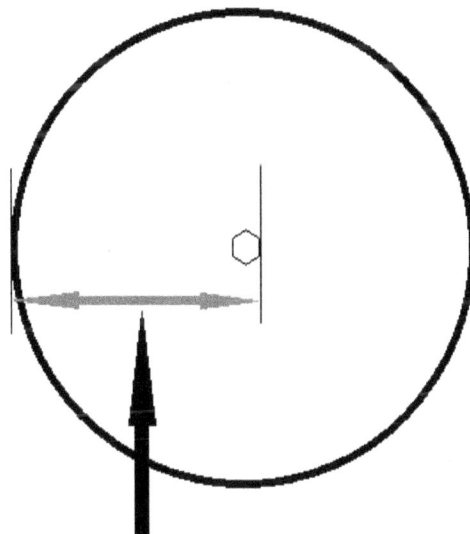

First Distance Measured

A more accurate circle centre finder is to put a set square across the round, and draw a line along the 45 degree mark. Repeat around the piece. Here's an easy tool to make for doing this.

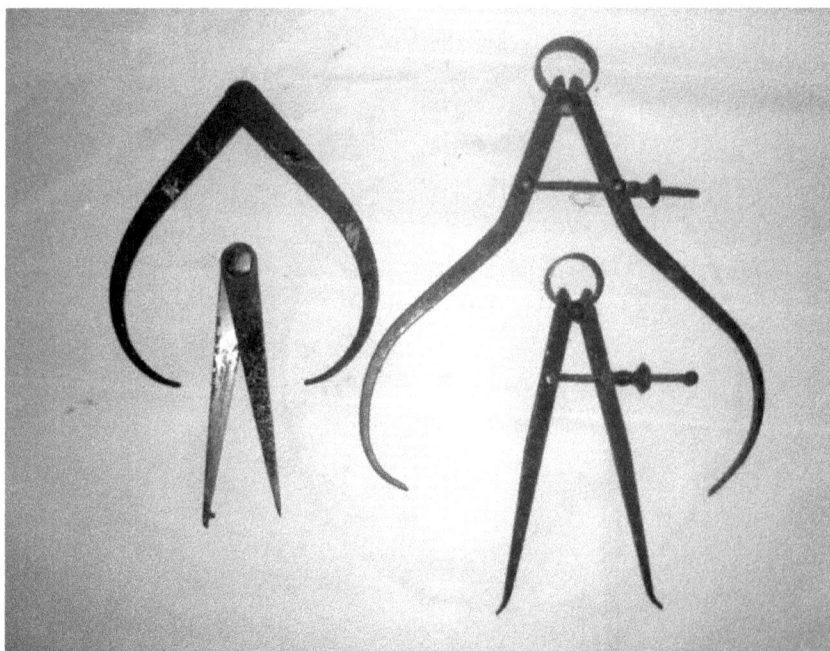

Here are some different types of callipers.

The two on the right have a spring at the top to force the legs out against the knurled nut on the thread, so they will maintain their setting very well. Largely used for comparing diameters from, say, the master copy of a chair leg to the one you're making, they're not often used for actual measurements. Use the top one for externals and the lower for internals.

The two on the left move freely, and will change their setting if you're not careful. However, the top left-hand side one will measure both inside and out, and the bottom left-hand side one is useful for centre finding, as shown below.

Set to about half of the diameter, and score a line 10 mm long in the middle.

Do this several times around the circumference. The true centre is in the middle of these lines.

A centre punch in the centre will avoid missing the mark with the lathe centres.

Dividing Heads

Once your piece is turned, you may now need to mark out the circle into an equal number of sections, with moderate accuracy (for instance, you have turned a stool top and need to know where to mark for the legs). It is assumed you have a centre point.

2 points is easy of course: just draw a diagonal through the centre point.

An easy way to mark 3 points on a small item is to use a 3 jaw chuck if you have lathe with one. You can hold the piece in the chuck and mark against the chuck jaws, being sure to mark on the same side, (so left or right) of each jaw, as shown below.

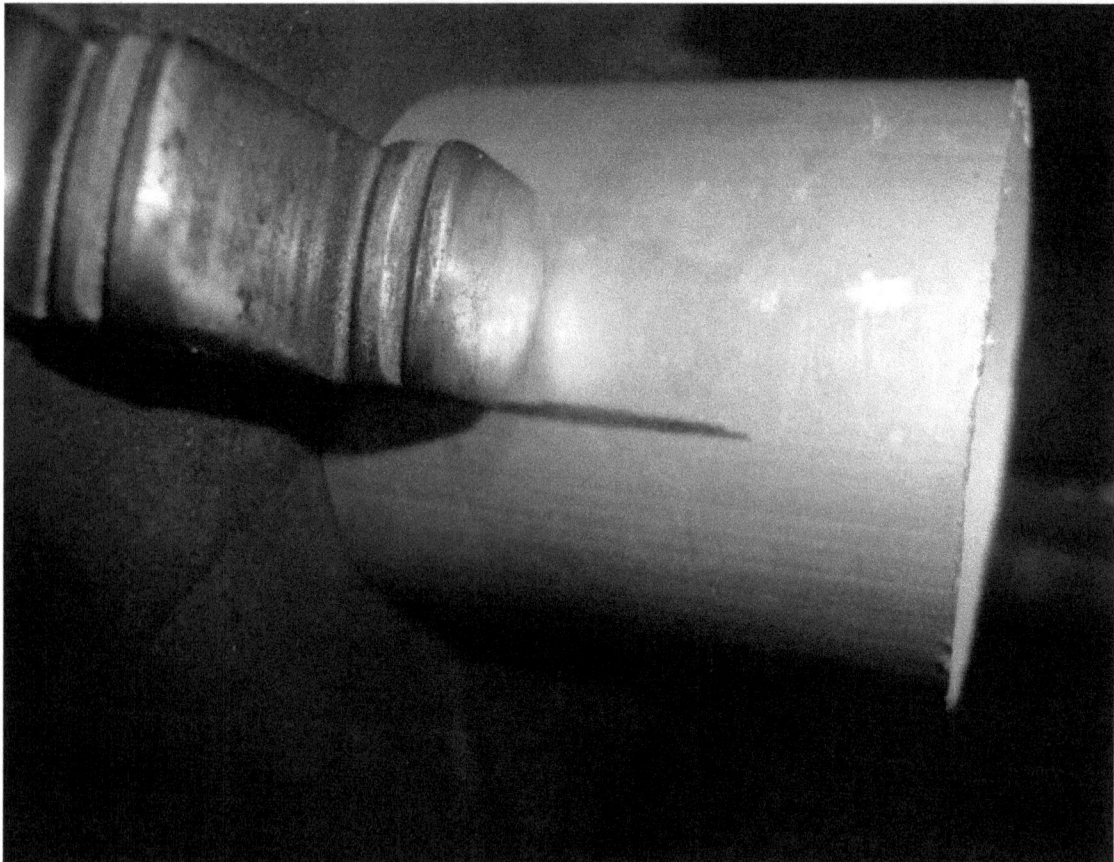

With no 3 jaw chuck available, you can use something that has already been divided into sections. Pulleys are sometimes divided by 3, 5 or 6 spokes. Sprockets have a number of teeth, and you can divide suitable sprockets into divisions that will work for you.

The pulley in the next photo will quickly give you divisions of 3 or 6.

A mark at the outer edge will be fairly accurate, marking with a vertical pencil (or scribe) to one side of the spokes will be more so. Of course you must mark on the same side of each spoke, always on the right-hand side, for example.

The change wheels found on older lathes make fine Dividing Heads, and will divide into a huge number of points.

Here, above, the work is being held in the 3 jaw chuck. A lathe change wheel, which has a suitable number of teeth for the divisions I require, is held against the work by the tailstock centre. So if I need 11 divisions I must use a wheel with a multiple of 11, say 55, teeth. 56 teeth would not do. The tool is mounted in the tool post, and is there to provide a steady and reliable reference point as I count the number of teeth around the wheel. A steel ruler across the teeth onto the work allows for an accurate transfer of the divisions.

This piece is too large to transfer the divisions across easily, so the tool on the right-hand side of the tool post is extended to be very close to the change wheel teeth to select the divisions, while a tool is held in the left-hand side of the tool post to allow an accurate transfer of the divisions.

If you have resort to measuring, either from the need for accuracy or lack of any quick guides, here are some helpers.

First you need to know that a chord is a straight line between two points on the circumference of a circle.

To find 3 points equally spaced on the circumference (as in an equilateral triangle), first measure the diameter, (draw and measure a straight line through the centre point) then multiply this measurement by the **sine of half of the angle** between the points. So for 3 points, which are 120° apart, multiply the diameter by the sine of 60°, which is .8660. E.g. If your diameter is 100mm, 100 x .8660 = 86.6mm.

Find the end of the chord from your starting point which is 86.6mm long and mark, (if you are using callipers, set your callipers at this amount and mark the next point where they meet the circumference).

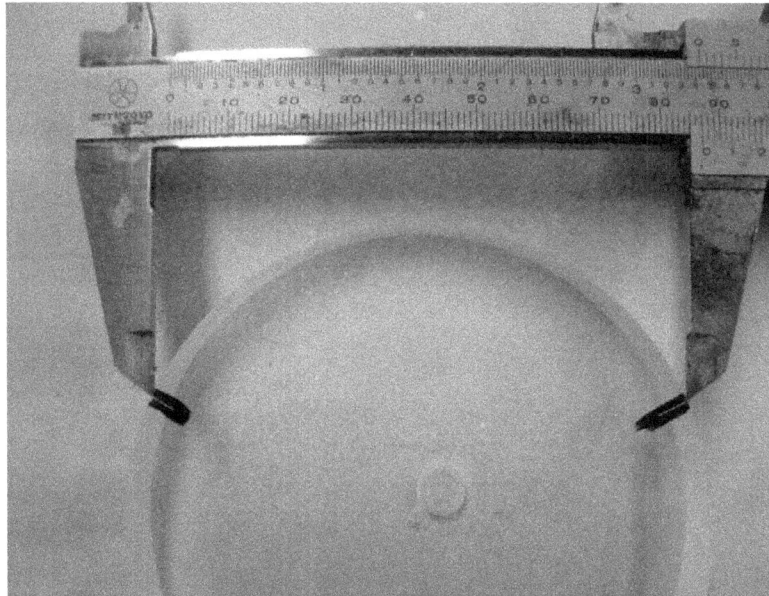

Here I have marked the second of the three divisions, using the scribe I made from the chainsaw file. Because it can be difficult to see the mark, especially on something like the acrylic disc seen here, first make a broad mark at about the right point with a felt pen or chalk, and then use the scribe to make an accurate scratch in the mark. The result as shown above, is very easy to see.

Use the second point to find the next end of the chord 86.6mm long and mark. Now you have three equidistant points marked on your circle.

To check, the chord between this third mark and the first mark will be 86.6mm.

For an equilateral triangle inside a circle : Diameter x .8660

For a square inside a circle (4 points) : Diameter x 0.7071 gives the length of each side.

For 5 points : Diameter x .5878   For 6 points : Diameter x .5000
For 8 points : Diameter x .3827

For ANY : Length of chord (distance in a straight line between points on the circumference) = sin A x diameter. A is half the angle at the centre. (so 45 for a square, 30 for 6 points etc).

Don't forget, it's the **Sine Value of <u>HALF</u>** the angle you use.

For example, the angle between 3 equal points on a circumference is 120 degrees, but you use the Sine value of half that, 60 degrees, which is .8660.
There is a list of some Sine Values in the Appendix, p203.

WORKSHOP TOOLS

Workshop tools are as diverse and varied as there are people to make them. Of course, there are some tools that are common, and found in every workshop, but there are thousands of 'special tools' that will never be found in any catalogue and are irreplaceable to their creators !!!

'Sets' of tools, such as sockets sets, spanners, and screwdrivers and various drill sets, files and sets of small tools often come with their own storage case. These are great. I like to keep them in the original case, though some are (oddly) designed to be kept horizontal!! Those, I generally find some way of mounting vertically, because I never have enough flat bench space for me, let alone for a set of spanners as well!! These cases not only keep the tools safe, but give good access as required and also an instant indication that one is missing.

Tools like Forstener cutters can become very hot during use. A set of them will generally come in a plastic case as you can see in the next photo, but wait before re-housing them till they cool. If you put a hot cutter into its slot, there's a good chance the plastic will soften, and the tool will forever after fall out.

For tools that are individual rather than part of a set, like hacksaws, hammers, shears, squares and many more that don't fit snugly into a display case, make yourself a shadow board.

A **Shadow Board** is a board of plywood or something similar into which you drive nails or screws to hold the tools. You then draw around each tool while it's in its place with a felt pen. The board is then mounted on a wall (or behind a bench) vertically. When the tool is not on the board, you can immediately tell, find it and replace it on the board.

It's a very easy and efficient way of keeping tools tidy, and close at hand, as well as keeping track of them.

GRINDERS and GRINDING

A **Bench Grinder** is essential in a workshop. And these days the price of really good, double ended single phase bench grinders has dropped so much and the range is so large, that you can shop around and buy the one that suits you best. Always try to buy one with the largest diameter wheels possible, the larger the diameter of the wheel, the flatter the surface presented to the work piece, and the big wheels can also have a greater width and a longer life. Start up can be slower though as they are often induction start motors.

Wheels come in a large variety of grit sizes. Grit is measured as to how many pieces of the grit fit in a given space, so 40 grit has bigger pieces than 120 grit. Finer grits, 80 to 120 sort of range, will give a finer cut, and also tend to work better on harder tool steels.

Wheels also come with different bonding agents. Common ones are grey, white and green. The difference is from a hard bond (grey) to a soft bond (green). Use a hard bond for soft metals, mild steels and alloys, white wheels for high speed cutters and drills, and green wheels for carbide. DON'T use you precious green wheel for a tent peg, or waste your time, and wheel, trying to grind a carbide cutter on a grey wheel. I like to have a grey wheel on one side for general work, and a white on the other for the lathe tools, drills and the like. A green wheel is safely in the drawer, and can quickly be mounted for those infrequent times (for me at any rate) I dress carbide tips. Good to have it there though.

Wheels can easily get either out of round, become contoured on the face, or both. However, re-dressing them is quite easy. There are two common types of dressing tools, and really, they are essential. You can try to repair a wheel's surface by grinding away on a piece of scrap steel, but it is very time consuming and is seldom satisfactory.

A **star wheel** dressing tool is a steel tool with a handle, that, at the cutting end, has a series of star shaped steel wheels, in between steel washers. The stars revolve once they are pushed into contact with the spinning grinder. The stars break off tiny particles of the bonding material, and so will reform the grinding wheel to its former state. The stars will wear away as well of course, but replacement star and washer sets are available; be sure to check if the brand of star dresser you intend to buy has spare stars available. However, while these tools are quick to use, they are somewhat inaccurate and it can be difficult to get the grinder exactly true.
Sparks when you're using the star dressing tool mean you should push the dresser harder onto the grinding wheel.

Another dresser comes in the form of a hard composite stick, about 25mm square and 150 long. You use it as you would a piece of steel you are grinding; that is you hold it against the spinning grinding wheel. It's perhaps not as fast as the star dresser, although nearly. It also has the advantage of having no moving parts, which makes it much easier to get the grinding wheel true and flat.

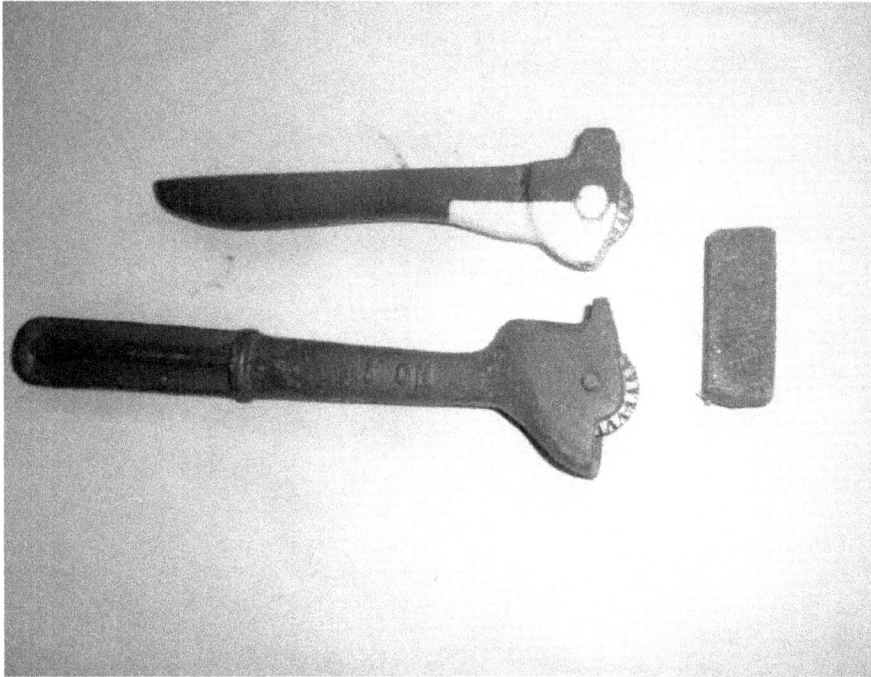

Here are two different sizes of Star Wheel grindstone dressing tools and about a half length of the composite stick dresser. The sticks last for ages, this one I have had for more than 20 years, whereas the stars wear out much more quickly. Either type of tool will dress any grit size or differently bonded wheels.

A Star type grindstone dressing tool in use.

The stick dresser is by far the easiest one to use if you want to form a wheel to a specific shape.

The grinding wheel shown above has been shaped to grind the radius of the larger tube. The small tube is then ground to that radius, giving a good fit to the large tube, essential for a neat braise or weld.

Grinding alloys can cause particles of alloy to become embedded in the grinding wheel, steels can 'glaze' the wheel, sharpening tools will easily form ruts in the surface, and heavy grinding can cause the wheel to become out of round, so a dressing tool is a really useful tool.

When grinding, keep the tool rest as close as possible to the wheel, and have a quench tank (really just a bucket of water) close by. Heat ruins the temper of the tools, so keep things cool with the water.

When you grind really thin material like sheet metal, use a piece of scrap material, (wood will even do, though it might burn a little), under the work piece to support the sheet right up at the grinding wheel's surface, as shown in the next photo. Otherwise, the sheet metal will be dragged down with the rotation of the wheel, and at that point you are in danger of ruining the piece and possibly of having it torn from your hands. Don't use gloves in this situation. Gloves can be a hazard if a finger of them gets caught, and bare hands will tell you when things are getting too hot.

Grinding sheet supported by a scrap of plywood.

When you are grinding a cutter of some sort, be it a drill or lathe tools, you need to have the leading edge as sharp as possible.

The grinding wheel sends streams of hot metal fillings and hot pieces of the wheel grit down and under the wheel. Most of it flies off under the wheel, but a certain percentage comes right round the wheel. When you are grinding a blade, you can tell it's sharp when the fillings that have gone around the wheel can no longer fit under the work because the blade is an exact fit to the wheel, and instead bounce off the tool in a visible spray, like you see in this diagram.

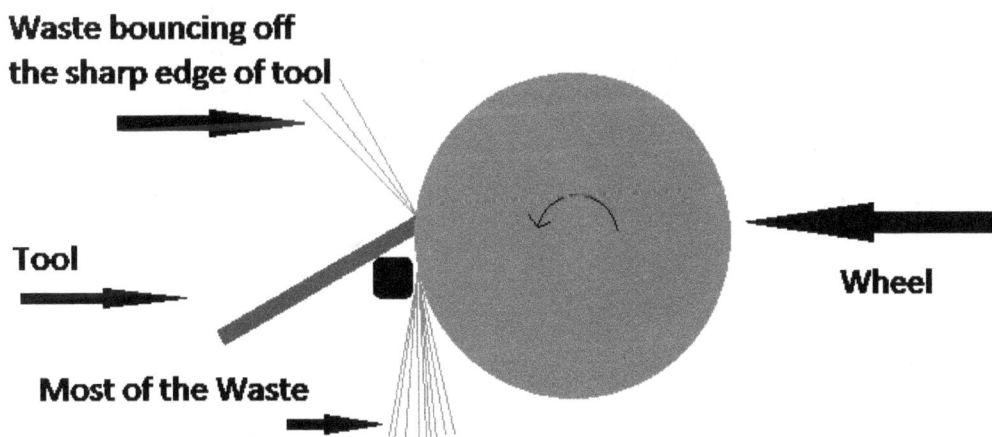

**Waste bouncing off
the sharp edge of tool**

Tool

Wheel

Most of the Waste

Practice is the only way to get really proficient when sharpening cutters, drills and wood lathe tools, but perseverance will win in the end. If you haven't achieved a sharp tool, try again; just remember to keep the heat down to avoid de-tempering.

30

DRILLS and DRILLING

The most commonly used workshop tool for drilling is the **Drill Press**. A half inch diameter (13mm) capacity chuck is the most common for the home workshop, and ½ to 1 HP is enough power.

Drill Presses come in either a bench model, or floor model, which, while more expensive, is much more versatile because of the extra height between the chuck and the foot plate, and also means that you don't have to provide a bench for it. Anchor it well to the floor. A tilting table can be a nice feature, but can also lead to inaccuracy: make sure the table has a tapered pin to guarantee the table will return to and is held exactly at 90 degrees. A crank to lift the table is nice too, though by no means essential.

 Most Drill Presses need little maintenance, the bearings are usually sealed for life, but the quill (the spline that allows the chuck to move up and down) should be oiled from the top periodically. Keeping the main pedestal shaft clean and with a slight coating of oil helps with the table rise and fall; an oily pad of fine steel wool is a nice way to do it.

I like to have the chuck key on a small chain, so I know where it is!!

There are loads of different tools for making holes, so we'll only consider the more common. **Twist Bits** are by far the most frequently used.

Using a centre punch to locate the hole exactly is essential, in any material. A **Centre Drill Bit** is a very stable one to use as a pilot, as you see below, though you don't have to drill beyond the small flutes. Now you can accurately re-drill to the required sized hole.

Twist bits range from very small, under .5 mm, to enormous. For the 13 mm chuck, however, a bit under about 1mm diameter is too small to be gripped, and even by using a stepped shank, over 20mm is too large for most materials as most home workshop presses won't have the power or slow enough spindle speeds for the really big sizes. Very large twist bits usually have a tapered shank, so won't fit the simple drill press.

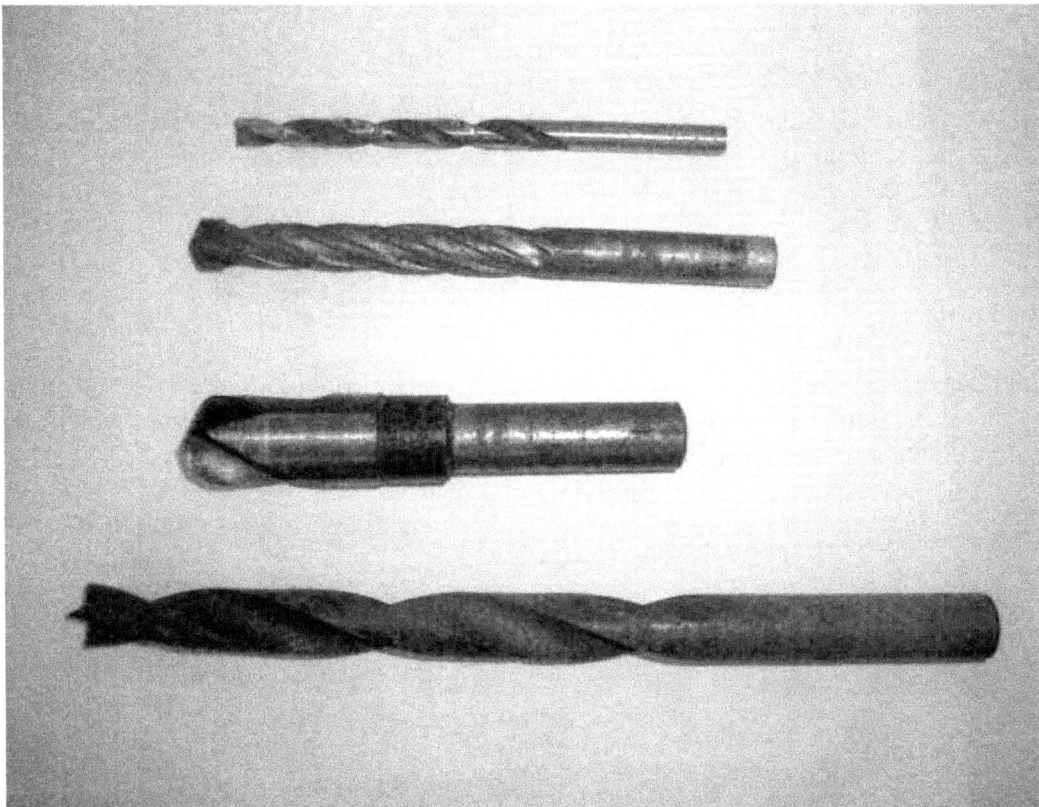

Unusual Twist Bits.

Here we see, from the top down, a flat ended bit for boring flat bottomed holes in wood, plastic or alloy, a masonry bit which has carbide cutters brazed to the shank which is not hardened at all, a stepped shank bit and a wood bit with a pointed end.

You can go above the 13mm chuck size with a stepped shank, and below 1mm if you wrap some electrical tape around the shank of the drill bit. Not pretty, but it works!!! Go very slowly though.

Twist bits are available in very small diameter increments, .1mm or less, and in a range of hardness. I personally think anything less than HSS (high speed steel) is a waste of money and so too are the various coatings you see advertised in the junk mail. Just stick to well recognised brands of tradesman quality bits.

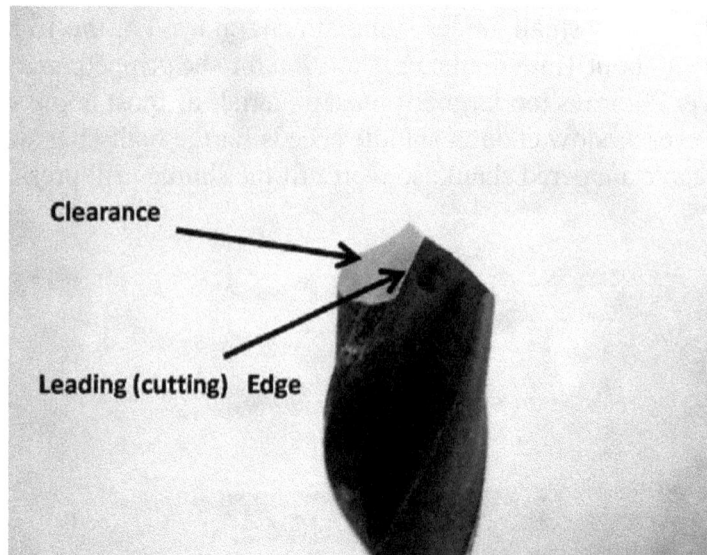

Clearance

Leading (cutting) Edge

While the 'proper' angle for the drill cutters is 59°, make the angle very steep for plastics (say 35°) with good clearance behind the cutting edge, and 45° for a countersink hole, if you don't have a countersink bit. You can measure the angles with a square for the 45° drills, and a protractor set to 120° for the regular drills.

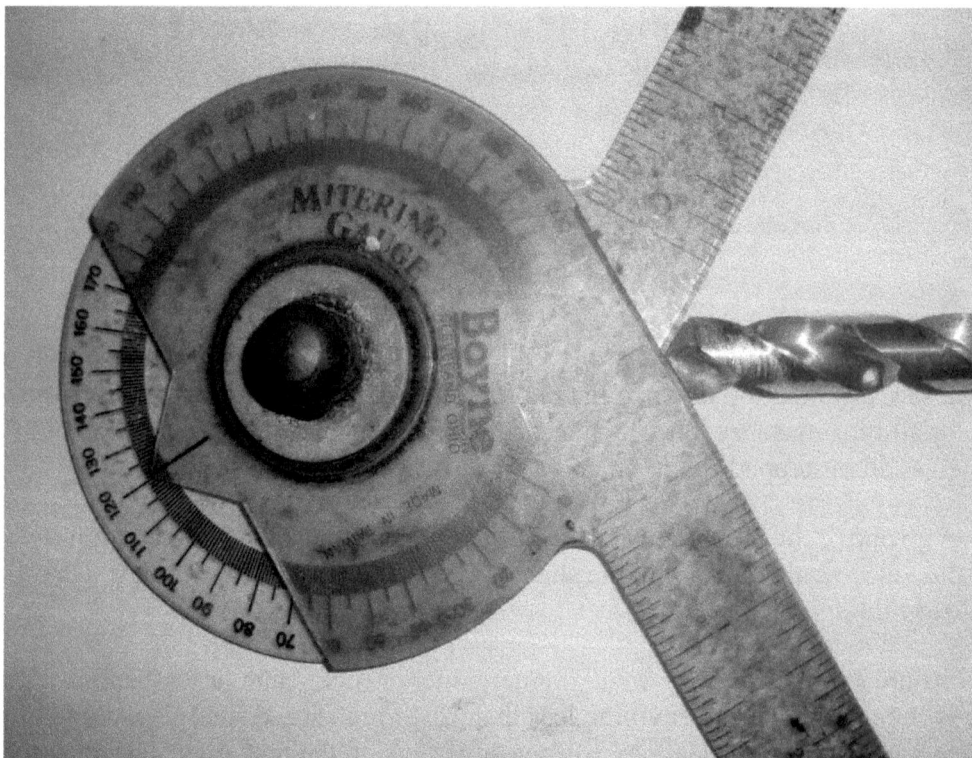

This helps, along with a mark or guide on the grinder, to not only get the angles right, but to keep them symmetrical.

Sharpen the bits on the grinder with the drill's cutter at 59° (60°) degrees to the wheel.
Put a line on the grinder rest, if it doesn't have one.
Sometimes the grinder tool rest has a groove to help get the correct angle. Grind the edge
true, and then lift the bit a little so the back of the edge is ground back to give clearance.
They are tricky to sharpen, but you'll get the knack. There are of course jigs available ....

This photo shows a groove in the grinder tool rest for sharpening drills at the correct
angle.

The swarf from the drill should emerge equally from each side of the drill flutes. If you
need a flat bottomed hole in soft materials, bore with a regular drill to the required depth,
and finish with a square ground bit, the top bit as shown in the photo on page 31.

There are several easily solved reasons for drills over-boring, and making holes that are
larger than the bit that bored them.
Firstly, make sure that the cutting edges are equal, so the tip of the bit is exactly in the
centre. Otherwise, the bit will tend to 'wobble' and so enlarge the hole. Be sure to
withdraw the drill bit frequently, to clear the swarf.
Once the flutes are full, the bit will be forced into the sides of the hole, and in an extreme
case, jam. Failure to clear the swarf will also cause undue heat, and in an extreme case the
loss of the drill bit's temper. Forcing the drill to cut faster than it 'wants' to, by pushing it
too hard into the work also will create oversized holes, as the bit will buckle, and once
again will cause extreme heat. Keep the cutters sharp and let the bit work at its own pace.

Hole Saws are useful for larger than 13mm holes. They go from about 19mm to beyond 100mm.

Once again, don't buy a toy. The ones with 3 cutters on a spiral centre are rubbish, as are the ones with multiple thin blades that fit into slots in the base. Buy the ones with an arbor that will accept different hole saws. The **Arbor** (see the photo below) has a drill bit, usually ¼ inch, locked in the centre. The hole saw fits a thread on the outside.

There are 2 kinds of arbors; below about 19mm diameter the hole saw is simply screwed onto the arbor, and the drill press holds the shank of the ¼ inch drill which passes right through the arbor. Above that, the drill press holds a hexagonal shank which is part of the arbor. The hole saw screws onto the arbor till it's nearly tight, but then you screw down 2 pins which take all the load of the work. Don't screw the hole saw until it's tight on the arbor; by the time you've done the job, it'll be so tight you will have huge trouble removing it from the arbor. Leave it a little loose, and use the pins.
Hole saws come in a standard and extra length size. The bigger the diameter of the hole saw, the slower it should turn.

The above photo shows the two different kinds of arbors. The left hand one has the two pins which screw down into the holes you can see in the blade when the blade has been screwed onto the arbor until it is very nearly tight, whereas the right hand one simply screws onto the arbor.

When using the hole saws, clamp the work firmly, and use a lubricant with metals, and some plastics. A thin penetrating oil or kerosene work well and are essential when cutting alloy.

The hole saw uses the central drill bit as it's guide. It won't work without a guide. However, for some applications, you can bore holes in a work piece with a ¼ inch drill, and then replace the drill bit in the hole saw with a ¼ inch diameter steel rod.

 If you need to cut less than a full circle, then clamp a waste piece where the guide bit will run, then you can cut a segment with the hole saw. Clamp the work piece too, of course, and work slowly. This is a time when setting the work piece and the waste piece up and just boring a ¼ inch hole with a normal drill first, then changing to the hole saw with a smooth steel rod in place of the usual centre drill can be quite useful. Cutting a segment is where you might expect a lot of chatter from the hole saw, and a drill in the centre can enlarge the centre hole because the flutes will cut, thus allowing even more chatter. A smooth centre guide will reduce this. The photo below shows a hole saw with a smooth guide, running in a previously bored hole, cutting a segment from a piece of aluminium. Both the scrap wood and the aluminium are well clamped to the drill press table.

Hole saws come in imperial measurements. You can put a hole saw in a lathe and reduce the Outside Diameter (OD) by grinding off a little of the set, or bend a few teeth out (use a small adjustable wrench) to make then a little bigger.

This will damage the teeth somewhat, and the finish of the cut will be rougher, but who cares if it does the job. Keep such altered saws away from your usual set!!!

They lend themselves to being made into special cutters as well, as shown in the photo below. The hole saw on the left has a centre guide for an existing hole (with a carbide tooth from an old saw blade brazed to it to make sure the guide doesn't bind, as it will if the original hole has gone slightly out of shape) and a large ring around the outside to act as a depth stop. There is also a cutter, just visible, inside the hole saw. The saw on the right has a forstener cutter inserted into the centre hole. The idea here is to have a hole the size of the forstener cutter with a slightly larger cut in the top. I could have done this with two forstener cutters, cutting the large hole first, but this allowed it to be done in one operation, good for repetitive operations.

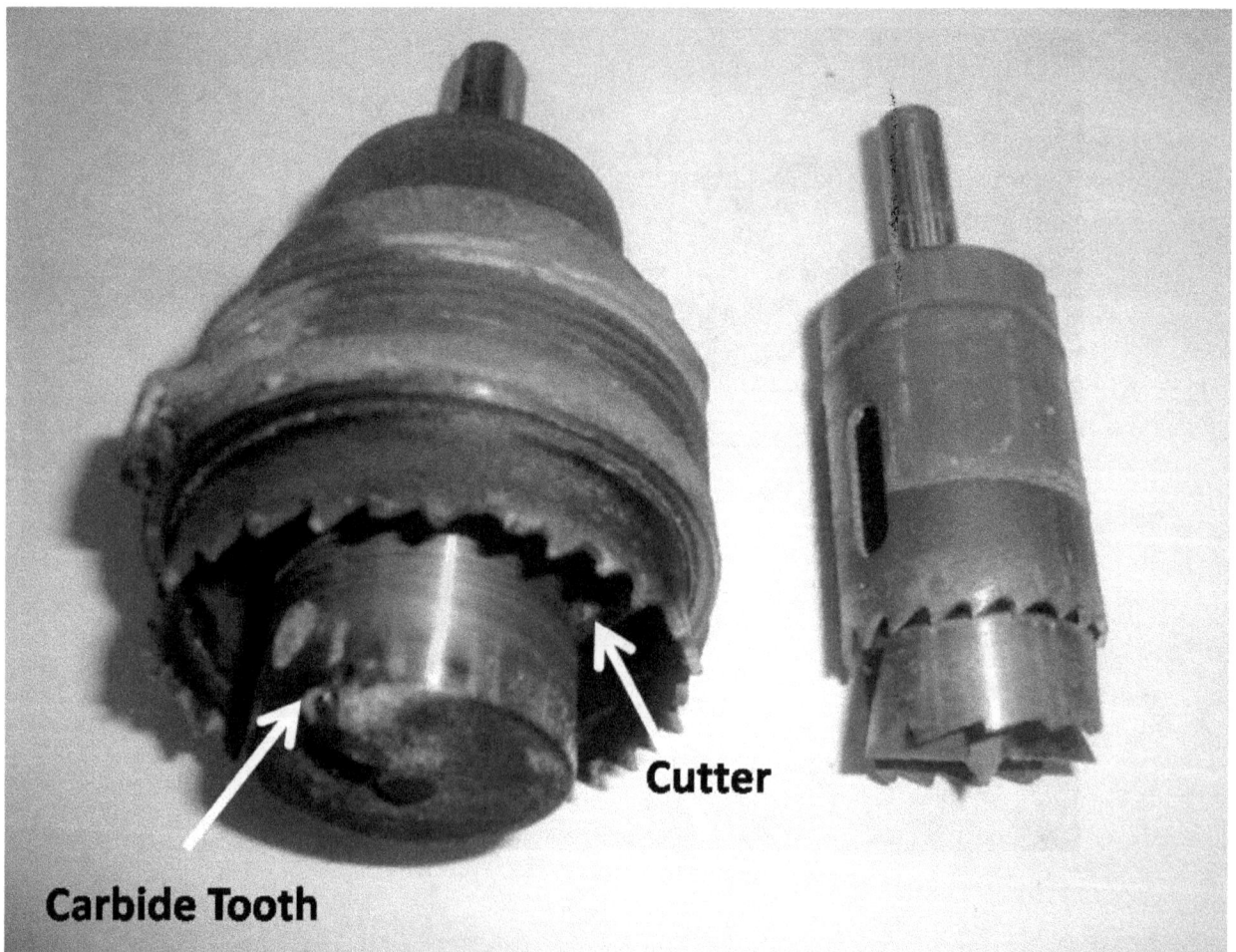

Cutter

Carbide Tooth

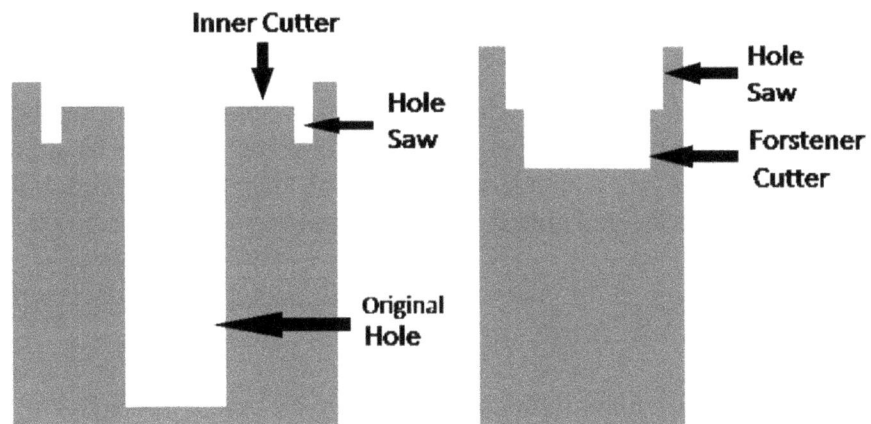

The Diagrams above show the different profiles cut by the two adapted hole saws in the previous picture.

'**Flat Bits**', or '**Speed Bores**' are great tools for quickly boring holes.

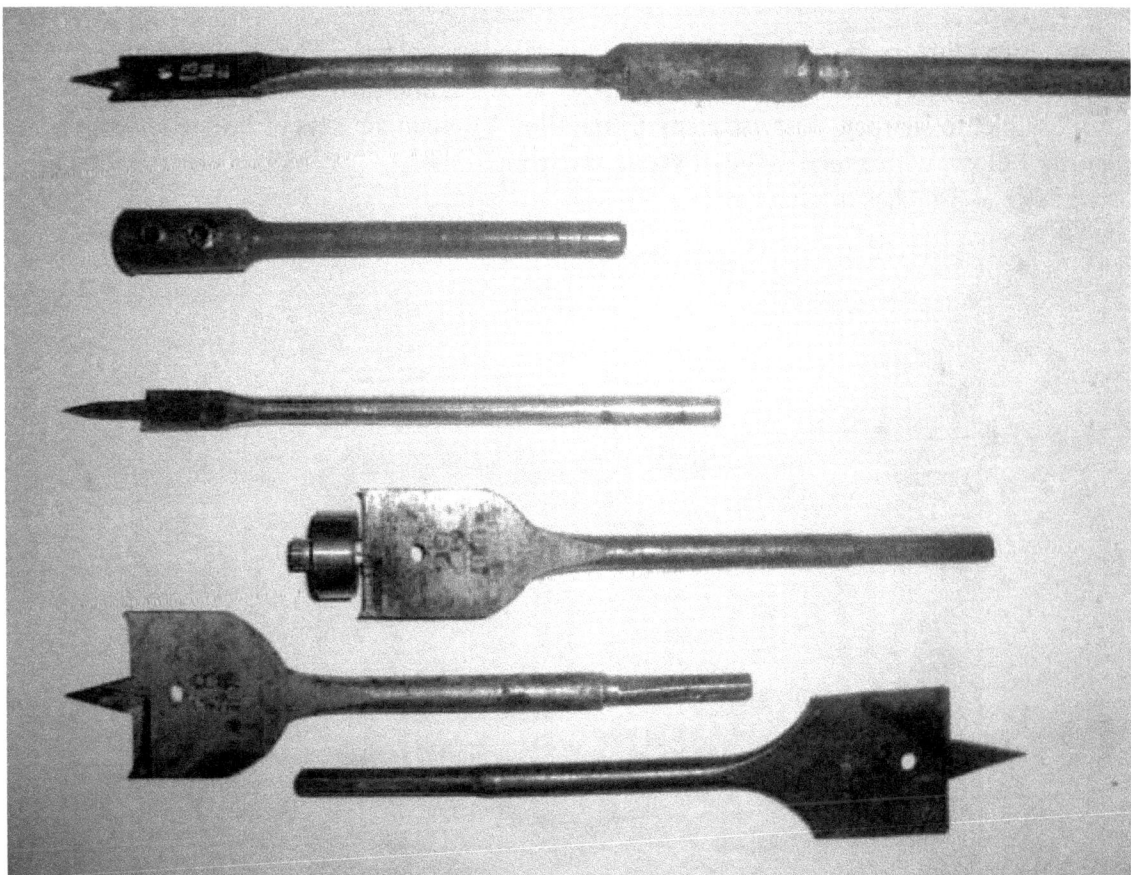

They are primarily used for wood, though they work very well with plastics of all sorts. They will also bore alloy quite well if you bore a pilot hole first. They don't like it very

much, but clamp the piece (it'll get hot), lubricate and use low RPM.
These bits are cheap, and lend themselves to all sorts of 'alterations'!!

Some have spurs below the cutting edge (second from bottom). For a flat bottomed hole, grind these off (bottom). It is relatively easy to change the sizes too, by grinding the edges down. Best to mark the bit on both sides first, so you keep the sides equal in width. They will bore a beautifully tapered hole if you grind the taper so it's wider at the top.

The third one down has had the point extended and shaped to provide a stepped hole in one operation.

You can grind the centre point right down (again, mark before you start) or even grind the point to a parallel spigot and mount a sleeve on it. The sleeve will follow a pilot hole (fourth one down).

They usually have ¼ inch diameter shanks, and readily accept an extension shaft. The extension in the top of the above photo has been braised onto the flat bit, and so is permanent. The shanks are ground to have three flats, one of which is where the grub screws seen on the short extension (second down from the top) should bear.

Forstener Cutters are fantastic, but only for wood and plastic. They are available in a large range of imperial sizes. They are also expensive, and difficult, though not impossible, to sharpen. Just use a small fine file. You can get sets of Forstener cutters, as shown below, with a nice range of sizes, say from ¼ inch to 2 ¼ inches, though they are available to 3 inches in diameter.

They bore a very clean and flat bottomed hole and because of their unique rim, are able to bore even when the centre point does not have contact with the material. Hence they will bore an angled hole quite easily or even a small segment of a hole.

This photo, above, shows a forstener cutter boring an angled hole using a press without an angle adjustable table.
The cutter's centre point has just started to bear.

Forstener cutters have no chip removal spiral on the shaft, so for full depth holes, or when you've added an extension to them for extra depth, you must frequently clear the swarf.

For **very small** segment cuts, if the centre point is not guiding, you must firmly clamp the work in the press. It can be easier to have the main body of the cutter (and so the centre point), cutting through a piece of waste, to prevent it wandering even a little.

They are really happiest cutting across the grain, but will bore with the grain if you need to.

For a large diameter hole, particularly when boring with the grain, run the finished size in first, but just for a few millimetres. Then run another cutter ½ inch or so smaller in diameter for another few millimetres, using the original cutter's centre point hole. Now do this again with a smaller bit, which, by now, may well cope with boring the full depth.

Then you can return to the second cutter, which will use the small amount it has already cut as the starting guide, and bore full depth. And finally use the finished size cutter in the same way. Now, you will have enough power to bore the large hole, which otherwise may be too much for the motor, and importantly, you will avoid generating lots of temper destroying heat caused by the cutter futilely trying to bore the hole.

Boring a large hole **with the grain** by 'staging' the cutters.

Forstener bits cut plastics quite well, though they do tend to generate heat, and as such can melt the plastic around the cutter head. If it **really** melts the plastic, you might well wind up with a problem, with the cutter locking onto the piece, and either stalling the motor or spinning the work piece. So go slowly, use a little penetrating oil, clear the swarf regularly, and often raise the cutter to give both it, and the plastic, time to cool. When you have finished the boring, run the cutter in and out of the hole several times, to clear any dags and be sure to have a good clean result.

Because the forstener bits are usually quite large, it's quite easy to add an extension shank to them. This is a handy thing to do, as the original shanks are quite short. A 3/4inch diameter mild steel bar is good, providing the cutter is larger than that. Bore a hole in the steel, to accept the round or outer diameter of the hex shank. One or two ¼ inch Allen head grub screws set into the mild steel, within the flat area of the forstener shank of course, will provide adequate locking. In the case of the round shank forstener cutter, insert the shank and mark where the grub screws will bear, and grind a small flat onto the forstener shank at that point. This will prevent any chance of the cutter spinning, because if it does, it will be almost impossible to remove it. The other end of the extension will need to be machined down for 50mm or so to ½ inch diameter to fit the drill press chuck if you are going to use it in the drill press.

If you wish to use it in the lathe, holding it in the 3 jaw chuck, leave the diameter of the extension at its original size. You get much better grip with a larger diameter shaft and there is much less chance of the shaft breaking at the point of the reduction.

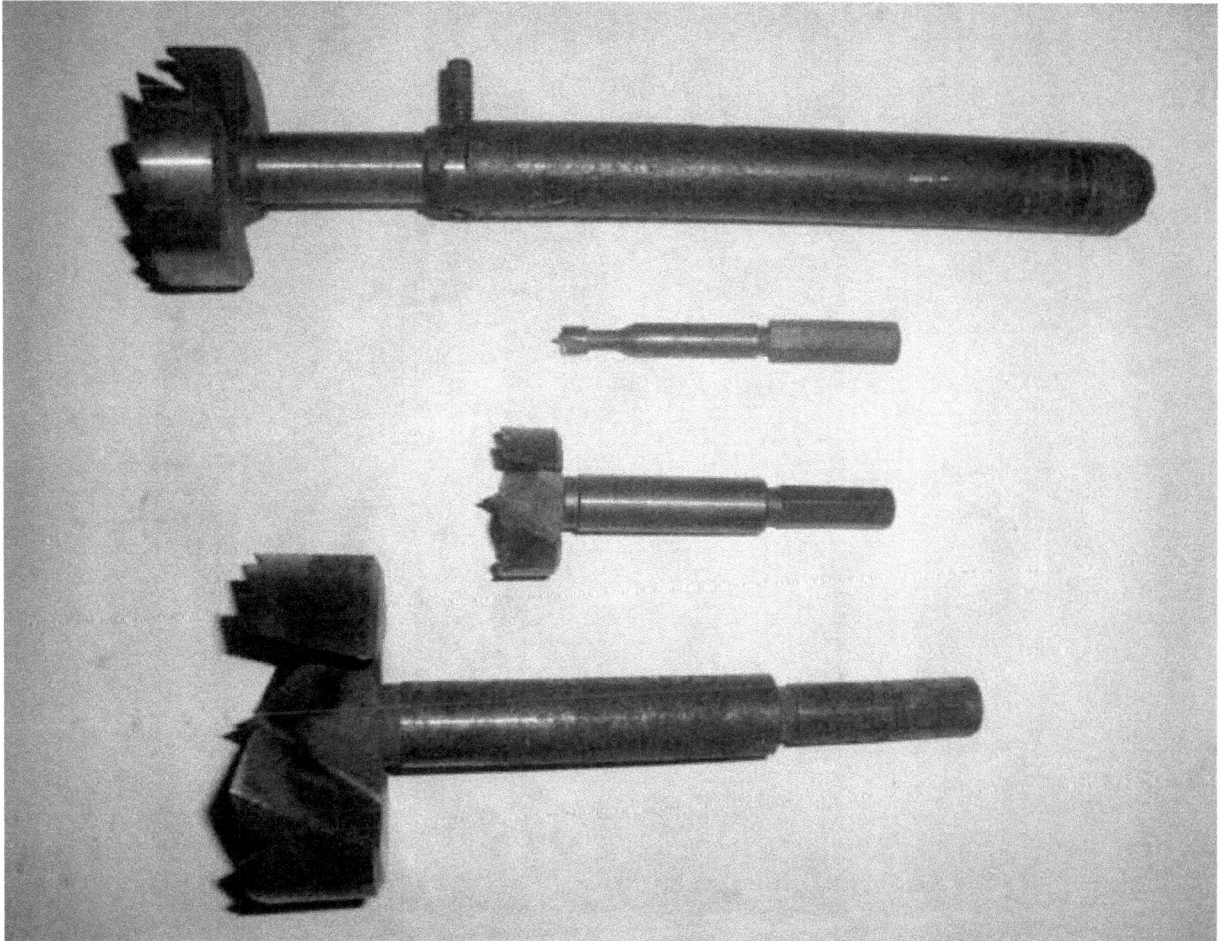

Different Sized Forstener Bits

The extension on the top forstener bit is designed to be held in a lathe chuck, hence the large shank diameter.

The grub screw is too long really, but is able to clear the sides of the hole and was all I had at the time!!

This next photo is a good example of a quick and secure jig for boring, with a forstener cutter, what is, from the cutter's point of view, a straight cut because the **surface** to be bored is at **right angles to the cutter**.

However, because of the angle of the turned piece, a jig was needed to be sure I didn't lose control of the drill, and ruin the piece. This jig is simply two pieces of waste wood, cut to the correct angle on the drop saw, and clamped to the drill press table. I've used two pieces of wood, one on top of the other, to give better support to the disc, as it was of quite a large diameter.

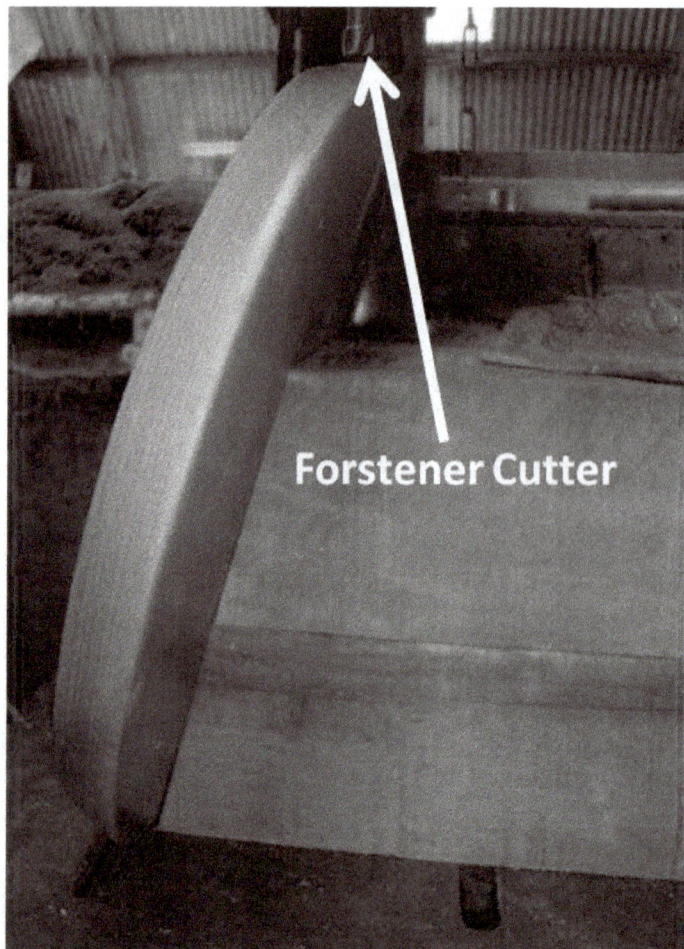

Forstener Cutter

Augers are wonderfully rugged, accurate and affordable boring tools.

They are available in a good range of sizes from 1/4inch to about 1 ½ inches in diameter, and come in a good variety of lengths.

You can add an extension shaft to an auger of course, but you will have to frequently raise the drill to clear the swarf once you are working below the top of the spiral. The spiral is often 'closed ' at the top, so swarf will tend to compact itself in the flutes. They make swarf at an alarming rate so you do have to clear it often. A long fully spiralled auger is better if you frequently bore deep holes.

A long auger, with its fly cutter intact and fully threaded centre point.

Augers are happy to bore with the grain as well as across it. However, when boring across the grain with a powered drill, either hand held or in a press, the threaded centre point can drag the auger into the work at such a rate, and with such power, that it is impossible to stop it. In a press, this may result in the work being lifted from the table, and the auger ploughing right through the piece whether you want it to or not, and in a powerful hand held drill can be quite dangerous, even to the point of being torn from your grip or injuring your wrists. You can avoid this by filing some (though not all) of the threads of the centre point away, leaving enough to keep the drill true, but not so much that they take over the operation, as shown in the next photo.

Above, an auger with some of the depth of the lead screw threads, and the fly cutter removed.
When boring with the grain, you can leave the full thread, it helps pull the drill along, and you won't lose control.

There is a fly cutter at the front of the auger, and this extends beyond the horizontal cutting edge. For a truly flat bottomed hole, you can grind the fly cutter away, as you can see in the photo above, otherwise your hole will have a deep groove running around it, deeper than the flat bottom of the hole itself.

Augers can be easily sharpened with a flat file with very fine teeth. You must keep the underside (the auger's surface that is in contact with the wood about to be bored), flat and slightly angled back to give clearance. The cutting edge must be a leading edge; if the steel behind the edge is proud of the cutting edge it will simply rub on the wood, prevent the cutter from actually cutting, and of course, summon the arch enemy; heat. Once you have filed the underside to a modest back angle, the front of the cutting edge can be filed so the edge is sharp.

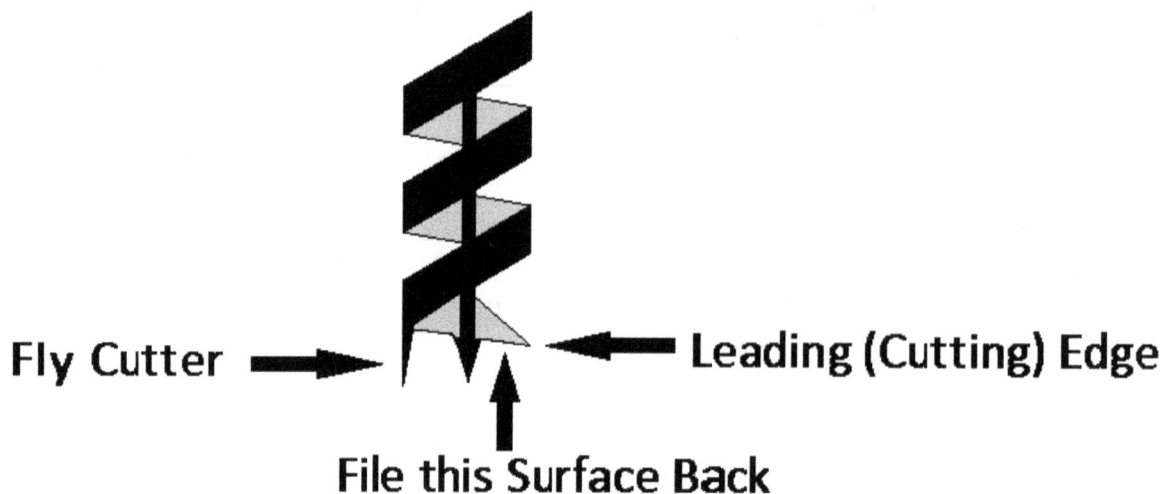

Fly Cutter ➡   ⬅ **Leading (Cutting) Edge**

File this Surface Back

A Diagram of an Auger.

The leading edge should be the only part of the cutter which has contact with the wood. File the underside surface back in an upward direction to make sure the surface doesn't rub on the bottom of the hole. Then file the top surface upwards, to get the edge sharp. The fly cutter can be removed or shortened to stop it undercutting the bottom of the hole.

Be very careful when using the augers. Because of the big open spiral, they will very easily pick up loose clothing, and that will **undoubtedly lead to serious injury**. So, as with any machine, keep all clothing away. Also be aware that the flutes on the auger are very sharp, and, when spinning, will act like a meat slicer on anything that comes in their way, like your hand for example. Be safe, and keep your hands well away from them when they are running.

The classic 'helicopter', where the piece is grabbed (often as the drill bit breaks through the underside) and spins round on the drill bit is a very dangerous thing. Even at a moderate RPM you will be hit several times before you can react. Blood may be the outcome!!!

For drilling, a **Flat Vice**, or **Drill Press Vice** is really useful; having the work piece well controlled gives not only a better result, but better safety for you too.

Drilling sheets, of any material, with a regular twist bit has the potential to be risky as the drill breaks through. The problem is that when the bit starts to break through, the material is thin enough to twist, and then 'ride' up the spiral of the drill. Once it does that, it's impossible to control, and it may well distort the sheet, as well as causing you harm.

The sheet should always be firmly held down, right up where the bit is working. If you clamp the sheet some distance away from the bit, there's still plenty of room for the sheet to bend up, and carve an elongated hole.

So clamp the sheet to the press table as close as possible to the bit; even better is to clamp the sheet to the press bed in the right place, and then clamp a scrap piece of plywood or waste over the sheet, right by the drill, with another clamp as demonstrated here.

Drilling sheet with the work clamped between two pieces of plywood.

The next photo shows a good jig for holding round section work. It can be quickly made by welding two Angle Plates to a base. The jig can then be clamped to the drill press table, and will accommodate a large range of sizes.

A simple jig for holding round work for drilling.

Short work should be held in the jig with slip jaw pliers or the like for the actual drilling operation; longer work can be clamped down to the jig.

To check whether a drill is diametrical (so will pass through the centre axis) to a round work piece, mount the round in a jig like is shown above, or in a flat vice, and rest a flat piece of steel across the top, as shown below. A short work piece can be held on the open jaws of the flat vice, like I have here.

Lightly push down with the drill, without turning it on of course, and if the tip of the drill is above the centre axis, the strip will be horizontal.

The strip leaning to one side or the other means the drill tip is too far to the lower side of the strip.

The first photo shows the work needs to be moved to the right, and the second shows the drill is correctly aligned.

When it's correct, you can lock the drill down with the drill press quill lock (it stops the chuck from moving up or down), to keep the flat vice or angle steel jig positioned while you clamp it to the press table. Release the quill lock, start the drill and drill the hole. You can first drill a small pilot, with a centre bit, and then change to and bore with a larger drill; all without moving the jig clamped to the table.

The round work jig in use. The clamp which holds it to the table also holds the stop at the back. This stop has been trued, so when the work is clamped to it, the work is not only securely held, it is square and true. A thick washer under the second clamp's foot allows firm clamping, despite there being a large hole in the work.

The next photo shows a situation where multiple pieces have to have holes placed in similar places.

For **repetitive work**, to avoid tedious marking out many times, centre punch the hole site in the first piece, and run a pilot hole through. Turn the drill press off, and lock the pilot drill into the hole with the drill press quill lock. Now you can clamp a straight edge along the back of the work, down to the drill table. Also, clamp a block at one end of the work to the straight edge you clamped to the drill table. If the block is over the drill table, make sure there is a small gap under the block. This will ensure that no dust or swarf can get between the block and the work, so changing the point of the hole.

Because you won't mark each individual piece, you also don't have a centre punch mark to guide the pilot drill. Use a centre drill bit to make the pilot hole in each piece, as the centre drill bit won't wander. Each work piece can then be quickly returned to the jig for every different drill bit used.

Note the gap under the stop to prevent waste accumulating and preventing the correct positioning of the work.

SAWS

The three most common machine saws in the home workshop are usually the **Band Saw**, **Rip Saw** or **Saw Bench** (also called a **Table Saw**), and **Drop**, **Mitre** or **Cut Off Saws**. As well, you'll find the various handsaws; **Hack**, **Fret**, **Coping**, **Back**, **Pull**, and **Tenon Saws**.

Generally, saws can either be a steel blade with teeth cut from it, or a steel blade with carbide teeth added. There is of course a major difference. A steel blade will have the teeth cut into the steel blade, at whatever pitch, or teeth per inch, you buy. The teeth are uniformly spaced along the blade, and each tooth is alternatively bent to the right or the left. This is called the 'set' and is there to provide clearance for the saw, it makes the teeth cut slightly wider than the blade thickness, to avoid binding of the blade in the material, and also to give good removal of the waste. The less the pitch (so the fewer teeth per inch) the greater the set, as the teeth cut a bigger piece of material, and need more room to expel the waste.

The steel blade, in the home workshop is the most commonly found blade for band saws, hack, fret, coping, back, and pull saws, used for cutting wood, metals and plastic.

Whichever saw is being used, hand or machine, it is very important to let the saw work at a pace that it is able to. Forcing a powered saw through material, or pushing down too hard with a hand saw will invariably cause the saw to wander. Let the blade clear the swarf easily, and the cuts will be much more accurate. Keeping the blade clean, and lubricated (candle wax is a good cheap lubricant) will make cutting easier.

When using a hand saw it is really important to hold it correctly. With the forefinger pointing down the handle like this, you have a far greater control over the saw. Seems strange, but try it and see. It will become automatic.

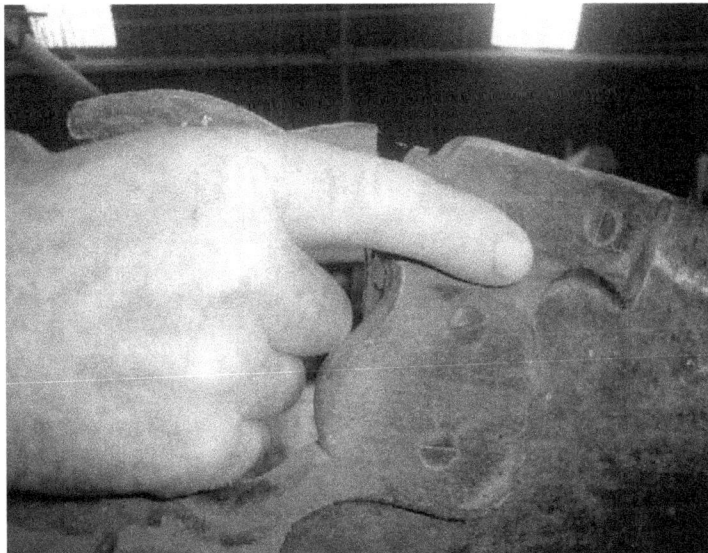

Joinery saws, such as the **Fret Saw** (with very fine blades in a hoop shaped frame for very fine work such a jigsaw puzzles) have a blade with tiny teeth (perhaps 40 per inch) with almost no set, which gives a very fine cut and will cut incredibly tight corners, right down to 3 or 4 mm in diameter. The blades are non serviceable, and held by a small clamp at either end, as are **Coping Saw** blades, but these, while still a fine blade, are much coarser and must face backwards, to cut on the pull. Coping saws too, will cut very tight corners, though not as tight as a fret saw, nor with as fine a result.

Back Saws have a strong steel stiffener along the top edge of the blade, to keep the thin blade straight. They cut on the push, have a small set, and give a nice accurate straight cut on wood and plastic; good for joinery, but definitely not metals. **Pull Saws** are the ultimate thin saws for straight cuts. As the name suggests, they cut on the pull, which means they can have a very thin blade, no top stiffener, no set, and give a very fine cut, ideal for fine joinery. A special sharpening stone is available from the saw's supplier, well worth getting as the local saw doctor probably won't be able to service it.

Hack Saws are the work horse of the home metal workshop. The blades are non serviceable, but are available in a good range of pitches. Use a course pitch for alloys and brass, fine for steel. Or go for say 32 TPI (teeth per inch) and cut everything with it, as I do. Works just fine!!! Use the orange blades if you can; black are fragile, blue better wearing with good hardness on the teeth, but orange are almost unbreakable, although with slightly less hardness. Worth some extra effort though, because you don't break so many blades!!!

A squirt of penetrating oil or candle wax on the blade really helps with accuracy and saves time and muscles!!

A home workshop may well have a **Band Saw**. They are available in a large range of sizes; some smaller ones have a third wheel to the left hand side to increase the swing without having to have huge wheels.
The band saw is a relatively safe saw, as the blade always works down, and the back of the blade is smooth. A band saw blade can easily be several metres in length. They give good long service, and are quite easily and inexpensively serviced. The saw doctor will just put it on his machine, and treat it as a very long hand saw.
A ½ inch wide blade is a very good size, it'll cut tight curves of 75 to 100mm, but is still wide enough for accurate straight cutting. Mind you, it is rare to fix a fence (a guide to keep the work straight when ripping) to a band saw with a blade as narrow as ½ inch, but for following a drawn line, ½ inch is fine. The finer the pitch, (in other words the more teeth per inch), the finer the cut, the harder the material it will cut, but the cut will be slower.
Personally, I never expect my band saw to cut steel: you need special fine toothed blades and very low cutting speeds and constant cooling liquid to do this effectively. However, a 6 or 8 teeth per inch saw will happily and quickly cut wood, plastic, alloy and brass, without cooling liquid, for a very long time.

If you need to cut tighter corners than 75mm diameter, you can use a narrower blade, but be aware that the teeth might start to run on your blade guides, not something that you want.

If you should want to 'rip' with your band saw, you can increase the blade width to the maximum your wheels will allow, and go for a courser pitch, say 4 or even 3 teeth per inch, clamp a piece of waste to the table as a fence, and use the band saw as a rip saw. Don't imagine you'll cut tight curves though!

Saw mills often run band saws, but the blades are huge.

Don't have the blade too tight. It shouldn't slip on the wheels of course, but there does need to be some flexibility.

Keep the top guide close to the work, a big gap above the work can lead to blade breakage. The blade should only rub onto and turn the rear bearing when cutting. When it's running free, the blade should barely touch the rear bearing. The top wheel has an adjustment for this.

Steel Band Saw blades are prone to damage that makes even cutting difficult. If you should strike a nail while cutting, say, an old fence post (they can have wonderful grain when turned), because the blade is so long it's likely that you'll only damage part of it. You might also only damage one side of that portion. So now the saw may 'pulse': when the damaged portion comes around, it may stop cutting completely, or it will cut to the side that has not been damaged. Obviously you'll need to have the blade serviced, but to finish the job you can even the teeth somewhat. Undamaged teeth will cut normally, while the damaged teeth won't, so the saw might cut to one side or the other, or not cut straight through. Run a piece of thick (2 inch or so) waste wood half way through so you can see exactly where the cutting edge of the blade is, and the blade is well controlled. Now you may be able to see the damaged area as it comes past. If the blade cuts to the right, the teeth on the left are damaged, so with a file, you can take some of the set off the right hand side. Not too much, just a gentle touch.

It will slow the overall cutting down of course, so work slowly and have the blade serviced as soon as you can. **Do not 'dress' tipped or hardened saw blades.**

'Dressing' a damaged **steel** band saw.

The **Table Saw** (saw bench) is the best way to rip wood, plastics and even alloys. Special blades are available for the various materials.

These saws will have an adjustable fence for cutting different widths, and a joinery bench saw usually will have an adjustable cutting height and tilt to just over 45°.

They will also often have a **Mitre Guide** which runs in a slot, so the work can have an angle cut on one end. While occasionally useful, this work is better done on a mitre saw or drop saw. With the mitre guide, it is difficult to pass the work through the table saw and keep it straight and level, while keeping the angle true.

The mitre guide in use.

For ripping long lengths, where possible have someone on the other side of the saw (called tailing out) to take the weight of the material as it goes through the saw, and help guide the work. Otherwise, you have to cut until the piece is able to be balanced on the table, and then walk around the machine to pull the work through and complete the cut.

Pivoting frames, called dimension saws, are available. They are attached to the table, and allow easy and accurate cutting of large sheets of plywood and the like.

The blade on the table saw turns towards the operator. It cuts down onto the bench top, but only for the front half of the blade. The back half is exactly opposite; it will lift the work off the bench if the work squeezes the blade. When ripping lengths of wood, internal stresses in the wood can mean that the pieces don't stay straight, either bending in or out. If they bend in, they may squeeze the blade and tend to lift the piece off the bench, cause drive belts to slip, or even stall the motor. Cut a small wooden wedge (the band saw is good for this) and hammer it into the cut, behind the blade, to keep the two pieces apart, as you can see in the next photo. Have the 'tailer out' do this, if you have one.

Smooth, easy and accurate cuts are made easier by keeping the tables clean and lubricated. Light oil rubbed in with steel wool is good, so is candle wax, again rubbed in with steel wool.

Carbide tips have almost completely replaced steel toothed blades on circular saws. These blades have a steel disc with carbide tips welded to the 'teeth'. There is no set as such, the tips are wider than the steel disc, and are shaped to a left and right configuration on their top surface.

Here is a quick, easy and accurate jig for cutting exact **Tapers** on a saw bench. The base of the jig is a rectangular piece of plywood. Its right hand edge runs against the saw's fence, and remains parallel to, and in contact with, the fence at all times. The piece to be angle cut is held between two guides, nailed to the plywood base. The right hand guide will determine the angle, the lower guide prevents the work slipping backwards, which would jam the saw in the cut. Moving the fence in and out will mean the cut piece changes in width, but the angle remains constant as that is decided by the angle of the right hand guide on the jig. Compound angles are easy too, simply by tilting the saw's arbour.

For ripping use a coarse, say 48, toothed blade, (though I have used a 12, and it ripped beautifully with really long shavings) and for crosscutting 80 to 120 or so is good. The greater number of (and therefore smaller) teeth give a better finish.

Blades for cutting alloys have a different tooth design, though a standard blade does quite well!! **Go very slowly, and hold very firmly.**

Carbide blades are best serviced by a saw doctor. Wonderful though they are, carbide blades are never as 'sharp' as a newly sharpened steel blade can be, because the carbide loses the sharp edges very quickly. This doesn't matter, of course, for most jobs, and in fact the longevity of the carbide tips is so good, it wins every time. Interesting point though.

While a really good joinery saw bench gives accurate rise and fall, and tilt, and is irreplaceable in the joiner's workshop, don't shy from making a break down saw bench if you are doing the sort of work that might need you to break demolition timbers or logs down to useable sizes.

I built and used a sturdy **BOLTED and GLUED** 100mm x 50 mm wood framed bench saw, below, with a 450mm diameter carbide blade run by a 5.5HP 3 phase (petrol would also do) motor for many years. I didn't have a machine lathe at the time, so had the spindle made, with simple 50mm diameter bearings, in plummer-block housings. No rise or tilt, just a fence, a 6 1/2 inch cut and loads of power. You need about 1HP per inch of cut depth.
My bench cost me less than $150 and was fantastic.

The modern **Mitre Saw** is a wonderful addition to the home workshop, effortlessly giving picture frame accuracy cuts, usually to 45°on both sides, plus 45° compound. They run Universal motors and are switched on for each cut, unlike the older drop saws with a bolt on motor which could be left running. Some have lasers to define, on the work, exactly where the cut will be. You still need to 'know' where your mark is though !!

The **Drop Saw** is a good robust machine, but it won't do a compound angle.

There's not much to say about either of them because they are so self contained, except for the usual maintenance; keep the blade sharp (you get better accuracy and less load on the motor) and lubricate any accessible parts, slides pivots etc. They can be permanently mounted on a bench, with long side supports to securely hold the material to be cut. When cutting pieces of the same length where a stop is used, either as a fixed hinge stop for often cut sizes or a clamped off cut, be sure to hold the cut piece, which is between the stop and the blade, to prevent the returning blade from pulling the cut piece upwards. It is often better to operate the saw with the left hand, and safely hold the cut piece with the right.
Feels a bit odd to start with, for a right handed operator who would usually operate the saw with the right hand, but it is very much safer.

This is a good example of a hinged stop, literally using a cut butt hinge bolted to the rear of the drop saw table.

This hinge has actually been cut into 3 pieces for 3 closely similar lengths of frequently cut sizes.

This is also where holding the work with the right hand and operating the saw with the left hand is good safe practice. Without holding the cut wood, the returning saw will lift the cut edge up, and it will jam between the blade and the stop.

Keep the stop raised above the bench, like you see below, to avoid a build up of waste gathering between the work piece and the end of the stop, so preventing the work piece from correctly touching the stop, resulting in the length changing.

The waste under the raised Stop would prevent accurate cutting if the Stop was at table height.

Power tools provide a good range of saws for the workshop, the **Jig Saw** being one of the handiest. As with all tools, buy the best you can afford. There is a good range of blades to fit jig saws, and it's important that you use the correct blade for the job. The blades have different profiles for different materials, wood, plastics and metals. They are incredibly good, even able to cut shapes in ¼ inch steel plate. They generally cut on the up stroke, so the work is pulled into the base plate, but reverse blades are available.

THICKNESSERS, PLANERS and MOULDERS

These machines all use a shaft mounted cutter block which has a number of knives bolted into it. The old style of a square block with slotted knives bolted to the outside are really very dangerous, the knives are prone to flying out and many serious injuries have occurred over the years. They should not be used. Replace the square block with a round one which has the knives held in slots machined into the block. They often have 2 or 3 knives. The piece must be put through these machines with the grain running back, or the finish will be compromised. However, sometimes with the surface planers and moulders, you have to run them backwards, to get a straight edge, before a final correct cut to get a good finish.

Machines which cut multiple sides and can take shaping knives and straight knives simultaneously exist as well, but are not often found in a home workshop.

A **Thicknesser** smoothes the top surface of the wood, making it flat and of a uniform thickness. It has a table with friction reducing rollers in it. The wood is supported on its underside by the table while the top surface is being planed. There is a drive roller with teeth to grip the wood in front of the cutter block, and a smooth roller behind it, both of which are spring loaded and bear on the top surface of the wood. These are driven by gears from the cutter block, which is driven from the motor.

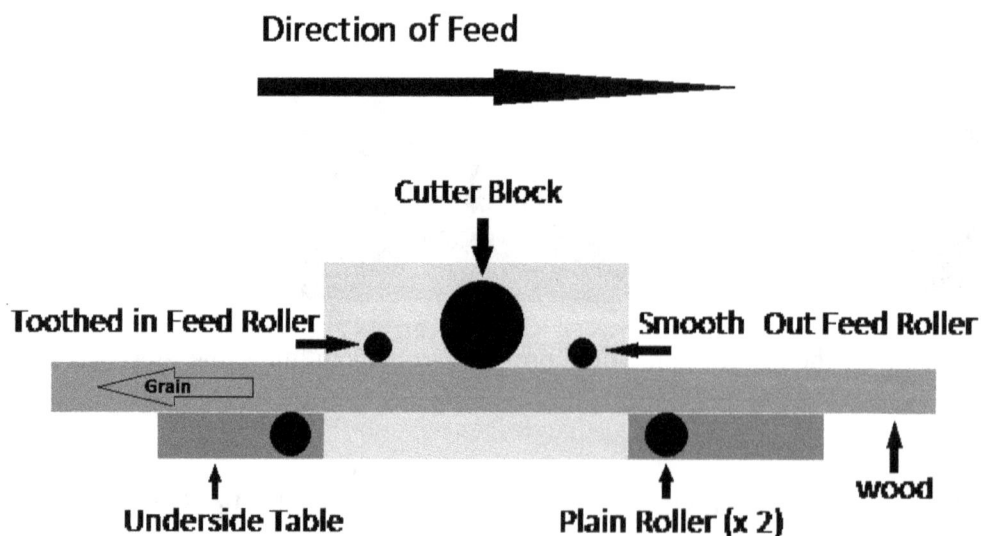

Direction of Feed

Cutter Block

Toothed in Feed Roller   **Smooth Out Feed Roller**

Grain

Underside Table   **Plain Roller (x 2)**   wood

Diagram of the essential parts of a thicknesser.

A piece of wood is fed under the toothed roller, and after the top surface has been machined, is fully extracted from the machine by the smooth roller.

A thicknesser has limited ability to straighten curves from a piece of wood (because the table is relatively short), and in fact can follow a gentle radius quite well. Straightening can be done, however, if the bent piece is mounted as shown below (in a very exaggerated diagram) on a true, flat, board, which is feed through the thicknesser with the bent piece on top. Provide stoppers front and back to control the work, and also underneath so the pressure of the sprung loaded rollers doesn't temporarily flatten it. Once the top side is true you can reverse the wood, and thickness it in the usual way. This way you can straighten boards too wide for the surface planer.

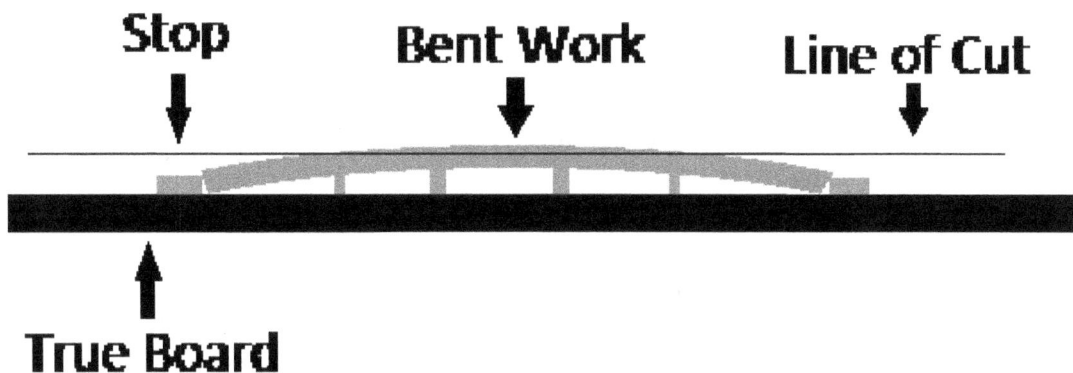

Straightening bent wood with a thicknesser

There is little maintenance required, other than keeping the bed clean and smooth, the bearings greased, and the knives sharp and correctly set. Most machines come with a set up guide for the knives, and all will have a removable cover over the top of the knife block to allow access to the knives. If you don't have a set up guide, then set the knives to the same height above the knife block surface at each end, with a projection of 3mm or so. When you run the first piece through the machine, measure the result and compare it with the gauge on the machine. From the difference, if there is one, you can work out the correct projection of the knives to coincide with the gauge.

A thicknesser can be used to cut pieces to the same width once they have been straightened on the surface planer. However, to gauge say a 4 x 1 can be awkward as the 1 inch side on the lower table doesn't really have enough stability, and can easily tilt off square. To give stability clamp it to a square block. Be sure to have the clamp low enough to pass the cutters, or put another clamp on at the out feed as it comes through, and remove the one on the in feed side before it goes into the machine.
If you try to plane several pieces at once, only a few of them will drive through so you can clamp them together and send them through as one piece. This will drive them all at once, and keep them square, with the same comments about the clamps as before.

Surface Planers or Buzzers

have the cutter block mounted between two tables.

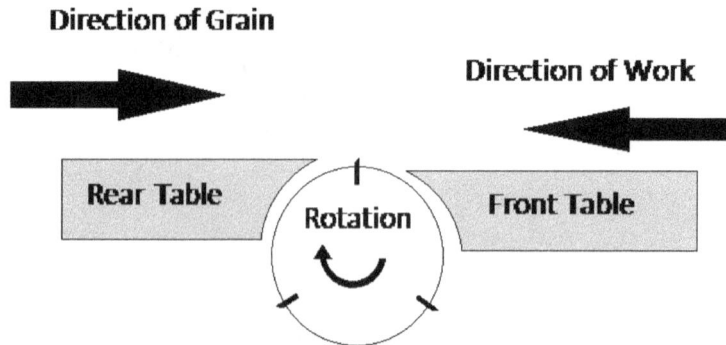

Often both the tables are on slides which are at 45° from the horizontal, and 90° from each other, though sometimes the rear table is fixed. There is a fence at the back (right hand side when using the machine) that will control the work piece. When the fence is at right angles to the tables (lengthwise) the cut edge will be at right angles to the surface in contact with the fence. The fence can be angled to produce angled cuts. As the cutter block is at least 6 inches and above in width, it is clear that while truing the edge of a 25mm thick board, at least 5 inches of the cutter block, and therefore the knives, is exposed. There is a safety cover which can be moved so that it covers the knives right up to the edge of the wood, and this must be correctly adjusted every time the machine is used.

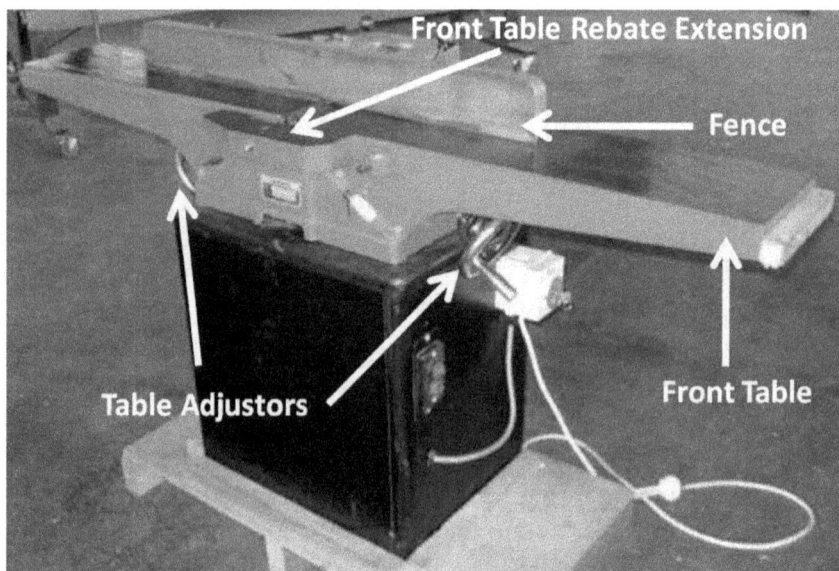

A Rebating Buzzer or Surface Planer

In this photo, the cutter safety cover on the left hand side has been removed to clearly show the rebate extension, see p 64. You can see the hole for the safety cover holder in front of the indicating arrow for the extension.

The rear table is the reference for the knife height, which, for most work, should be set to a fraction of a mm above the table height. If the rear table is adjustable, set the knives at table height using a steel ruler on edge along the table and projecting out, over the knife, and adjust the table afterwards. If not, a piece of paper on the table surface and under the steel rule will give a good amount of extra height to the knives.
The depth of cut is determined by lowering the front table. The work is pushed from the front table to the rear table.

Buzzers can perform a wide variety of tasks.
If you want to join several planks together to make a table top, for example, you must first straighten the edges of the pieces.

To straighten a bend in a very badly bent piece, as shown below, you will need to start in the middle and cut through. You can do this as often as you need, with each cut being
 longer than the one before.

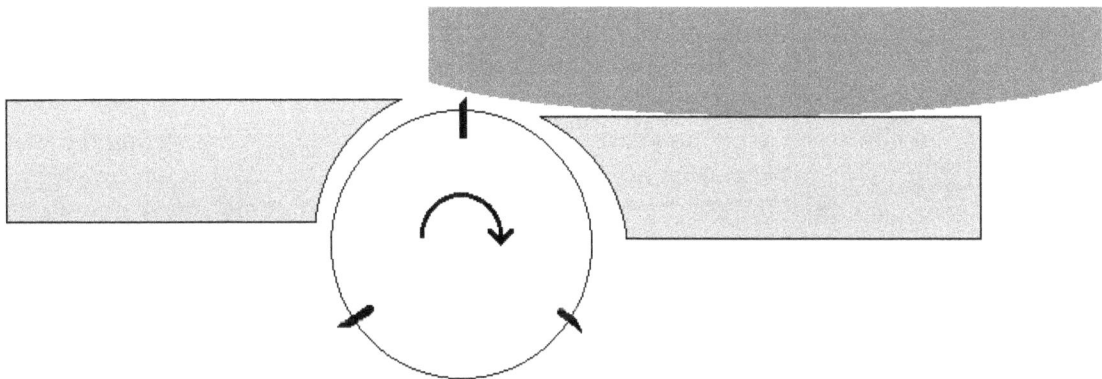

For a piece bent the other way, start as shown below, cut through, reverse the piece and do it again until you can cut all the way along, in the right direction, in one pass.

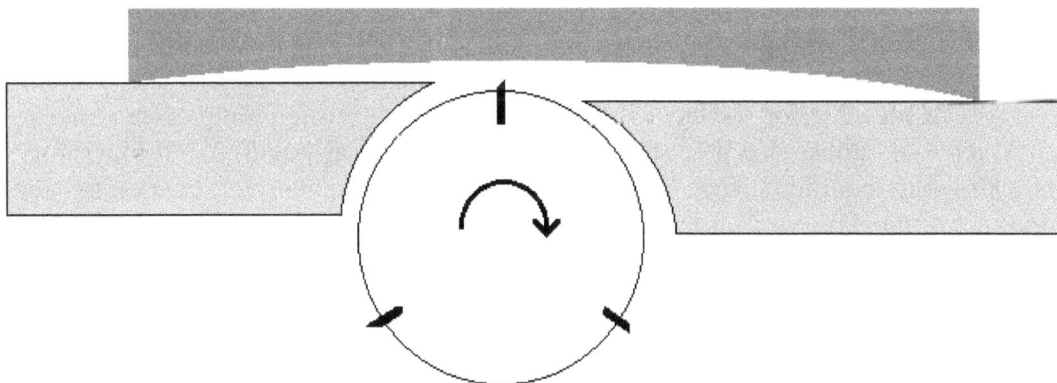

Once you have a straight edge, you can use that edge as a reference for the table saw (or thicknesser if the pieces are not too big), to cut the other edge straight. Then, if you've used the saw, you can plane the second edge smooth.

Fence ——→ ←—**Rear Table**

**Front Table
Extension** ——→

←—**Cutter Block**

Wood——→

←—**Front Table**

Finished Rebate

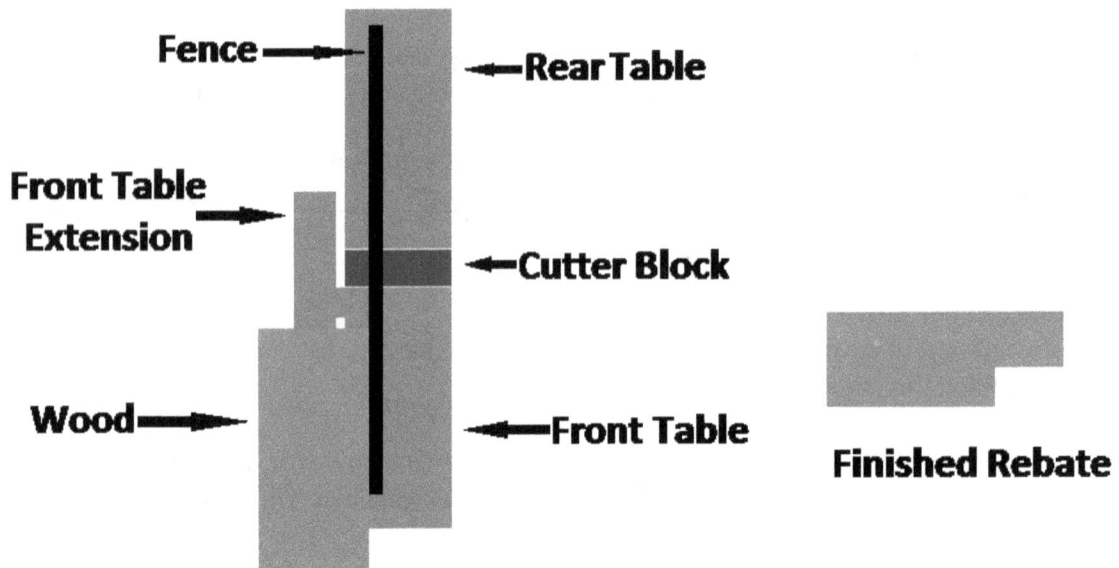

A diagram looking **down** on a Surface Planer cutting a **Rebate.**

The front table on a planer sometimes has an extension to the left hand front side. This extension is to allow you to cut a **rebate** in the edge of the wood, by supporting the work when most of it would otherwise be off the table entirely.
The fence is brought in to the required amount, and the front table lowered to give the correct depth to the rebate. If it is a deep rebate, lowering the front table and rebating in several steps, will prevent tearing and give a better finish than a single big cut.

A **Shaper** or **Spindle Moulder** is like a buzzer with the cutter block spinning vertically, instead of horizontally, with the shaft bearings below the table. There are no bearings on the top of the cutter block, just a large nut for tightening the cutter block onto the shaft. The shaft is in the centre of a large strong table, and can be raised or lowered. Different cutting blocks can be mounted on the shaft; straight cutters are used as you would the surface planer, for straightening the edges of a piece of wood, shaped cutters accept shaped knives to allow you to make all kinds of mouldings instead of just straight vertical cuts.
The work slides on the table of the machine, with front and rear fences at the back, standing vertically up from the machine table. They are adjusted **front to back** in the same way as the tables on the buzzer are **raised and lowered** for depth of cut, but can be moved left and right so that they support the work as close as possible to the cutters, while allowing room for shaped knives. Spring steel pressure bars can be used to keep the work back against the vertical fences, and an adjustable safety cage covers the block.

For straightening edges, the knives are set up in the same way as those of the surface planer, on page 63.

The photo below shows these features. The rotation of the cutting head is **into** the direction the work is pushed, the same as surface planers and thicknessers.

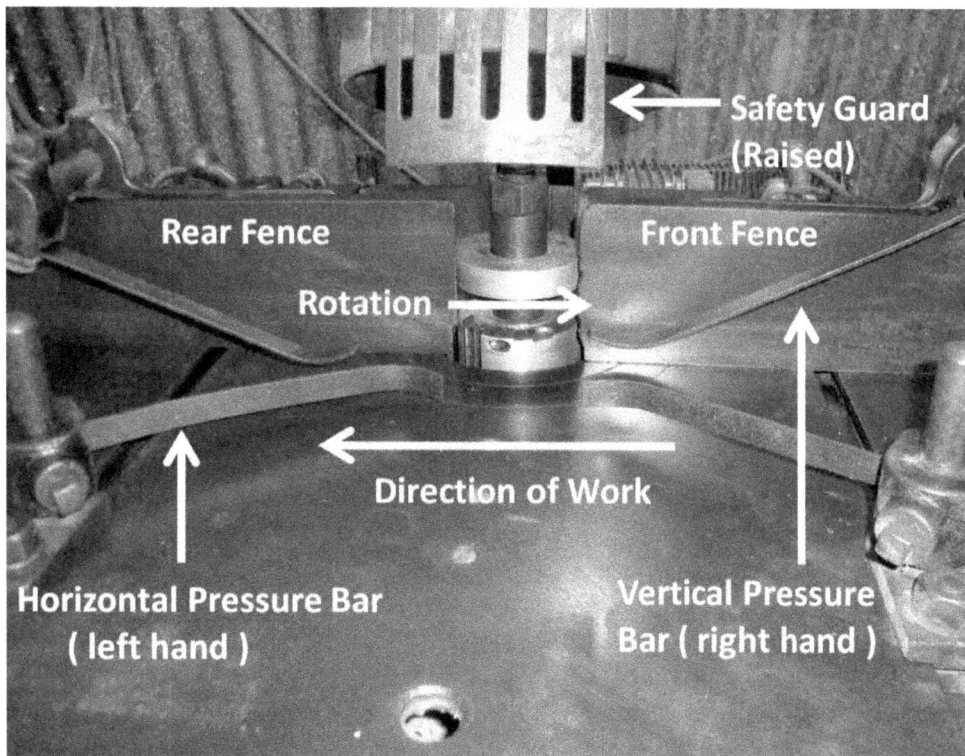

Rebating

The shaft can be lowered in the table until only a small amount of the cutter block is showing above the table, and with correct fence adjustments, a rebate can be cut into the wood.

The fences, which run either side of the cutter block, are positioned as shown in the diagram below.

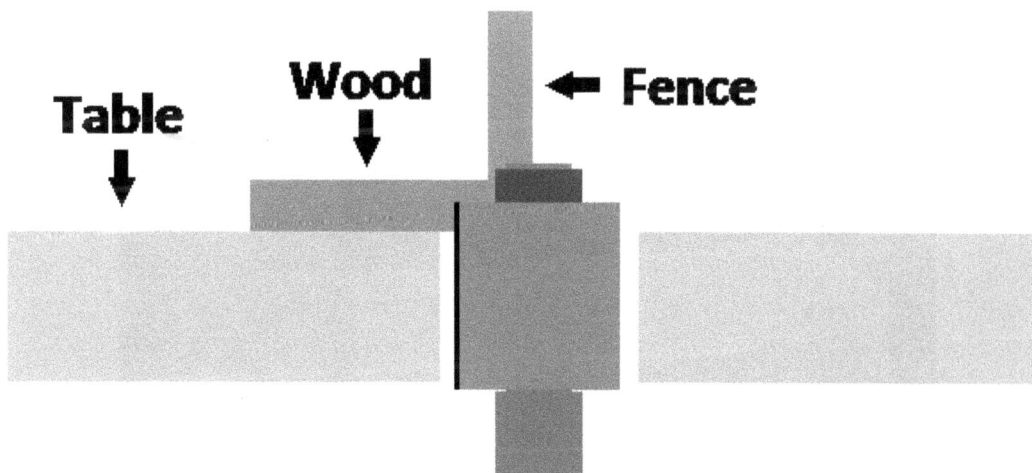

Surface planers and spindle moulders can also cut accurate **Tapers** and **Blind Rebates**.

In the photo above, the moulder's rear table is set to the usual height for a straight cut, and the front table to the amount of **Taper** required.

The leading tip of the work is rested on the front edge of the **rear** table, and the end tip of the work on the front table. The taper will be cut to the depth of the front table height. For longer work than the front table allows, a straight piece of wood, or something similar, can be clamped (above the work height) to the front table. The depth of cut must, of course, allow for this extra width, though the rear table remains at the same setting. Clamping a raised stop, as shown, to the front table is essential, as it prevents an accident if the leading tip of the work is put into the cutting head **at the full taper depth**, instead of resting on the rear table. In such a case, the work will be violently thrown back towards the front table. The stop will also allow for exact repetitions of the taper. The setup is identical for the surface planer.

Blind Rebates can also be accurately and safely cut on the moulder or buzzer too.

In the photo above, you can see a **blind rebate**, cut on a spindle moulder.

Here, the front and rear tables are set to the same height, which is the depth of the rebate. The front stop is **absolutely essential** to avoid a nasty throwback, and also to accurately determine the starting point of the rebate. The rear stop is required to determine the end point of the rebate. When starting the cut, make sure the rear end of the work is in solid contact with the front stop and front table, and then swing the work into contact with the cutter, until the full depth is reached. Go slowly, and firmly hold the work; the cut is largely uncontrolled at the start because the work is unsupported at the cutting point until the front edge of the work is in contact with the rear fence. The full length cut may then be made. Keep the stops above the table to avoid waste building up at the edge, and changing the cut length.

Below is a diagram of the set up, at the start of the cut. Note the raised stops. If you view this diagram from a horizontal perspective it is a surface planer setup. Viewed from a vertical perspective, it shows the procedure on a spindle moulder.

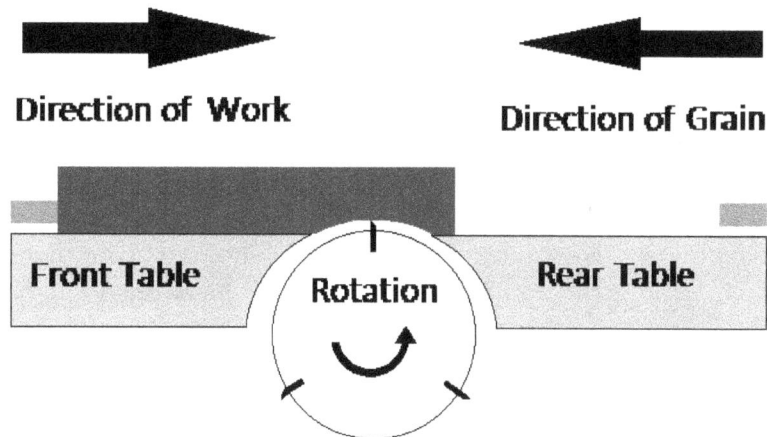

Direction of Work   **Direction of Grain**

Front Table   **Rotation**   **Rear Table**

The next photo shows an interesting variation on a blind rebate with flats being machined onto a turned piece. This one is actually a mid-section of a longer assembly.

The usual stops are used to control the start point, to ensure the flats begin inside the small diameter of the 'vase' shape, and also the end point, to avoid running the flat into the next section where the join (see page 90) will be. Because I want the six flats to be equidistant around the diameter of the piece, I've screwed an hexagonal ply pattern to the end, with a screw long enough to reach the bottom of the join hole. At the other end, the oversized spigot is required to keep the work at the chosen angle for the flats. Without this, the rear table would bear on the top of the 'vase', and the angle of the taper would be steeper. I will now remount the piece in the lathe and machine the spigot to the right size to join the next piece.

Another extremely useful feature of the spindle moulder is the ability to follow patterns.

Here, the front and rear fences are removed to allow 360° use of the table (other than where the safety guard mounts), and a bearing (or disc with a bearing fitted to the inside) is placed above the top of the cutter head, separated from it by a spacer, and secured with the cutting head nut. The work piece is roughly cut to shape, on the band saw for example, and an exact plywood pattern is screwed (where the screw holes won't matter) to the top surface, again with a spacer. The bearing on the top of the cutter block runs against this pattern, and so the cut follows the pattern exactly. It's easier if the outer diameter of the bearing is the same as the cutting diameter of the knives, as this means the pattern is made to the exact finished size. If your bearing is of a different diameter to the cut diameter, the pattern has to be sized accordingly.

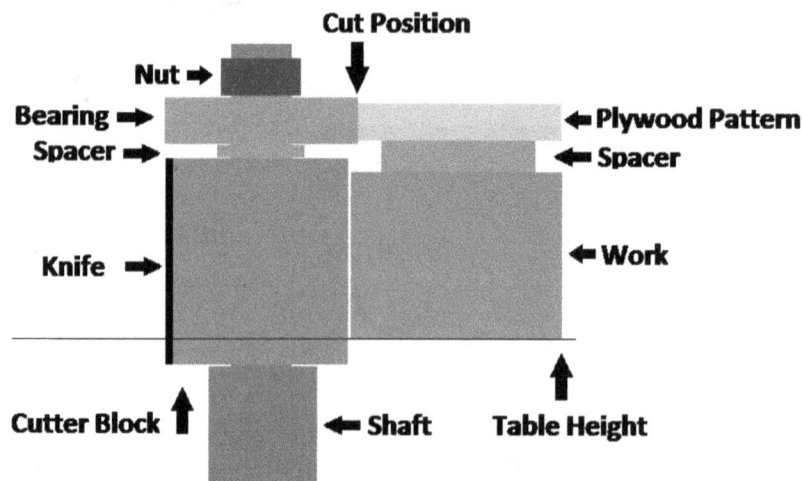

Here is the set up for following a pattern.

The work is pushed into the cutting block until the bearing prevents it from getting any closer. You then work your way around until all the sides of the wood have been cut to size. It will follow almost any shape exactly, and with sharp knives a very good finish is possible.

The next photo also shows this arrangement.

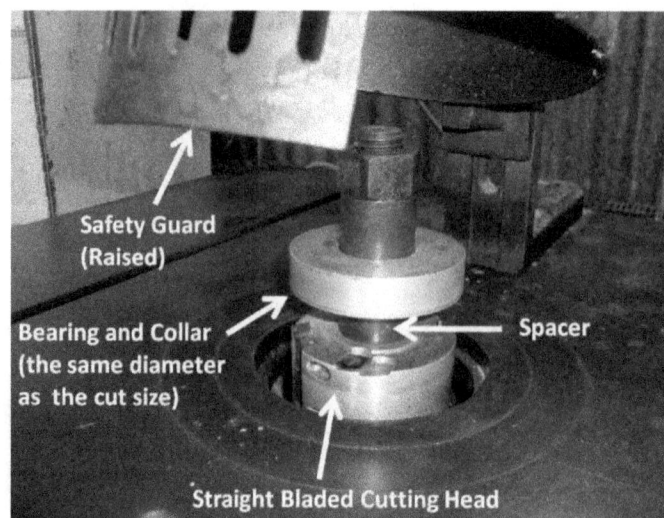

WOOD LATHES

A Lathe is one of the most useful machines in the home workshop, either a wood lathe, a metal lathe, or preferably both!! As there are endless good guides available for techniques of lathe work, we'll just concern ourselves here to general comments and hints.

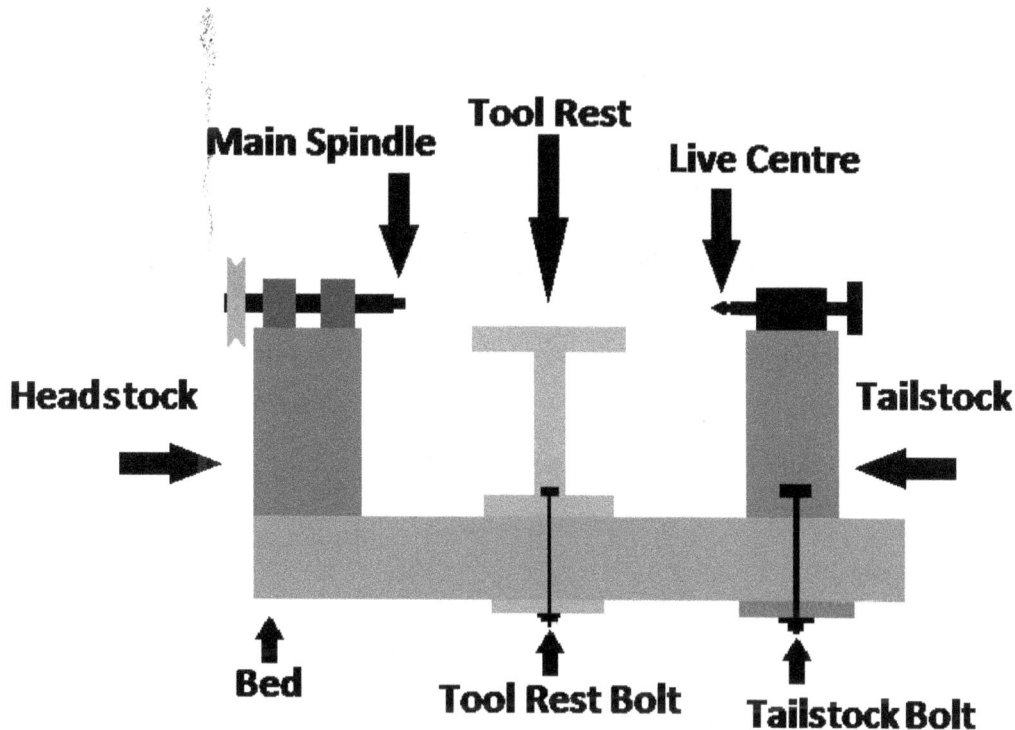

Parts of the Wood Lathe.

The **Wood Lathe** usually drives the piece to be turned, when working between the centres, with a Spur Centre, with either 2 or 4 blades. The Spur Centre has a tapered shaft which fits into a tapered hole in the end of the main lathe head stock spindle. The outside of the main spindle will have a course thread on it, (photo page 99) which will accept a Faceplate and, if possible, a chuck. The Spur Centre gives good drive to the wood, and doesn't get in the operators way, as a chuck can.

If you file a small edge off one of the blades on the Spur Centre, then remounting the piece in exactly the same position, should you need to, is very easy, as the indentation in the end of the wood is 'indexed', and avoids any mis-alignment which may be caused by the Spur Centre not being exactly symmetrical.

This spur centre has had a small angle filed off one tine or blade.

Here are a variety of taper-shank spur centres.

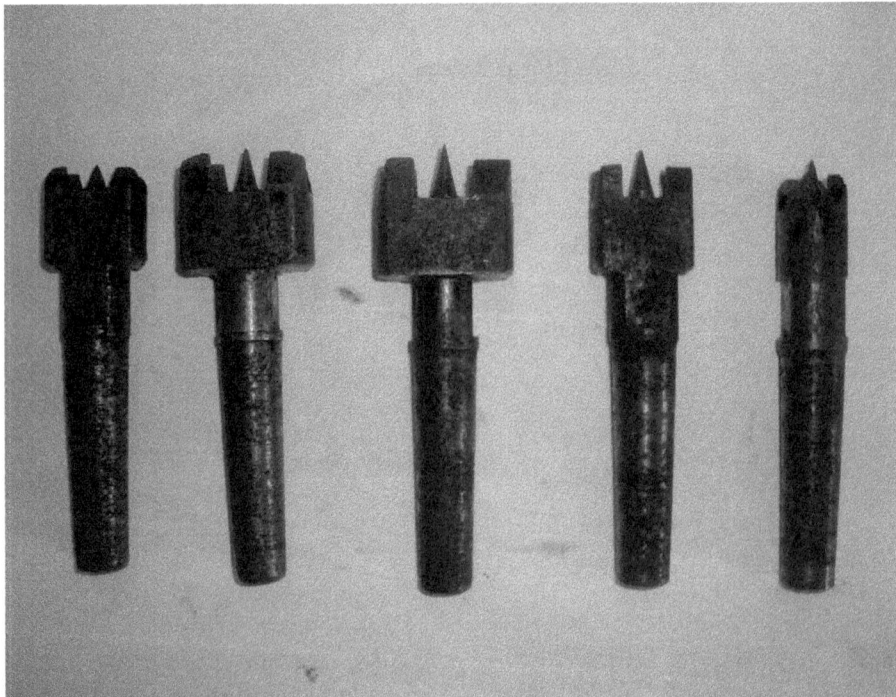

At the other end of the piece of wood, you have the tailstock. In my opinion, a 'live' or 'running' centre (one where the point is mounted on bearings and can spin with the wood) is essential. A 'dead' centre requires constant lubrication, (and may burn anyway), and it will inevitably loose thrust and allow chatter. Don't bother with one.

Be sure to remove it when you're working with the faceplate, a jab in the right elbow with the tailstock point is unpleasant.

A ½ inch drill chuck mounted on a taper to fit the tailstock, for drilling holes, is a good idea for a wood lathe, and these days not an expensive tool.

A **gap bed** lathe has a removable section near the headstock, to allow extra diameter work 'in board'.

With the full bed.

With the Gap.

Because of the extra distance from the end of the permanent bed to the work face, support the end of the tool rest with some blocks down to the bed, as you see above.

A Faceplate is a must for work not supported by the tailstock, but of course, if you have a 3 (or 4) jaw chuck that fits on the Main Spindle, you can use this in some cases instead. Generally, it's O.K to screw the work piece directly to the face plate. Where possible, I like to place those screws where they will be hidden. So for example, on a stool top, I'd like to have the screws placed where the holes for the legs will eventually be.
Don't hesitate to drill extra holes in the Faceplate to accommodate specially placed screws, though this one of mine has plenty to choose from.
Always use holes at as large a diameter on the Faceplate as possible.

Alternative Mountings.

For large items Screw a piece of thick plywood or particle board to the Faceplate, and then you can effectively have the 'Faceplate' as large as you like. Do make the board thick though, to reduce the chatter.

You can screw a piece of scrap on the Faceplate, true it, and then, with a soft glue like PVA, glue a piece of paper to the scrap wood, and then glue the work piece to the paper. Once cured, you can turn the piece, and when done, separate the work from the scrap by tearing the paper apart by inserting a knife, for example. Residual glue is easy to scrape off the finished work.

In the case of a bowl, where both the in and outsides of the work will be turned, you can make and use a **Friction Chuck**, where, as the name suggests, friction holds the work in place.

Turn the outside of the bowl first, allowing a small shoulder as the base. Now mount some scrap wood on the Faceplate, machine it true, then cut a recess into it so that it is a tight fit around the shoulder on the outside of the bowl. That way you won't have to remount the chuck and it will be running perfectly true.

Here is the finished outside of the bowl with the shoulder ready for the chuck which is on the Faceplate.

The next picture shows the bowl blank mounted in the chuck, ready for the inside hollowing out operation.

When the bowl is hollowed out, you can carefully nudge the bowl from the recess with the ball of you palm. If it's very tight, and you're nervous about damaging your work, split the scrap wood with a chisel to free it.

Various steel chucks are available that will do this, but I always preferred to make wooden friction chucks like I've just described, not only because they are easy to make, but also because they are so cheap, and a 10 inch diameter steel chuck isn't!!

Don't worry if you make the recess a little too large - a very easy thing to do!! Just wrap some insulation tape around the bowl shoulder, to get a good fit. Make sure you have some of the last circle of tape wrapped right over the bottom edge and underneath, so you don't simply push the tape up when you push it into the recess. Insulation tape is good, because it is a little spongy, and so grips well.

The wooden chucks work well for things like goblets and egg cups too, but whereas a bowl has a large diameter and so a shallow recess will do, the smaller diameter goblets need to have a little more depth to the recess.

A **Screw Chuck** is also a valuable tool for turning Faceplate mounted items, and is both quick to make and extremely cheap, though commercial ones are, of course available.

One came with my lathe when I bought it which fits into a tapered hole in the end of the main lathe head stock spindle, but it's often too small.

 Essentially, a **home made** one is just a wood screw driven through a (face trued) scrap piece mounted on the Faceplate, and which extends for some distance out. The work piece is simply screwed onto this screw until it's tight against the scrap. Use a strong, large, course, and fully threaded screw.

This finished disc was mounted on the home made Screw Chuck and the (what would become the rear) surface trued and finished. Then it was re-mounted the other way round and the edge and front face machined.

You do need the surface of the work to be fairly true as well, so there is good friction between it and the scrap.

For small items, I like to first rough the wood out between the centres. That way you can easily prepare long lengths, maybe a metre long, so that when you cut the goblet sized pieces on the drop saw, the end cut will be nicely square to the sides. Always bore a pilot hole the size of the unthreaded portion of the screw shank (preferably in a press to keep it true) because, as you're using the screw along the grain instead of across it, a pilot hole will give the screw a better bite.

When you're finished, just unscrew the work.

If the screw becomes loose in the scrap, screw the work to it by using a screwdriver from the inside of the back of the Faceplate.

Don't worry if the screw isn't **exactly** in the centre, as long as you have enough diameter on the work to be able to lose a little bit. It will turn to a true axis, irrespective of where the screw is. You will, of course, have a screw hole in the bottom of the piece.

Don't dismiss the 3 Jaw Chuck as a way to hold suitable pieces of wood, on a wood lathe.

Here, the inside of this piece has been finished, and put over the chuck. The jaws have been extended to grip the inside edges.

Holding a hollowed out blank with a 3 jaw chuck with the jaws inside the work, and expanded to grip the edges.

If you want to work both the front and some of the way round the back of a piece which is smaller in diameter than the faceplate, without the trouble of remounting, screw a very thick piece of scrap to the Faceplate, perhaps 2 inches thick. Then turn it down until it is less in diameter than the minimum diameter required on the back of the work piece. You can then make this into a Screw Chuck with a long screw. The extra distance between the Faceplate and the thick scrap will give you the room needed to easily turn around the back of the piece.

It is almost impossible to quickly remount a piece with screws, say to work the other side, and have it run exactly true.

You can do this by cutting a recess, as discussed before with the Friction Chuck, (page 73) but instead of having the fit tight enough to machine the other side with friction holding the work in place, you use the recess as the centring guide, and secure the work with screws from behind.

Alternatively, you can glue and screw at least three scrap pieces to a faceplate mounted disc of plywood or particle board, and when cured, use a parting tool to cut the inside edge of these pieces to the correct diameter for your work, which is then secured by screws from behind.

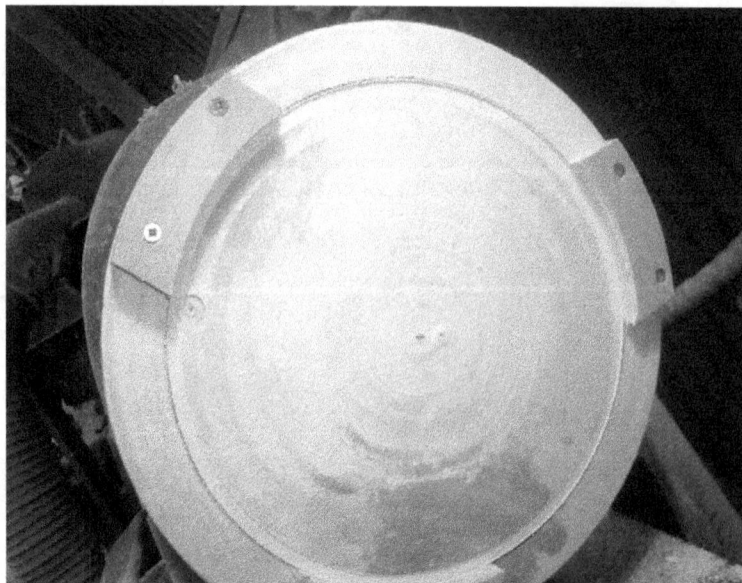

Ready for the work piece to be mounted, and screwed from behind.

This next photo shows what was a fun project to make: a wooden Corinthian Column to be used as a mould for some concrete ones to adorn a new building.

Built up and machined particle board ends were added later.

The tube itself is a laminate of 2 x 4 pine, cut with an angle on each long side, with temporary ply ends for mounting in the lathe.

I have joined two lathes together (the right-hand side one using the outboard side of the headstock) to achieve the extra length, clamping a 12 x 2 to either bed. For extra peace of mind, homemade 'hose clamps' are at each end, just to be sure it wouldn't delaminate.

It didn't!!

The main drive is from a Faceplate. The tool rest looks quite inadequate, but it was only there to machine the end section. For cutting the main body, I assembled a long single piece of angle iron for the tool rest. Also of interest in this photo is the use of the wooden pulley on the headstock spindle (wooden pulleys are discussed later), a second electric switch at the tailstock end for convenience when turning long lengths, and a clear view of the construction of the wooden lathe, which is also discussed later.

Finishing.

Of course, keeping the tools sharp, and making the final cuts very light will give the best finish to the wood. However, almost always sandpaper, or sand cloth is used to get a really fine finish. Naturally, you start with a course grit, (measured in the same way as the grinding stones, so 40 grit is courser than 150 grit) and finish with fine grit, or perhaps even steel wool. There are a large number of kinds of sandpaper and abrasives available, and to get the best results you need the right stuff.

The major points are what the abrasive actually is made of, what the backing is made of, and what the adhesive that holds the abrasive to the backing is made of. Inevitably, some of the grit will be embedded in the wood, so using tools again after sanding will blunt the tools very quickly. Unavoidable if you've made a blunder.

Of course, the term 'sandpaper' harks back to the days when sand was used, but **Garnet,** a hard mineral, is a great abrasive and gives good service. I can no longer source the 'E Type Backing', which is a shame as it had a very durable paper, and an adhesive which would stand the high temperatures generated by wood lathe sanding. The '216 Type' backing is almost as good. Do be careful before you buy a 50 metre roll!! Ask your supplier exactly what the paper is designed for, and if it's suitable for lathe work. Try a small bit before you buy a full roll. Paper designed for low temperature hand sanding will not stand the rigors of turning work.

Also available is cloth backed sheet, the sort of thing that is used on sanding belts for power sanders and machine sanders. The cloth is very flexible and tough, but it is more difficult to have a hard edge to it, because it's a cloth rather than a hard paper. I prefer paper for hand sanding turning work because that hard edge, even better when you fold the paper over, is just the thing for getting into deep beads, and will roll agreeably to maintain your hard worked for radii on your beads and vases!!

A final polishing with steel wool is a good way to finish. Steel wool is available in a range of coarseness, so having a course and a fine is a good idea. You can get it in either pads (large or small, I prefer the large) or in a long length, which you can cut into smaller more easily managed sizes. The long strands of the steel wool are able to catch on the work, particularly on any rough unfinished parts at the ends of the work where the centres are. If this happens, it will try, (and often successfully!!), to wrap the entire pad around the work, ripping it out of your hands in the process. So do be careful with steel wool on revolving pieces. Short pieces cut from a long length are more prone to this; the pads have fewer loose strands.

Strangely enough, hand sanding on a wood lathe is easier if you reverse the direction of the spindle. When you do this, the paper is taken away from you, rather than pushed towards you. It's easier to keep the paper tight when it is taken away, than it is to stop it bunching up when it's pushed towards you.

 A STRONG WORD OF WARNING here though, for sanding Faceplate work in reverse. Faceplates screw onto the spindle so that the action of turning will tighten the Faceplate to the spindle. Reversing the direction will mean the Faceplate will UNSCREW when the drag of the sandpaper is applied or even with just the force of starting up. Unless you have a way to lock the faceplate onto the spindle so it CANNOT unscrew, do not attempt to reverse the direction of rotation when using a faceplate. A 300mm diameter bowl running at 800 rpm will hit the floor (and maybe you as well) at nearly 50 kph, destroying the bowl, and maybe whatever else is in the way.

MORE COMMENTS:

Removing the corners off pieces that are intended to become fully round saves roughing out time, allows tool rests to be closer right from the start, and makes lots of fine pieces of kindling or glue sticks! Quite a time saver on very large diameter pieces. Similarly, mount a bowl blank on the Faceplate, attach the Faceplate to the lathe, and **BY HAND** turn the blank and draw a perfect concentric circle on the BACK of the bowl blank. You can then cut to the circle on the band saw, with the Faceplate still in place. The piece will run true from the start, and you won't have to slowly take off the corners. No band saw? Use the table saw, hand saw or even chain saw for very large pieces to cut the blank into an octagon (or more) based on the circle you've drawn. It all helps speed up the roughing out process.

A range of tool rests of different lengths is a great thing to have, especially if you are doing a large run of spindles or balustrades for example. You can make them quite easily, by welding a length of 'L' angle steel to a short piece of steel that will fit into the tool rest hole. Make them sturdy, 40 or 50 X 6mm or so, and for the long ones, support the ends with a tightly fitting piece of scrap, wedged between the lathe bed and the underside of each end of the new tool rest. You have to have the rest set up in the one position for the whole run, which does mean that the distance between the tool rest and the work face will increase as the work proceeds.

This can actually become quite a large distance. On a 3 inch square piece, the rest is about 2 inches from the centre axis at the start, to avoid the square edges. If you then turn parts of the piece down to, say, 1 ½ inches, you are 1 ¼ inches from the tool rest and the work face. Quite a long way, so keep the tools sharp, and take small, slow cuts. Taking the corners off before you mount the work means that the rest is considerably closer right from the start, as mentioned above.

Long pieces are very prone to chatter. The work will move away from the tool until the elastic nature of the wood makes it spring back in. So you get a terrible cut, and in an extreme situation with long thin pieces, even breakage. A work steady can be mounted on the lathe bed to support the wood and prevent the vibration. They are rarely satisfactory. You have to machine a true section on the work where they can run, and then have them tight enough to prevent the chatter. The friction will burn the wood, even with waxing the contact area, and then of course, it will be loose enough to start the whiplash all over again. By far the best solution, in my experience, is to hold the tool in the right hand, as per normal, and just rest your left hand thumb on the very end of the tool, right up where the cut is, for control and guidance. Then, you can wrap the 4 fingers of the left hand gently around the work. With a small amount of practice, you'll control the chatter perfectly, with no discomfort. On thin pieces, say 1 inch square or less, it's quite O.K to rest your hand there as described when roughing from square.

For all my work, I just sharpen the tools with an electric bench grinder, running a white wheel of about 100 – 120 grit. I prefer the 200 mm diameter wheels, because the radius it grinds is, for most of the working life of the wheel, larger.

You can spend a long time honing the tool with a hand held stone to a very sharp edge, only to lose it in the first few seconds of work.

The SIDES, not just the front, of the parting tool and the skew chisel are also very good cutting edges. They are just as sharp as the front tip, and are very stable. So, for example, to cut a flat angled face on a spindle, you could make a straight cut with a parting tool, and then use a skew chisel to make the angle. Or you could stay with the parting tool, and use the edge to cut the angle. The finish is usually very good with the edge cuts.

Using the edge of a parting tool.

A **Scraper** is a flat tool with only one bevel. It is very difficult to persuade a scraper to give a good finish, they are prone to chatter, and are poor at creating nice shapes.
You might employ one if you need to turn a lot of chair legs, and want a quick way to make a long spigot to fit into the holes in the bottom of the seat. Here, the finish doesn't matter (in fact, a rough finish will glue better). The spigot is always at one end or the other of the lathe, well supported by a centre, so will be less likely to chatter.

The Headstock is the sturdiest end of the lathe. You will find it easier if you work from the tailstock towards the headstock. This is because you will have the greatest amount of wood still on the piece between the tool and the headstock, and there will be considerably less chatter. So with a chair leg, have the square section (if there is one) at the headstock end, rough down towards the tailstock, and then work back towards the headstock with the decorations. At the finish, you'll have the square section, maybe 2 or 3 inches square and 3 or 4 long at the headstock, and the foot of the chair leg, which may be as small as 1 inch diameter, at the tailstock end.

If you have some chatter marks that, try as you might, WON'T go away, try changing the speed of the spindle. Sometimes a harmonic is set up, and the tool simply follows it, and changing the rpm of the piece can disrupt this basic harmonic, and allow a proper cut.

Spirals are often done on a lathe, and some fancy jigs for holding routers and cutters are available. To make a spiral by hand only the preparation requires the 'normal' use of the lathe. Mount the stock (the wood) in the lathe, and rough down to round the section where the spiral will be. You may have square sections at either end, or a foot at one end. Mark 4 straight lines down the work, at 90□ to each other. If you have a square section, use this to give an easy guide. Now decide on your 'pitch' and mark down the length at this division, say every 60mm. Run the lathe and make these 60mm (or whatever they are) apart marks go right round the wood. Turn the lathe off, and use some sticky tape to mark the spiral by winding the tape around the wood, with one edge of the tape going from the intersections of the long axis lines with the circumference lines, so marking out a regular 'thread'. By using tape you can keep the edge straight. Now draw a pencil line down that side of the

tape, and remove it. This line is the centre of the spiral. Now you use handsaws, rasps files and sandpaper to create the spiral profile either side of it. You could do this on a bench, but held between the centres as it is, you can easily turn the piece round and round. Running the tape in the other direction gives the anticlockwise spiral.

Sanding Drums

A simple and cheap sanding drum (expensive pneumatic ones are available) for sanding curves can be made on the lathe by holding a piece of wood between the centres, or bolted to the Faceplate and roughing it down to a flat and smooth cylinder. A dedicated Faceplate can be made (just a nut welded to a disc) and used for frequently used drums. If you are careful with the diameter (including allowing for paper thickness) you can make **very** exact shapes. The paper can be simply glued on. You can use a contact adhesive, and, if the diameter is not crucial, when the paper is worn out, glue another one on top. Eventually, it'll become too thick with old papers, so you'll have to rip them all off and start again. Disc cement will allow you to remove the sheet easily, and add another to the wooden surface. Either way, make sure that if you have an overlap that it's in the right direction, so that when the drum turns, the work is not able to lift up the edge of the cut end of the paper. So for a lathe turning in the normal direction, i.e. towards you at the top, attach the paper at the top and go in the **opposite** direction to the rotation so that the **last** end of the paper to be stuck down is **over** the first end. You'll have to put a bit of glue along the grit side of the paper, where the final end will go. An overlap will mean the diameter is not exact though. You can, instead of glue, put a fine saw cut along the drum, say 25mm deep. Now push the end of the paper into the cut, and stretch it around the drum. You can push the other end into the slot as well, or even leave it loose. Once it's spinning it'll be O.K; it'll flap about a bit when running free but will behave itself when working. See page 86.

You can make the drums in any size you want. For **between centre** drums, if you've 'indexed' your spur centre as I mentioned before, the drum will be mounted in its original position and so will always run true.

If you want, say, an 8 inch diameter drum, and decide to use a piece of tree branch or fence post or some large piece of wood for the job, be careful when you mount it. Run the lathe slowly at first, as the wood may very well not be of uniform weight around the circumference. It may have more heart wood on one side than the other, for example, and getting a smooth running drum at a good rpm may be impossible, not to mention dangerous.

If you have trouble finding a balanced piece, build one up. 4 pieces of 8 X 2 will make a nice 8 X 8. A piece of ½ inch plywood glued and nailed to the centre of each end of the wood before you start will give a firm cross grain for the centres to bite on, similar to the photo on page 89. If you repeatedly put drive centres into the same marks **with** the grain, they will forever be driven further and further into the wood. Finally, make sure to use a high temperature paper, the same as for lathe sanding.

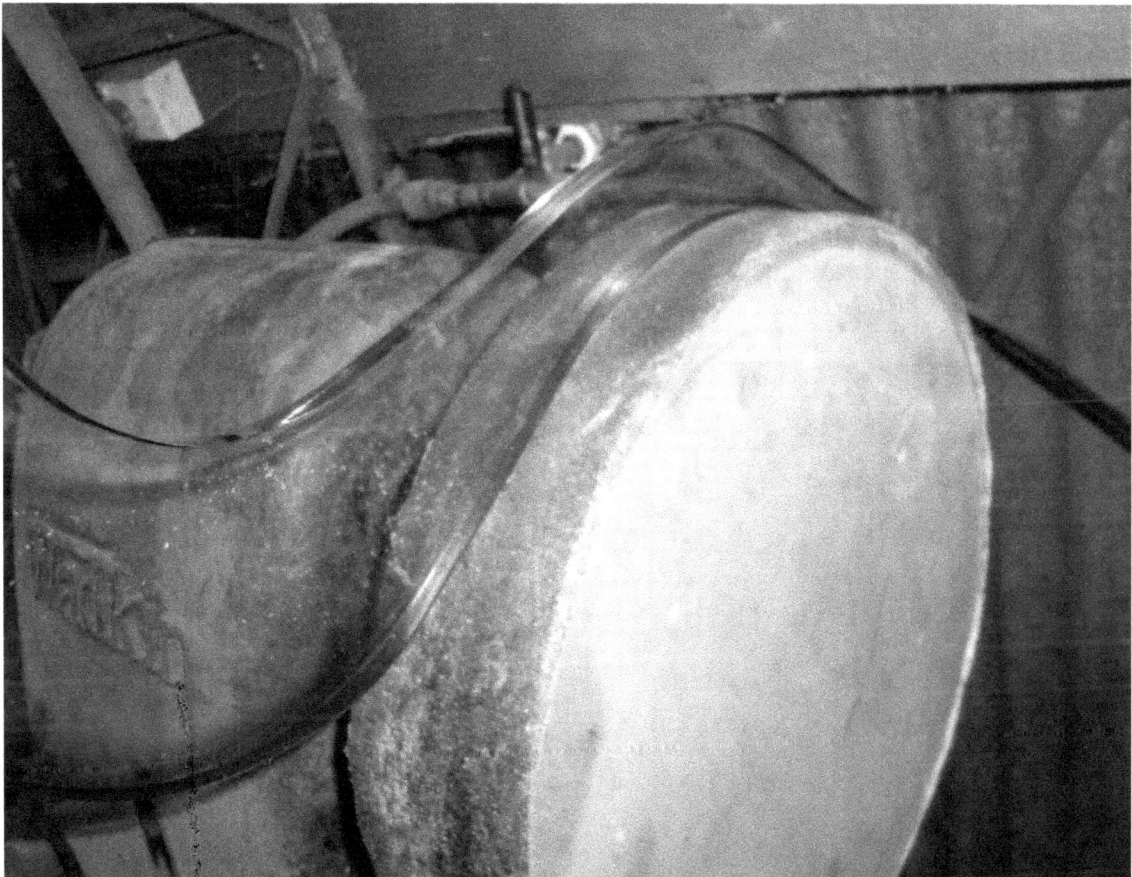

A Face Plate Mounted Drum Sander.

Plywood and particle board are great for faceplate drums. This drum is made from several layers of particle board glued and nailed together, then mounted on a Faceplate and turned to an exact diameter for sanding this acrylic piece.

This little sanding 'drum' (above) is nothing more than a steel tube with a slot cut into it, the rough edges filed off both sides of the slot, and one end (though you can do both) of the sandpaper fed through. No glue is used at all, no overlap. You can tell from the direction of the paper that the lathe was set to run clockwise from our view, so the reverse of normal.

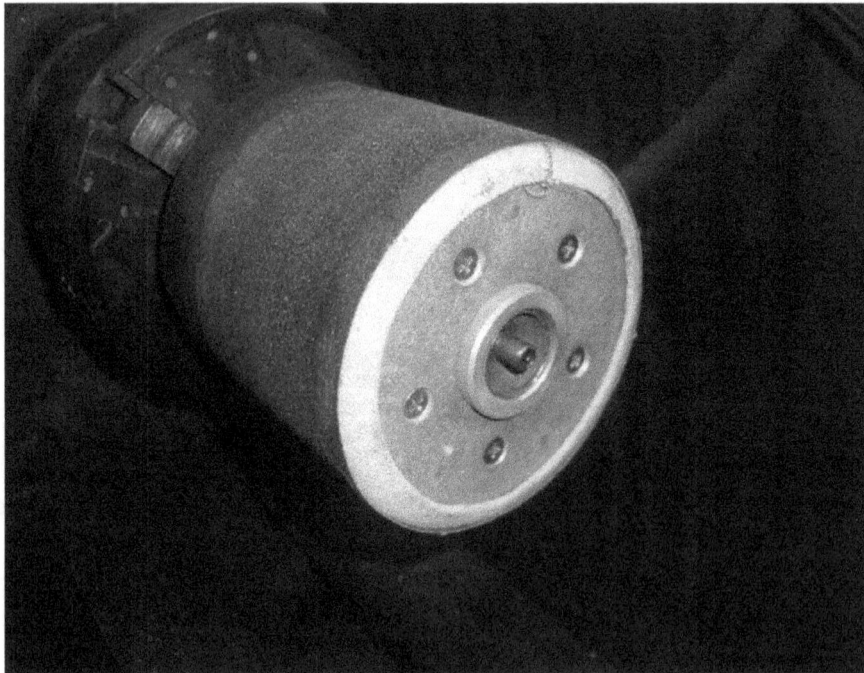

A pneumatic sanding drum.
The sleeves for the pneumatic drums are available in a variety of grits, and the drums in a variety of diameters. The air valve on the end is a standard vehicle tyre valve, so you can pump it up to whatever pressure suits the job at hand.

Slotting and Joining Turned Work.

You might want to have a flat board slotted into a turned piece, like on a cabinet or the foot of a bed perhaps.

A Footboard of a Four Poster bed.

Cut the slot while the wood is square.

It's easier to do while it's square, and you won't risk breaking edges of the decorative turnings.

You can use your table saw for this by setting the height of the blade to the required depth, (which has to be deep enough so there is always some slot under the minimum turned diameter). Start at one edge of the slot, make the first cut, then reverse the wood and do the second cut. This way, the slot is always exactly in the centre.

Move the fence slightly less than the width of the kerf (the width of the saw blade cut), so 3.5mm movement for a 4mm kerf, until you reach the desired width. Of course, you can cut the slot with a router, moulder or whatever you like.

 You now cut a piece of wood to fit into the slot, and secure it with countersunk screws, not nails as they might pull out when the piece is whizzing round in the lathe. You must keep the screw heads lower than the finished diameter, or you'll hit them with the tools. Put them where you know the finished diameter is the greatest, and have them every 6 inches or so on a long piece, closer on a short one. When the piece is finished, remove the screws and the waste wood, and you will have a slot with nice sharp tight edges, and a piece of wood with the profile on it, for copying to the next piece, or using in a decorative way on another project!! Be sure to have the slot in the centre of the wood, and the wood accurately mounted, so the slot is diametrical. It won't fit well to a foot board if the centre is not exact.

If the slot is so deep, and it may be, that the spur centre has nothing to drive on, add a piece of plywood to the ends, as shown in the next photo, and drive on that.

The prepared blank.

The finished shape. Note the plywood ends for the drives.

The separated sections, with the plywood ends for the drives removed.

When you need to **join a turned piece**, as you might if your lathe is 1200mm long but the 4 poster bed you're making is 1800mm high, bore a hole the same size as the outer diameter of your spur centre in the end of the square piece before you turn it.

Don't make the hole so deep that the spur centre can't reach the bottom; the idea here is that the spur centre will drive from the bottom of the hole which will then become the mortise for the tenon of the join to fit into. You can always make the hole deeper later; the important thing is that by driving the spur centre in the hole, the turning will be concentric with the hole. I like to have the join in a sequence of decorations, so one side of the join is, say, a 40mm diameter flat, and the other side a 50mm bead followed by another 40mm flat.

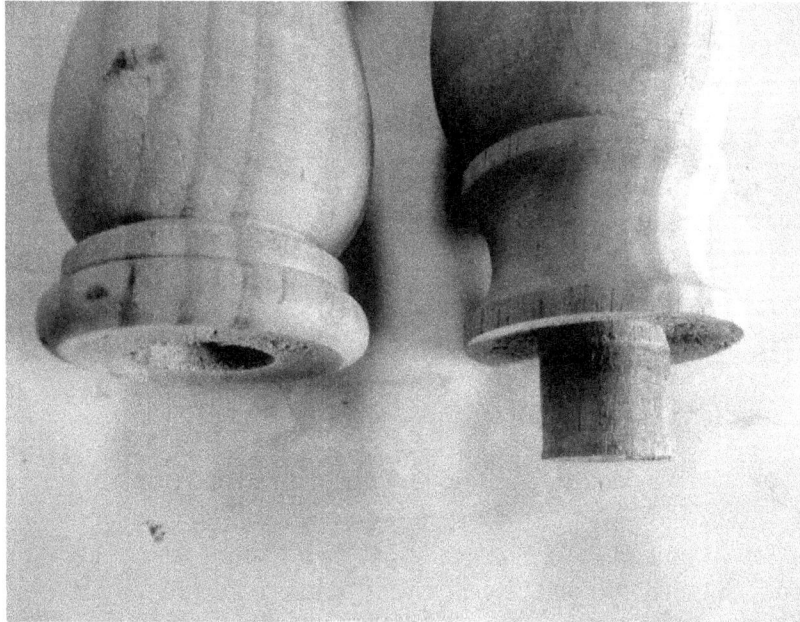

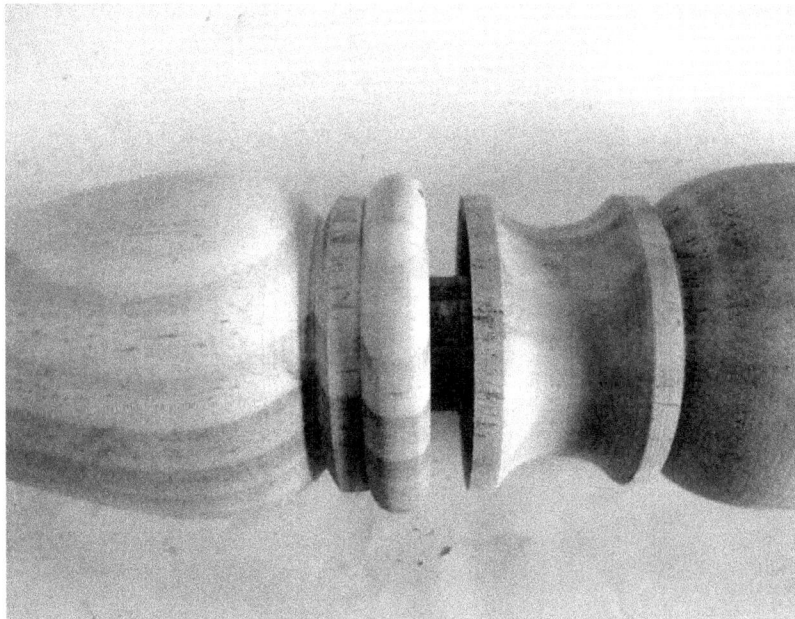

Have the flat surfaces of each side of the join slightly undercut towards the centre, so the outside meeting point is tight.

There's nothing special with turning the tenon, it's done in the usual way, to the same diameter as the hole in the other piece.

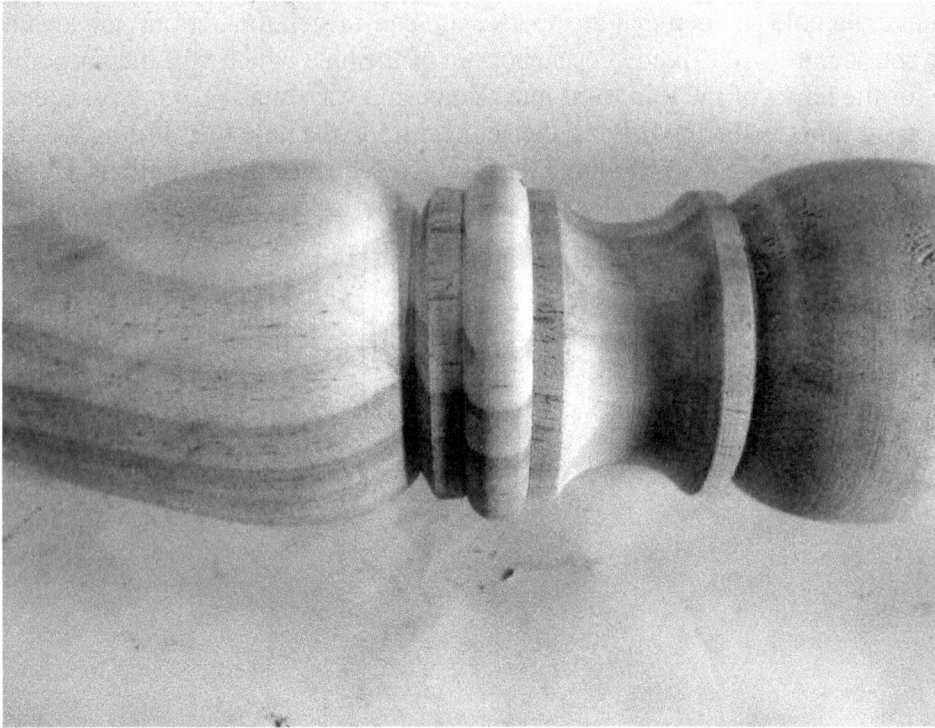

The end result is an invisible and strong join.

When turning tenons on pieces to fit holes, it can be a tedious task to get them all the same diameter. The holes will be uniform, but if you turn the tenons down to about the right size, you can then use an open ended spanner as a **Form Tool** (page 140) to quickly produce the final size for the hole. Don't use an adjustable spanner, just a regular open ended one, which are available in a huge range of sizes.

Wood almost never comes with a totally uniform density across or along it. So if you edge glue say 10 pieces to make a table top that you're going to turn round, there's every chance the un-turned blank will be out of balance. Over maybe 3 feet diameter, if you have a gap bed lathe, you'll have to turn it out board, that is to say on the other side of the headstock than usual. To check the balance, remove or slacken the drive belt, spin the blank by hand, and the heaviest side of the blank will go to the bottom. Screw a weight to the top, and try again. When you first try turning it under power, start at the slowest possible speed, and only run the motor in small spurts, until you know it is in balance enough for working. If you are truing it round from a considerable out-of-round/balance shape, the weight might need adjusting, or removing, as you go.

With the large laminated tops, you attach cross grain braces to the back side to increase the stability anyway, so do it **before** you turn the table top. NEVER glue these braces to the table top, the top must be able to 'breathe' or change size slightly in response to changes in atmospheric humidity. Use screws in elongated holes. See the picture of a large table top being turned on page 100.

Mandrels

A **Mandrel** is a very useful way of holding work in a lathe when there is no easy way to simply hold it in between the centres, on a faceplate, or with a chuck, perhaps because there is a hole through the work, where the centres would normally bear.

A Mandrel is often just a round rod or bar which will run through this hole, and could be held by a drive or chuck at one end, and the tailstock centre at the other.

The mandrel in the previous photo passes right through the pre-bored blank. The mandrel has a stepped section at the headstock end, and you can see it's of a larger diameter there, and that the blank sits right up against this larger section. The blank is prevented from spinning on the mandrel by brads at each end.

Split Pin

In other cases, you can have modified drives in the headstock and tailstock as you can see above.

This two piece variation of the mandrel is where the headstock drive grips one end of the hole in the work, and a modified tailstock centre holds the other. Thrust from the tailstock alone (so no need for the brads used previously) can be used to provide drive to the work from the headstock. Here, for turning a kaleidoscope body, the headstock drive will centre on the hole in the blank and achieve its rotational force by use of the split pin that has been run through the across the drive, so it indents slightly on both sides of the hole in the wood. The modified tailstock centre will run into the 10mm hole which will later serve as the kaleidoscope eyepiece. Thus the centre hole of the blank, which is not necessarily true to the axis of the square piece of wood when it's bored, is held true to the axis of the lathe.

The resultant body will then have its outside decoration concentric with the centre hole.

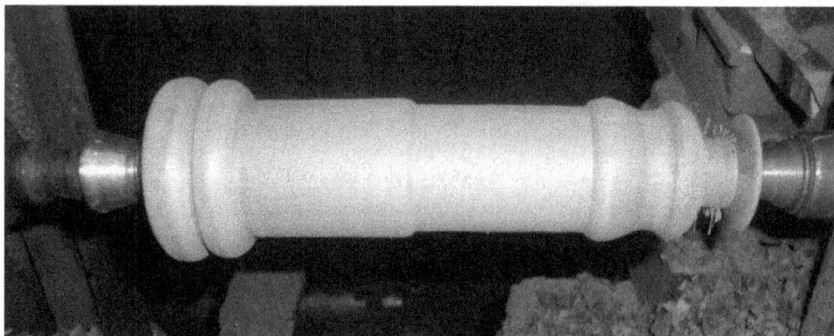

The turned Kaleidoscope body, still mounted on the mandrel shown above.

Sometimes the work is asymmetrical in nature, and so out of balance. Therefore it must be turned slowly. Great care must also be taken to avoid having the spinning work hit you or your tool.

Here, in the photo above, I'm holding a very awkwardly shaped pre-bored piece with a two piece mandrel, in order to machine the right-hand end to fit a small brass cap. Obviously it has to be turned very slowly because of it being so off centre, which makes it a little harder to get a good cut. Equally as obvious is the need for safety!! Thrust alone is enough here to provide adequate drive.

If sufficient thrust cannot be applied by the tailstock to give reliable drive to the piece via the headstock, then you must use a mandrel which runs right through the piece and is driven by the headstock and held by the tailstock. The thrust from the tailstock is not transferred to the work. Therefore, the work must be secured to the mandrel, either by having the mandrel very slightly thicker in the centre than at the ends, very slightly tapered so it 'locks' onto the work, or by securing the work to the mandrel with a screw or nail, placed where the tool won't strike it and it won't interfere with the final design, as seen on page 93.

The same principle is used for machining work on the engineer's lathe.

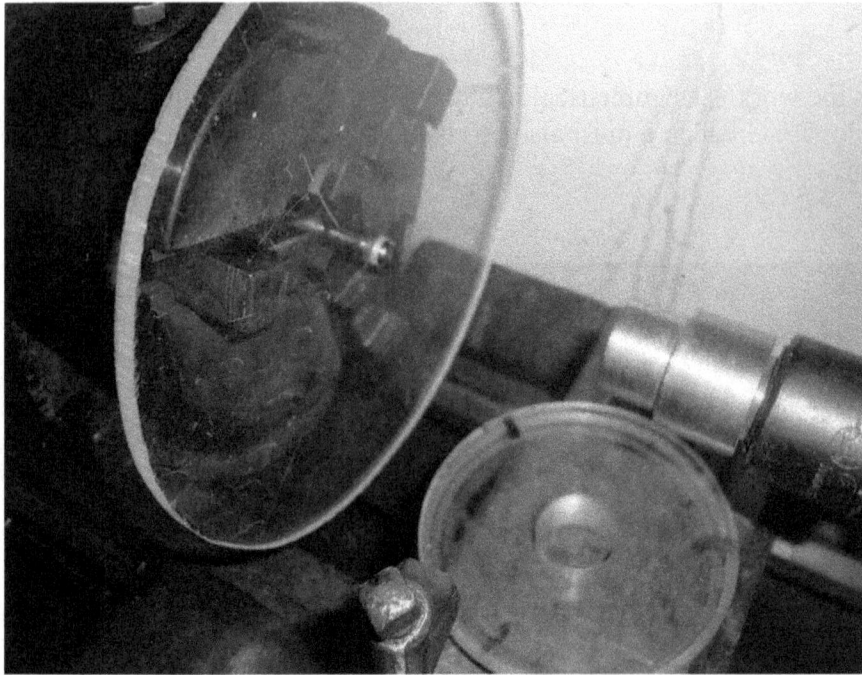

Here's the mandrel assembly.

The mandrel in this case is an 8mm rod, and I'm going to true the thin large acrylic disc.

The jaws in the chuck have been changed for the outer jaws (as described in the metal lathe section) in order to support the disc of a larger diameter while still gripping the mandrel in the centre of the jaws. The modified revolving tailstock centre will accept the thick acrylic disc to provide thrust. The completed set up is seen in the next photo. The thrust is applied and the machining operation can begin.

Safety:

The lathe is a wonderfully versatile machine, capable of producing a huge range of items, and at the same time allowing great scope for creativity. However, it is also quite capable of creating mayhem in the workshop, and causing damage and injury. One of the most common injuries caused by wood lathes is when loose clothing is caught by the revolving spindle. A 2 inch diameter stool leg, for example, spinning at a very modest 800 rpm, will reel in the loose strands of a frayed jersey sleeve at around 2 meters per second. This means your face will be up close and personal with the STILL SPINNING spindle in 1/3 of a second, depending on how long your arm is. This is one of the easiest situations to avoid.

Don't have any loose clothing, frayed or otherwise anywhere near the turning work. Keep your arms bare to the elbow, especially when sanding.

Another favourite way of having accidents with a lathe is to set the rpm too high, particularly when starting a new piece, and even more so with irregular things like tree branches, and built up work like spinning-wheel wheels. Start slowly and safely, and once the piece is roughed out and spinning smoothly, you can increase the speed.

It can be tempting, especially in the absence of a band saw to pre-cut the discs, to mount a square piece of wood to turn into a platter, perhaps, and run the parting tool into it from the front to cut the corners off. At 800 rpm, the corners will come off a 10 inch disc at over 35kph, and in a very random fashion, possibly bouncing off walls, the lathe bed, and your head. It's a very dangerous practice, and also often tears away the rear of the disc as the final few millimetres give way.

Lathes throw chips all over the shop, and many a day has been ruined by having waste lodged in an eye. Also a very simple one to avoid.

Wear eye protection.

The fine dust generated by turning and from sanding in particular, is a poor substitute for clean air in your respiratory system. Some wood dusts are just irritating, but some are toxic; like resin bonded particle boards and wood treated to stop rot.

Wear a dust mask.

The resin and rot treatments are also very hard on the tools, because of the hard crystals they contain.

Build Your Own Lathe

Making your own wood lathe is a fun and rewarding project, and can give you a larger lathe than you might otherwise be able to afford.

Use something sturdy for the bed and stocks, like an 8 X 4 inch, hardwood if possible, or similarly sized box section steel beams. If you're going to bother making a lathe, make it a good length and have a nice high swing. So a 6 feet overall length will give over a 4 feet working length, and a swing (the distance between the spindle centre and the top of the bed) of 1 foot will give a diameter of 2 feet. Both are minimums, I feel.

You can have the spindle, spur centre, faceplate and tailstock shaft made for you if you don't have an engineer's lathe. Be sure that the thread to take the faceplate is not undercut on the inside face, it weakens the shaft too much, see page 100.

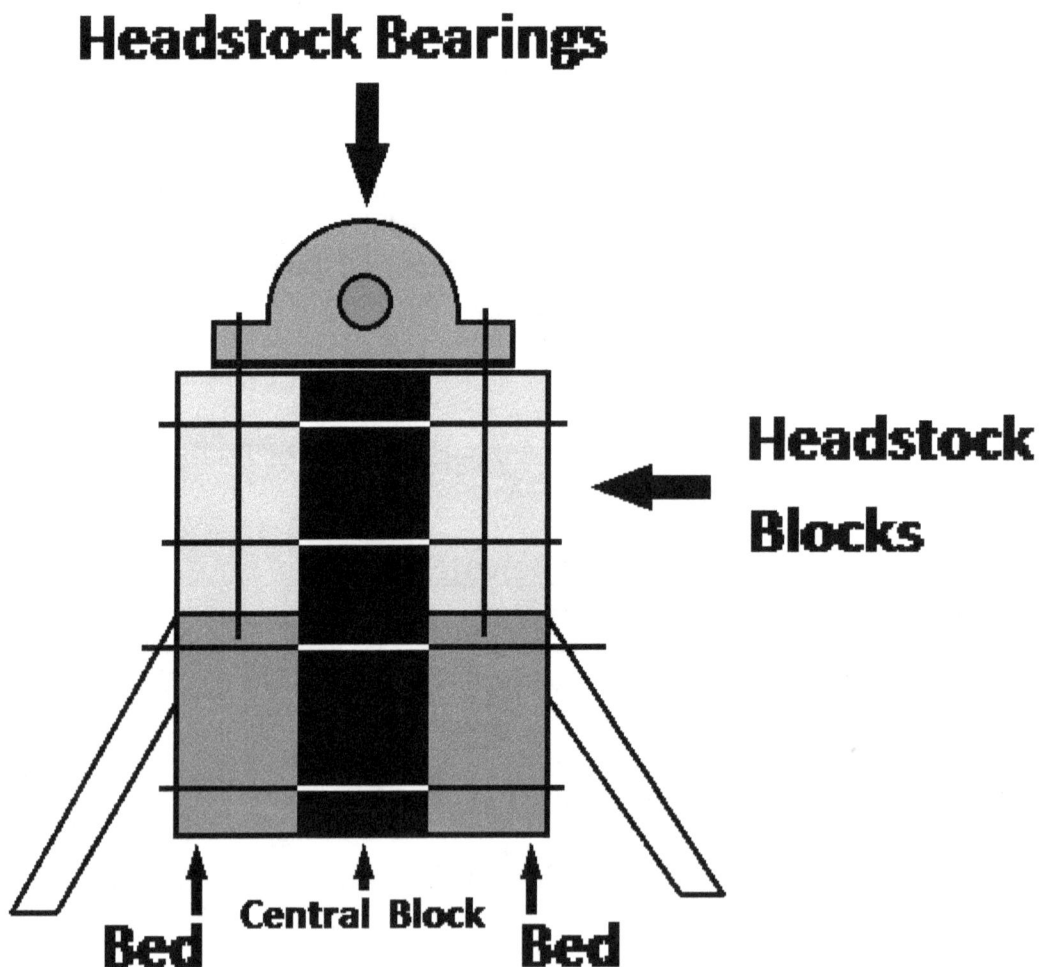

Headstock Bearings

Headstock Blocks

Bed **Central Block** **Bed**

Here's a diagram of a home built headstock and bed.

Bolts are represented by the black/white lines. Never use screws or coach screws if you are making a wooden lathe, they will work loose.

The headstock blocks and central block are bolted together horizontally. The two lengths that make up the bed of the lathe are bolted horizontally to the central block. The headstock bearings should be bolted vertically to the headstock blocks. If you're going to go to the trouble of making a lathe, you might as well make it as big as you can, so have a large swing (at least 300mm) and ideally you should be able to comfortably fit a 1200mm long piece into it. The central block provides a good gap between the lathe bed lengths (also called ways) for the tool rest securing bolt to run in.

The tailstock is essentially the same as the headstock, but with the central block only reaching down to ¾ of the height of the bed, so that a single vertical bolt can be used for locking the tailstock into position against a piece of wood or steel which runs under and across the bed, the same way as the tool rest bolt does (page 69).

Note in the photo below, that where the thread on the headstock main spindle finishes near the bearing, there is no undercutting of the shaft. An undercut makes it slightly easier for the thread to be cut, but seriously weakens the shaft, which may then break at that point.

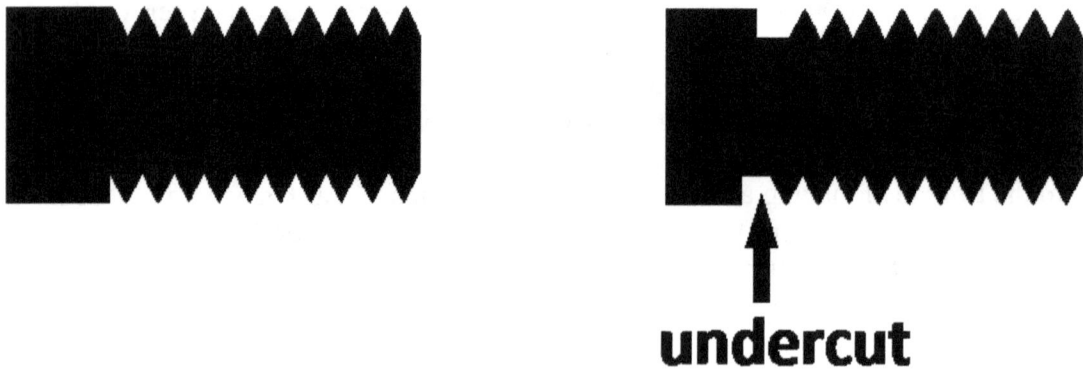

undercut

A diagram of an undercut shaft on the right, and the correct shaft on the left.

A comfortable height for the top of the lathe bed is about bent elbow height when you are standing.

 Go for a good sized main spindle, 50mm or so, and make sure you have a ½ - 5/8 inch hole running right through the axis. This is useful for removing stubborn spur centres, and for bolting out-board faceplates.

 The picture below shows one of my early homemade lathes turning a 5 foot diameter dining table top using a bolted up out-board Faceplate. The Faceplate has a central bolt which runs through the hole in the main spindle. There is a thick washer under the nut to prevent damage to the thread on the spindle.

Use self aligning taper lock bearings, and always bolt them as per the diagram on page 98.

For a lathe running a large diameter spindle, and required to machine quite big pieces, a 1 hp motor is the minimum. Even then, in very cold conditions the bearings will need to be warmed at up at slow speed, before full rpm can be achieved.

Here is part of my collection of drives and tailstock centres, some for the wood lathe and some for the engineers lathe. Most of them are taper shank, some for the tail stock, and some for the head stock spindle.

It is just an example of how you should be prepared to make tools like these, to easily and safely carry out the wide range of tasks that might present themselves to you. As the collection grows, you'll find uses for them that you didn't think of when you first made them.

THE ENGINEER'S LATHE

My small machine lathe is an essential tool in my workshop. There are so many jobs that require its precision and unique capabilities - from making extras for the wood lathe like special drives, to extensions for drills and forstener cutters, cutting threads, winding springs and of course any other turned work in steel, alloys, brass and plastics.

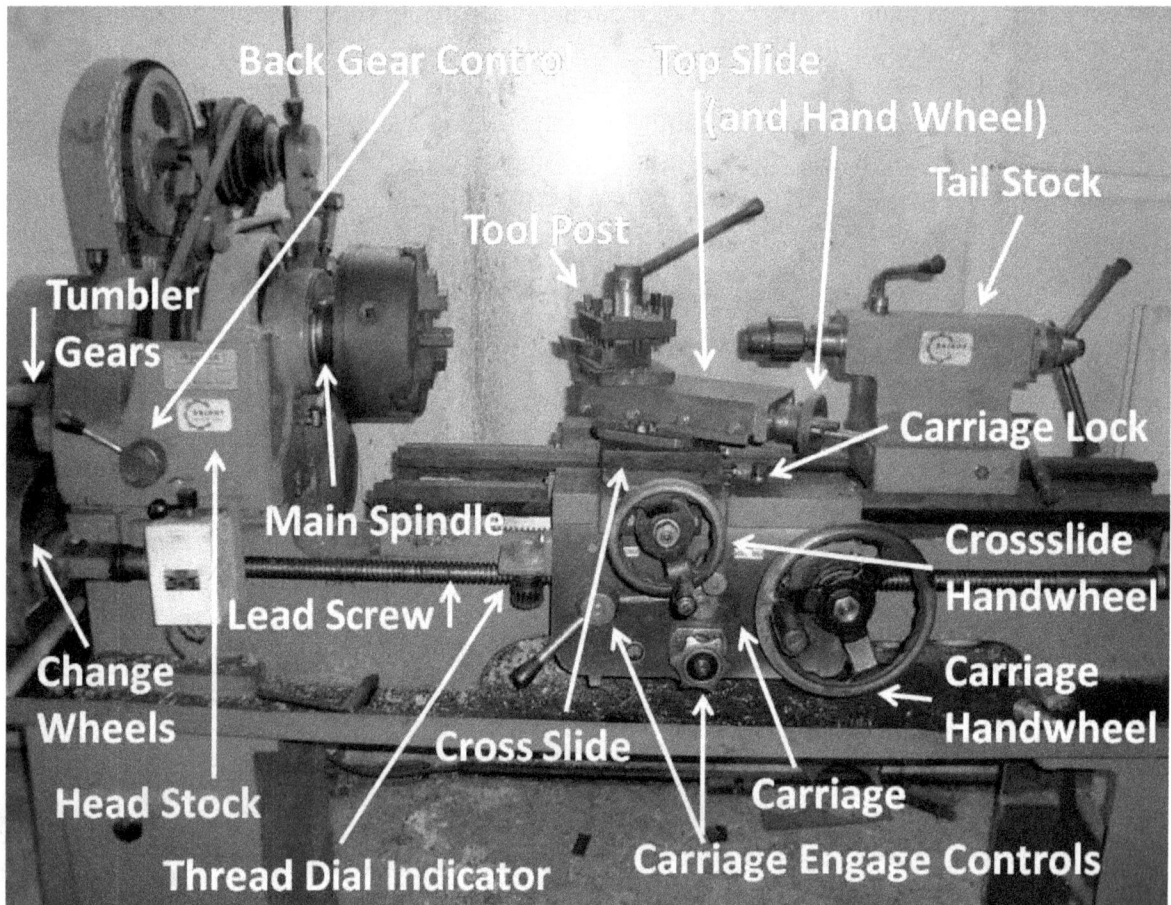

A typical small Engineer's lathe, with a 3 jaw chuck.

These lathes usually come with a 3 jaw chuck, and often with a 4 jaw chuck and driving (face) plates which all screw onto the main spindle, and a 'live' or 'running' tailstock centre and a ½ inch 3 jaw chuck , both with a tapered shank, which fit a tapered hole in the tailstock shaft. If you're lucky it will have work steadies (which, unlike the wood lathe are essential for some operations) and even collets and some 'special tools' that a previous owner has made.

Another small lathe, with 3 jaw chuck, running tail stock centre and both fixed and travelling work steadies.

A 3 foot bed is fine for a home workshop, though a 4 foot even better!! Only a very old lathe will not have screw cutting capabilities, which is an essential feature of a home workshop lathe.

Also essential is the **Back Gear Assembly**, which allows a great reduction in chuck speed, often 5:1 or so, and can also be used to lock the spindle, which is a help with removing a chuck or collet adapter from the spindle. The Back Gear is a large gear immediately behind the headstock chuck. It is usually locked, by a pin, to the main spindle, so the spindle speed is the same as the chuck speed. However, if you release the pin, the chuck is no longer directly connected to the spindle. When you engage the Back Gear Assembly (with the back gear control), the chuck speed is then much less than the spindle speed, essential for getting the low chuck speeds necessary for screw cutting.

A **Set Over Tailstock** allows you to alter the alignment of the tailstock with the headstock. It has set screws on either side of the tailstock casting, which, when the main tailstock clamp is released, can be adjusted to move the top half of the tailstock either way across the lathe bed, see photo page 138.

A **Gap Bed** lathe has a removable section near the headstock, to allow for extra diameter work in board, the same as the wood lathe on page 71.

Try and have a lathe that has a large diameter spindle, as the hole running through the spindle will be larger, to allow lengths of stock to be passed through.

If you buy a lathe without a bench or stand, be sure to build a very sturdy, well braced one, and, as with the wood lathe, make the top of the bed height about the height of your bent elbow height, when you're standing upright.

The lathe has a long threaded rod along the bed, called the **Lead Screw**. The lead screw runs the entire length of the lathe bed, and gives movement to the carriage. While you can move the carriage along the bed by using the hand wheel, it is always an irregular and jerky movement. Using the lead screw and a combination of drive gears gives a very controlled movement, resulting in a smooth cut, and accurately cut threads. The ratio of movement of the carriage to revolutions of the spindle is controlled by gears, either loose and fitted in various combinations to the head stock, or in a gearbox. This means that for every revolution of the main spindle, irrespective of the speed of the spindle, the carriage will move along the bed a pre-determined amount. You can think of the tool, therefore, always cutting a thread on the work as it is drawn along the work as the work revolves. The **Tumbler Gears** change the direction of rotation of the lead screw, and therefore the direction of movement of the carriage.

For general cutting, the amount of carriage movement is so small, compared to the revolution that the 'thread' is finer than the tool tip, resulting in a smooth finish to the work. When cutting 'real' threads, the carriage movement is much greater, and so, for example, the work will only revolve 20 times, say, while the carriage has moved an inch, giving a thread pitch of 20 to the inch.

The lead screw can also be made to drive the cross slide as well, to give a controlled cut across the face of the work, at ninety degrees to the axis of the lathe bed.

It's a good idea to remove the tailstock centre when you're working with the faceplate or the chuck where the tailstock is not required, a jab in the right elbow with the tailstock point is unpleasant.

Chucks

The most common type of 3 jaw chuck is the geared scroll type, where 3 square key ways are arranged around the chuck body, any of which will operate the jaws. The jaws are numbered, 1 – 3, and must be installed in the correct order, starting with 1, so that the jaws are equally distant from the centre axis. The chuck will have 'inside' and 'outside' jaws.

The preferred method of storing chucks, sitting upside down on their jaws, with the keys kept in the Chuck Mounting Threads. An **Independent** 4 Jaw chuck is on the right.

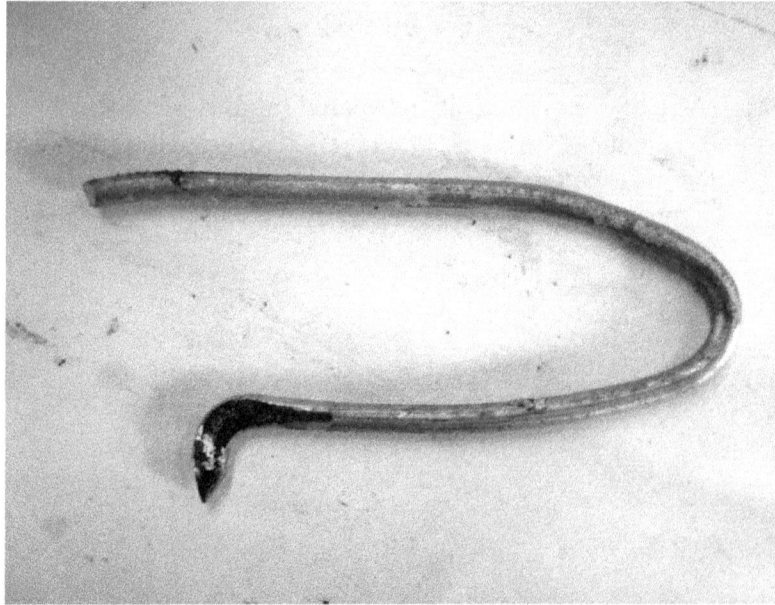

This little tool provides an easy and efficient way to keep the chuck mounting threads clear. You can make it from a thick piece of wire. The method of use is shown in the next picture.

Thread Cleaning Tool

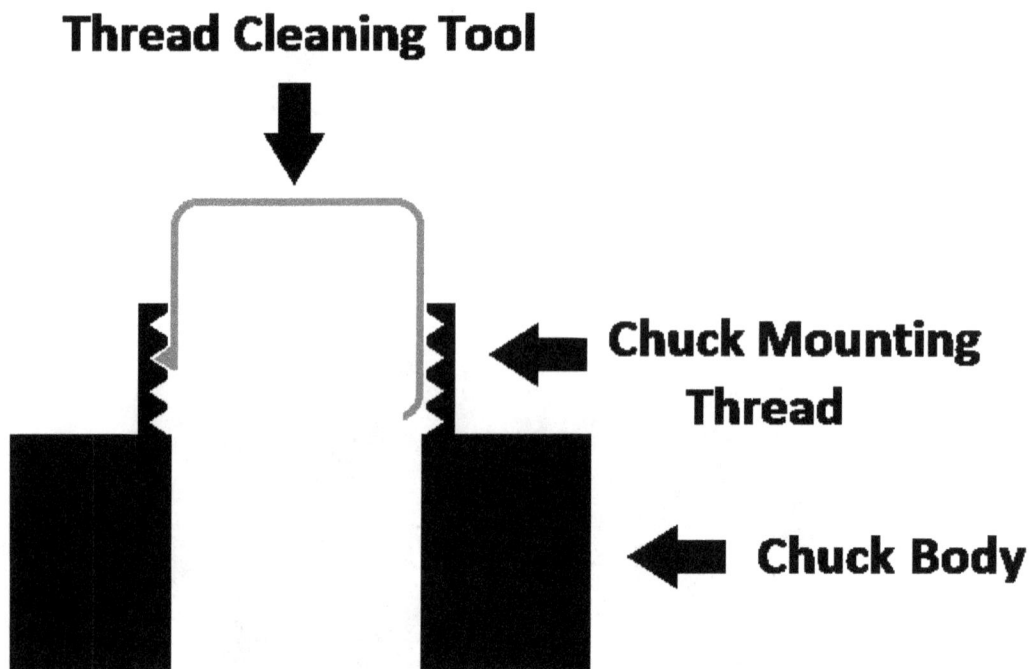

How to use the home made Chuck Thread Cleaning tool.

It will 'screw' into the Chuck Mounting Threads, cleaning them as it does so.

The 3 jaw chucks are known as self-centring, as the jaws are moved together with the one key.

A rod passed through the spindle hole will be held by the inside jaws, a ring, by the outside jaws. However, it is possible to hold rectangular pieces in the 3 jaw chuck as shown below, which will allow facing off the front surface, or for a hole to be bored to a precise measurement.

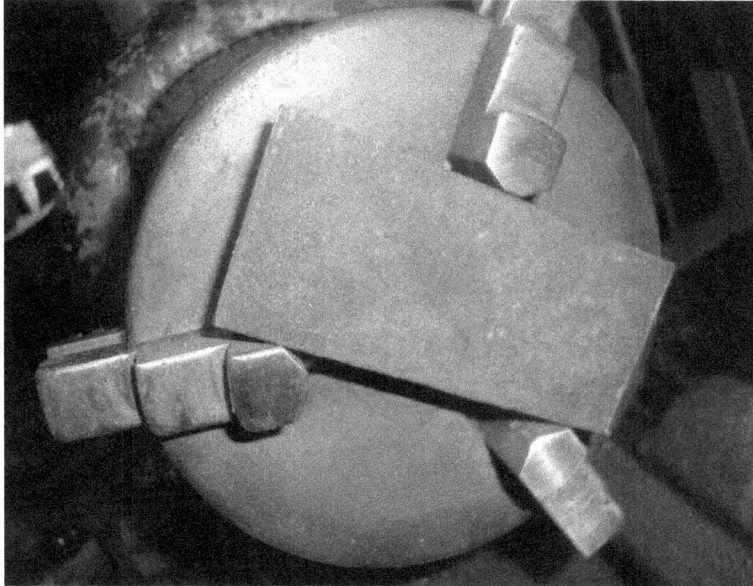

The centre of the work, however, won't be in line with the lathe axis, so it's rare to mount work like this. Still, you can if you need to .....

It is also possible to safely hold a piece off centre in the chuck by deliberately allowing a full rotation (or two) of the scroll gear without jaw 3, and then fitting the jaw next time round as you can see in the next photo. This will only provide a very limited amount of off-set variation though, which may not always suit the job at hand.

Offset by inserting Jaw 3 (here the upper most one) one turn late.

Another way of doing this is to put a piece of metal between one jaw and the work. This way, a very accurate amount of off centre can be achieved, because, by measuring the piece of metal, you know exactly by how much the work is off-set. Be very sure the jaws are **all** tight against the work, not just 2 of them

Offset by the thickness of the inserted nut.

The **4 Jaw Independent Chuck** is useful for holding irregular or 'off centre' work. The jaws are controlled independently of each other, each having its own controlling keyway, and are also reversible. They are robust chucks, because each jaw has its own gear, and can hold a wide variety of shapes.

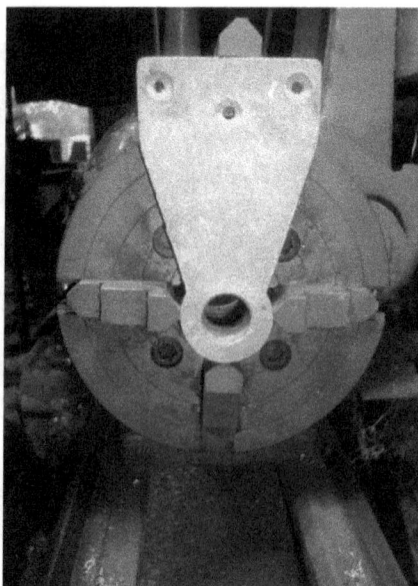

An odd shaped piece in the 4 Jaw chuck, ready for boring the centre hole. Note the top Jaw has been reversed for greater grip.

Mounting Squares in the 4 Jaw Chuck

For repeated mountings of identical square sections in the 4 jaw chuck, start with a round section of the same diameter as the square section. So for a 2 X 2 inch square section, use a 2 inch diameter round piece. It need not be very long, just long enough to be easily held in the 3 jaw chuck to have a centre drill make a small hole in the exact centre. Now transfer it to the 4 jaw chuck, and use the **Centre Finder** to centre it. See page 114 for how to make and use a centre finder. Once the round piece is centred in the 4 jaw, release 2 adjacent jaws, remove the round section, and insert the square section. Tighten the loosened jaws, and the square section will be true, as long as you didn't move the other two jaws, of course!!

<u>WARNING !!!</u>

This is a very dangerous practice. Don't leave the chuck key in the chuck, you'll forget one day and switch the lathe on with possibly disastrous consequences.

Faceplates

Of course, there are shapes and sizes that simply won't fit the 3 and 4 jaw chucks, and these can be held on the Faceplate. With the wood lathe the work can simply be screwed to the Faceplate; with an engineer's lathe, the work is bolted to the Faceplate. In some cases the work can be bolted directly to the Faceplate and turned. The assembly shown is a good example.

A ring which has been trued in the 3 jaw chuck (so it's a uniform thickness) is held under the work piece. It must have an internal diameter larger than that which you are going to machine into the work piece. Hence, you cannot see it in this photo. It allows clearance behind the work, so the tool doesn't touch the Faceplate as it comes through. The work is tightly bolted so the ring is squeezed onto the faceplate and will remain in place throughout the operation, (even though it may not run particularly true to the centre). Here, also, the use of the **Centre Finder** is helpful (page 114).

The hole can be simply machined out.

This is also a good example of using a **Boring Tool**. These tools need to be quite sturdy, and usually have a carbide tip braised to the end, though a cutter held by a grub screw can be used, especially with the larger tools. Clearance is the key to successfully using a boring tool. If the pilot hole in the work is quite small, then to have the cutting tip at the centre point and not have the lower face of the tool rub the inside edge of the pilot hole can be quite difficult. You may need to have a small tool to start with, and change to a larger one as the hole is increased. Mounting the tool so it is higher than the centre point will help with clearance, but makes the tool more inclined to grab.

This close up shows the angles ground on the boring tool to give clearance

Various Ways to Mount Work on the Faceplate

Say, for example, we want to accurately machine out the hole in an irregularly shaped piece. The work is tightly held by the clamps. The clamps also squeeze a ring under the work piece, as above, firmly onto the faceplate, to give clearance behind the work. The clamps are easy to make, simply being short flat bars with a hole in them. Use as big a bolt as will fit the Faceplate, and do them up well.

Another good use for the **Centre Finder** (page 114).

A piece of Angle Plate (or Iron or Steel) is a good way to bolt difficult shapes to the Faceplate so they can be machined at right-angles to their fixing. Turning out the central hole in this bearing block is a good example.

Gap left after the removal of the Set-Up Block

Another view of the Angle Iron jig and Counterweight.

It's very important to make sure the Angle Iron is, in fact, a good 90°. Otherwise, the bore of this bearing block won't be parallel with its base. Having the Angle Plate made true by a machine shop with milling facilities is very worthwhile. Commercial Angle Plates are also available. Lightly bolt the work to the Angle Plate and the Plate to the Faceplate. Set up the operation by using a block (removed before the lathe is switched on) which has been face trued (perhaps by holding the block in the 3 jaw chuck as shown on page 107) to provide a parallel space behind the work which will allow the tool to come right through without touching the Faceplate. As we need the original hole to be true with the lathe axis, you can use a centre finder to centre it correctly.

The block underneath must now be removed, as there's nothing to prevent it flying out when the lathe is turned on.

Now you can tighten the bolts and proceed with the work. If you make your own Angle Plate, just be sure to use a sturdy piece of Angle Steel for the job, and some gussets across the ends help with the rigidity too. With the weight all on one side you may wish to use counterweights, like you see in the previous photo. Here some brass discs are bolted to the Faceplate, to allow reasonable spindle speeds without unworkable vibration from the out of axis centre of gravity. The amount of weight and position (the further out they are the more effective they are) are both determined by trial and error. Start with a low rpm, as always.

In the previous photo, the mounting plates are set up on small blocks almost the height of the work, to give good grip. Without the blocks, the plates would be at a very steep angle, with the chance of slipping. The blocks keep the plates almost horizontal.

There is a trued ring underneath, once again, to allow clearance for the tool to cut right through and not hit the face plate. Unlike the set-up block we used before which had to be removed as it would fly out when the lathe was started, the ring here is firmly clamped to the face plate by the rectangular plates, and will not fly out. Again, the ring must be of a sufficient diameter to not have any contact with the tool when the tool comes right through the work.

Making and Using a Simple Centre Finder.

A centre finder is a useful tool when mounting strange shapes that need to be exactly centred. It is simply a central ring with a short rod through one side, and a long rod fixed to the other. The rods are in alignment. The diagram below is the 'side on' view.

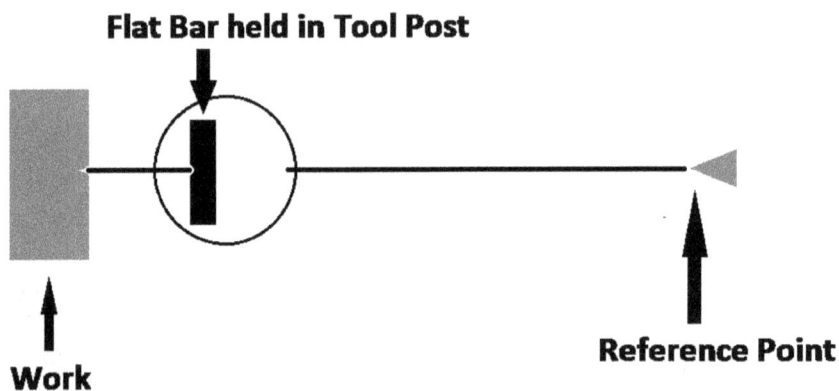

Flat Bar held in Tool Post

Reference Point

Work

Centre Finder

It works by the right hand end of the short rod being held in the shallow hole in a flat bar, mounted in the tool post. The left hand end of the short rod is put in the shallow hole in the work piece, which is mounted in the lathe. Any discrepancy between the axis of the two holes, and therefore the axis of the short rod, and the axis of the lathe bed is greatly magnified by the long rod, which will travel in a circle around a reference point, often simply the tailstock centre.

When the hole in the work is in the same axis as the hole in the flat bar, the small rod will also be in this axis; so therefore will the axis of the long rod. This means the end of the long rod will no longer travel in a circle around the reference point, but will stay in alignment with it. This tool makes it quick and easy to centre a piece in the 4 jaw chuck (or that matter an off-set piece in a 3 jaw chuck) or on a faceplate, and it is simple to make.

A homemade centre finder in use.

PVC Collar

To centre the likes of the assembly shown above, first turn a collar (this one is made from black PVC rod) to fit the large hole in the work. Put a small hole in its exact centre, for the small rod of the centre finder.

When you make the centre finder, start by mounting a flat bar in the tool post, and run it into a **Centre Drill Bit** held in the main chuck, boring a shallow hole by moving the carriage sideways to the left. It's vital to mount the flat bar in the tool post in exactly the same way each time you use it. When you remount the tool to use it, align it by once again holding the centre drill bit in the chuck, mounting the bar in the tool post and adjusting the Cross-slide so the pre-bored hole is exactly in the right place. The height is automatically set by the flat bar being held on the bottom of the tool post in the same way as it was when the hole was originally bored.

To use the centre finder, first hold the flat bar in the tool post and align it with a centre drill as described. Now mount the work piece in the lathe (4 jaw chuck or Faceplate) as close to the centre as you can by eye. Hold the short rod of the centre finder between the pilot hole in the work piece collar and the small hole in the flat bar held in the tool post, by moving the cross slide gently towards the headstock.

When it's nicely held, rotate the head stock chuck **BY HAND**. The end of the long rod of the centre finder will swing around the tailstock centre unless the work piece centre hole is exactly in line with the lathe axis. Have something in the tail stock to use as your reference.

Now adjust the position of the work, until the long rod remains in alignment with the tailstock centre as you turn the chuck, once again, **SLOWLY BY HAND.** In the picture, page 114, I've used a centre drill bit for a reference, and the long rod is very nearly in perfect alignment with it.

 The bar can be of any metal, this one is aluminium, but the two rods are steel and the ring is brass, as the rods are soldered to the ring. True each side of the ring in the lathe, the width is largely irrelevant. Now hold the ring in a drill vice or the round section jig mentioned before, and, using a centre drill, make a pilot hole in the top surface. It is important that the hole is diametrical, so check the alignment with the thin strip trick as shown on page 48. The diameter of the rod is not very important either, but so it will fit any size of work, don't make it too big. Around 3mm is fine. Whatever you choose, bore that size of hole through the ring, and carry on and pass the drill through the underside wall as well. Cut a small piece of the rod (say 40mm), and put a slight taper on each end of it. Now hold the **long** rod (say 300mm) in the lathe chuck so only ½ an inch projects, and the **short** piece in the tailstock chuck so that ½ inch projects. This ensures the two rods are exactly in alignment. Put the ring in place, with the long rod just through the inside surface, and the short rod a little more because it extends to be held by the flat bar, and solder them firmly into place. You could of course thread the rods and tap the ring, but whichever way you do it they **must be in alignment**, and holding them in the chucks and soldering them is an easy way to do this, as you can see below.

Collets or Split Chucks

Collets or split chucks are a great addition to the lathe, as they have a very positive grip, and are quick to operate.

The collets can be held in an adapter fitted into the main spindle taper. A tube with a threaded end is passed through the spindle hole, then through the adapter, and screws into the collet. The collet locks when the tube is tightened by a hand wheel or lever. Alternatively, an adapter is screwed on to the main spindle thread and accepts the collet, which is locked by an external threaded collar.

Collets will grip almost anything: round, rectangular, square, triangular, hex, octagonal and more. It's rare, however, to find them above 1 inch diameter in the home workshop; mine, in fact, run from $1/16^{th}$ to ¾ inch, with increments of $1/16^{th}$ inch.

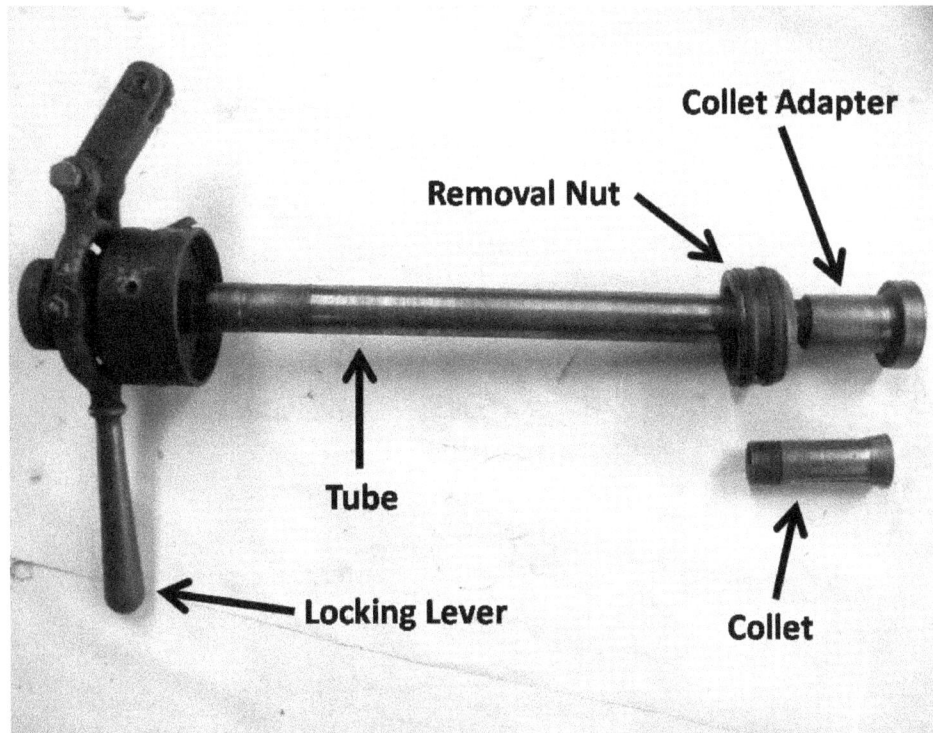

Here is a complete collet set up. From the left: The lever which tightens the tube and locks the collet. The tube runs through the hole in the headstock spindle, then the adapter, and screws into the collet. The large round nut is screwed onto the headstock spindle thread and is used to remove (with a ' C ' spanner) the collet adapter which sits inside the headstock spindle taper. The collets fit inside this adapter.

A collet in the adaptor, mounted in the main spindle taper, with the removal nut behind it.

Holding a square section in the collet.

Using the Lathe Steadies

A **Fixed Steady** (so called because it is bolted to the lathe bed and so doesn't move with the carriage) is used to hold the end of work too long for safe holding in the chuck by itself, if the piece is too thin for vibration free machining, or when the tailstock has been removed to allow the end of the piece to be machined. Don't have the steady jaws too tight, and use plenty of lubricant. You can apply lubricant in an economical way by having a cup of oil on hand and using a small brush to transfer the oil to the work.

It is vital that the steady holds the work exactly parallel to the lathe bed, both to and fro, and up and down. Work which is out of line will create huge stress in the chuck and head stock, and the piece will inevitably work its way out of the chuck.
The simplest way to align the steady is to drill a centre hole in one end of the work by holding it in the chuck with the majority of the work inside the head stock spindle hole, and a small amount protruding to the front. Face the piece and bore a centre hole with a centre drill held in the tailstock chuck. Then, remount the work by holding only a small amount in the chuck, and the other end with the tail stock centre using the hole you just bored, and set the steady according to this. If the work is too long or too large in diameter to allow this, then set the steady up by eye, and use a dial gauge to check the distance, at either end of the work, vertically between the lathe bed and the underside (or topside) of the work, and horizontally between the tool post and the front of the work. Without a dial gauge, mount a tool and or a piece of wire in the tool post, and check the distances at either end, both to the front surface, and the top.

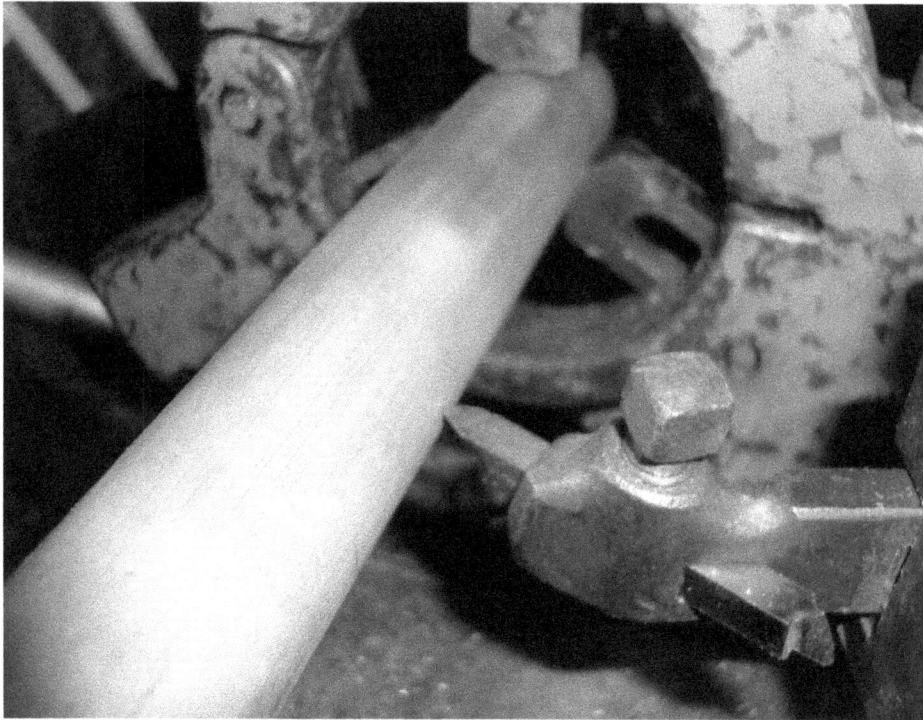

Checking the horizontal front to back adjustment with the tool in the tool post.

Checking the vertical up and down adjustment with a wire in the tool holder.

When the work is true, a centre hole can be bored.

A **Travelling Steady** is bolted to the carriage, and so travels with the tool. It bears on the work from behind, and prevents 'whip' of the work due to pressure from the tool. Thin stock can easily be bent out of shape by the steady being too far forward, or allowed to chatter by having the steady too far back. Adjust the steady to the work right up as close as possible to either the chuck or the tailstock, where the work is unlikely to flex. As before with the fixed steady, lubricate well. A photo of the travelling steady is below.

Temporary (because they will wear) **Steadies** can be made from a block of hard wood bolted to the lathe bed.

Marking the centre point of a temporary steady.
The front edge of the wood must be held firmly against the front edge of the lathe bed, so later aligning it at any point on the bed is possible.

The temporary steady in use.
Before the bar was inserted, the inside of the hole was well coated with candle wax.

Screw or Thread Cutting

Screw or thread cutting is done by linking the main lathe spindle speed (rpm) to the speed of travel up the lathe bed of the Cross-slide carriage, and therefore the tool. In other words, for every revolution of the spindle, the carriage moves a certain distance. There is a lever on the Cross-slide carriage which will engage the Lead-screw with the carriage. The various combinations of gears for the change wheel lathe, or gear lever selection for the gearbox lathe is written on the lathe itself.

A set of **Change Wheels** and the legend plate, which is riveted to the cover plate.

THREAD CHART

WHITWORTH THREADS

THREADS	2	3	4	5	6	7	8	9	10	11	12	13	14	15	16	18	19	20	24
A	60	30	60	30	30	30	30	30	30	30	30	30	30	30	30	30	30	30	30
B	–	–	–	–	–	–	–	–	–	55	60	65	70	75	80	90	95	80	80
C	–	–	–	–	–	–	–	–	–	50	50	50	50	50	50	50	50	40	30
D	40	30	80	50	60	70	80	90	100	100	100	100	100	100	100	100	100	100	90

METRIC THREAD

PITCH	1	1·25	1·5	1·75	2	2·5	3	3·5	4	4·5	5	5·5	6
A	30	25	30	30	40	30	30	60	80	60	75	30	90
B	127	127	127	127	127	127	127	127	127	127	–	127	–
C	50	75	75	70	75	100	90	70	75	90	–	110	–
D	100	100	100	80	100	80	60	80	100	80	127	40	127

CHANGE GEARS FURNISHED

25 30 30 40 50 55 60 65 70 75 80 90 95 100 110 127

To set up the change wheels with the correct amount of clearance, put a piece of paper between the gears when mounting them. Turn the spindle by hand to remove it.

Right hand threads are cut from right to left

Now select the slowest spindle speed.

The tool is shaped to fit the thread to be cut, with a thread gauge if you have one, or by comparing it to an existing thread. Set the tool to just touch the work, then move the carriage off the work towards the tail-stock and advance the tool by a very small amount, using the cross-slide. This will be the first cut. Take careful note of the **Cross-Slide Index** number.

Cross Slide Index.

A **Thread Dial Indicator** is a great help when cutting threads as it allow the tool to be engaged in exactly the same place on the work, every time.

Engage the indicator (they usually are held in position by a locking nut. Loosen the nut, and swing the indicator down, so the gear on the indicator meshes with the lead-screw) and run the machine without engaging the carriage drive. You will see the indicator turning, and the numbers on it slowly passing the static mark.

Engage the carriage drive when an indicator number, and it doesn't matter which one, lines up with the static mark. Now the indicator stops turning as the carriage travels down the bed. Quickly withdraw the cross-slide when you reach the end of the cut, and stop the lathe. Release the carriage drive, and return the carriage to the start point at the tail-stock end by hand, or you can leave it engaged and run the motor in reverse. Return the cross-slide index to the original setting, and advance it by a small amount, to deepen the cut. Run the lathe without engaging the carriage drive until the original number on the thread dial indicator is in alignment with the static mark, and immediately engage the carriage drive. This means that the second cut will be in exactly the same place as the first.

It is imperative, of course, that the work is not moved in the chuck, or the tool in the tool-post in-between cuts.

It's a good idea to run the tool twice at the same depth of cut, every now and again, to keep the thread clear and accurate, and at least twice when the finished depth has been reached.

A left hand thread means the lead-screw is turned the other way, by the use of the tumbler gears at the head-stock.

A slot must be cut to the finished depth at the extreme end of the threaded portion at the head-stock end, before the left hand threading is started, to allow access for the tool. Use the thread dial indicator as before.

Internal threads are cut in exactly the same way. Firstly, bore the hole to the diameter of the external thread minus twice the depth of the thread itself. Then follow the same procedure as for the external threads, but, of course, moving the tool towards you to increase the depth, rather than away for you. Internal left hand threads are more easily done by reversing the spindle and having the carriage travel right to left but with the tool set up to cut on the back face of the work, rather than the front. **Make sure the chuck is tight enough not to unscrew!**

With no thread dial indicator, you can leave the carriage engaged and reverse the motor to run the carriage back to the start, advance the tool, and cut forwards again, all once again without disengaging the carriage drive. Alternatively, marks can be made on a spindle gear tooth and headstock, and a lead-screw gear tooth and lathe bed with a marker pen or chalk. Before the second cut is started, the tool is advanced and the lathe run, without engaging the carriage drive, until the marks are in alignment. The lathe is stopped, the carriage drive engaged, and the lathe run again.

Boring Bars

A simple boring bar is an easy tool to make, and allows for boring down the line, (down the lathe bed), of awkward shapes or long pieces. First bore a pilot hole in the work to be line bored. To make a boring bar, take a length of round steel, smaller in diameter than the pilot hole. Hold it in the chuck, and if it will fit in the spindle hole, protrude a small amount of one end and drill, with the centre bit, a centre hole for the tailstock end. Reverse the steel, and true it for an inch or so for the chuck end. If the steel won't fit into the spindle hole, you'll have to use the fixed steady (page 120) to make the centre hole, and the true section.

The work is mounted on the Cross-slide with the boring bar through the pilot hole, and the cutter to the headstock side. Hold the boring bar by the true section in the chuck, and the centre hole by the tail-stock centre.

A **fixed size** boring bar, for use with wood, is shown in the next photo. The cutter can be brazed to the bar, and ground sharp. A fixed cutter will cut the finished diameter immediately.

A metal cutting tool will have a much smaller cutter, with slow carriage travel.

For an **adjustable** one, use the round section holding jig (page 47) to support the bar in the drill press, and bore a diametrical hole right through. This hole will hold an HSS cutter. Make a simple cutter from a piece of HSS square section tool steel fitted in the hole. You can use a smaller hole if you grind the edges off the square HSS. Bore and tap a hole to accept a locking grub screw at right angles to the cutter. Use a slow rpm, and slow feed. Adjust the cutter to take a very light cut, return the work to the tail-stock side of the cutter, extend the cutter a little and continue, measuring after every cut, until you reach the required diameter.

Boring a block of wood with a very large (because it's cutting wood) fixed cutter boring bar. The block has been raised on packers of the correct height, and then clamped to the empty tool post.

Turning Discs

Sometimes you need to make discs, with or without centre holes. This can be tricky, especially with very thin material.

With a thickness over about 3mm and below say 10mm, if a centre hole is allowed, bore a pilot hole in the work. Hold a thick round block (anything will do, wood is fine) in the 3 jaw chuck, preferably close to the finished size of the disc to be turned, and face it true. The work is then pushed against the block by the tailstock centre bearing in the pilot hole. The pressure provided by the tail stock centre has to be enough to provide sufficient friction between the block in the chuck and the work to make it turn without slipping.

Over 10mm, the work is likely to be strong enough to withstand the pressure of the thrust without distortion. You can still have a block in the headstock, but you can also have the disc push up against the jaws. Outside jaws will give you a greater diameter. With a centre hole, use the tailstock centre directly into the hole. Without a centre hole, use a block to take the tip of the tailstock centre, or a modified centre.

Here a washer is providing the thrust and preventing the centre's taper from burying itself in the work, enlarging the hole, and losing thrust. In the above photo, I'm making a disc from Foam PVC. I chose a washer whose centre hole was large enough to allow the point of the tailstock centre to project through and be a tight fit in the pilot hole in the PVC, to keep it true.

A folded over piece of fine (400 grit) sandpaper between the disc and the block will help give good drive to the piece, if you need it.

If the material can be band sawed, marking a circle and cutting close to it speeds things up. Even cutting just the corners off a square blank will save time.

The centre hole can be enlarged later, if required, by holding the piece in the chuck and re-boring it, or if it is too large for the chuck, clamping it on the Faceplate with a spacer under the work to allow for the tool to come through (page 110).

If there is no centre hole, the tailstock is put into a hole in another block thick enough so the point doesn't come right through, and the pressure applied.

Almost anything will do for this block as it is only there to provide thrust to the disc, and its diameter is largely irrelevant.

Turning a disc with no centre hole, using a modified tailstock centre holding another disc and providing thrust.

This acrylic disc, with centre hole, was thick enough to mount directly between the slightly opened chuck jaws and the standard tailstock centre.

For thin material always use a block at the tailstock, as well as one in, or over, the headstock jaws. Folded sandpaper as mentioned above will increase drive friction. Make the blocks that are in or over the chuck jaws and held by the tailstock very close to the finished size. Supporting the disc very close to the finished edge will help control the work; otherwise it will just bend around the tool without actually being cut. Plywood or particle board make good blocks as they are easy to have in any size, and don't have a grain which may cause the block to bend when under pressure. If there is a centre hole in the work of say, 8mm, have an 8mm hole in the ply discs as well. Hold an 8mm rod (in effect a mandrel) in the chuck, with the sandwich of ply/disc/ply mounted on it. In the next photo you can see the tailstock taper is pushing onto a brass block. It too, has an 8mm hole. Have the 8mm mandrel come through the ply/disc/ply sandwich enough to have the brass block securely located on it, but not so much as to touch the tailstock taper. That way you can have the maximum amount of thrust; if the tail stock centre taper tip touches the mandrel it will be prevented from delivering maximum thrust to the sandwich.

The centre hole can be enlarged later, in the drill press or by holding the disc onto the faceplate with metal plates (p 111).

If you want to make a ring out of your disc, (once the outer diameter has been cut with a regular tool), and you have a centre hole and are using a mandrel, you can hold the disc against the headstock block with a new block, slightly smaller than the diameter of the hole you wish to cut, mounted on the tailstock point. The hole is cut out at the finished size using the parting tool. Because the ring is parted off, the waste is left under the tailstock block. Turn slowly, as the ring you care about will become free when the tool cuts through. It can't escape because of the presence of the tailstock, but could damage itself.

Be careful with measuring the cut size, you can't cut it twice!!

With no centre hole leave the original ply/disc/ply sandwich in place after cutting the outside diameter, and cut right through; first cut through the tailstock block, and then the disc you are making into the ring. If you disturb the ply/disc/ply sandwich with no centre hole you will never get the disc to run true again, so your ring will be inaccurate. You must rely on the friction of the pressure (you can use folded sandpaper) to stop the disc spinning and coming out of the lathe, so take the cuts slowly.
Photos next page.

Outer ring diameter finished with the regular tool, no centre hole.

The Tailstock block turned down, and the ring parted off with the parting tool.

A similar principle is used in the next photo for cutting the centre out of a spun cap (see page 142) to make a shouldered ring.

In order to provide thrust to the cap, a **VERY** useful modification to a tail stock centre is shown, which gives the required thrust and rotation to the work and allows plenty of room for a conventional tool set up. It is a process I use often, so I've made a dedicated mandrel for the headstock end from an aluminium rod, and set up time is just a few seconds.

The tool (diagram above) has been ground to a narrow tip, slightly tapering towards the rear to give clearance between the tool and the sides of the cut. The tip has been ground back so that when the cap is parted off, the waste stays with the centre disc, and the ring, which I want, has a nice clean inside edge.

Using a modified revolving tailstock centre to provide thrust and room at the same time for the tool to cut this small cap.

Turning Tapers

Using the Chuck

Tapers are often required, not the least for making special drives to fit the wood lathe Headstock spindle taper. For these short pieces the **Top-Slide** will usually have enough movement.

Here, you can hold the work in the chuck, and then set the Top-slide to the required angle. Keep the tool tip at the vertical centre height, see below.

The taper, may, at its minimum diameter, represent far more of a depth of cut than is possible in a single pass. Use the Cross-slide to regulate the depth of cut. As you approach the final sizes be wary of taking off too much material, a tight fit can quickly turn into one that's too small.

If you're making a taper to fit the spindle taper of the engineers lathe you're actually working on, remove the entire chuck, with the work undisturbed, to check the fit in the spindle taper. If you remove the work from the chuck, it'll never go back in exactly the same position.

The picture below shows a small V belt pulley being modified. The Top-slide will be set to the same angle for each side.

Working Between Centres

Work cannot be held in the chuck at the head stock end and be off centre at the tail stock end. For long tapers, the work must be held **between the centres**, (in other words between two points) in order to allow the work to be at the lathe axis centre at the head stock, and off-centre at the tail stock end, and still revolve.

Unlike with wood, however, a drive cannot be simply pushed into the head-stock end of the work.

A centre hole should be bored in each end of the work to be turned (using the chuck and/or the fixed steady mentioned with a photo on page 122) with a centre drill bit.

Then a pointed centre is held in the tapered hole in the end of the main spindle. A live centre is mounted in the tail stock. The work is held between these points, and a driver attached to it. The driver is in turn driven by a stop bolted to the Faceplate or Driving Plate. See the diagram and photo below.

The driver has a hole large enough to fit the work, and a grub screw or bolt to fix it to the work, firmly enough so that the turning operation can be carried out without the driver slipping. This means the work is free to revolve around an axis that is NOT the same as the axis of the lathe itself, because it's on a sharp point at either end. The driver ensures a good rotational force.

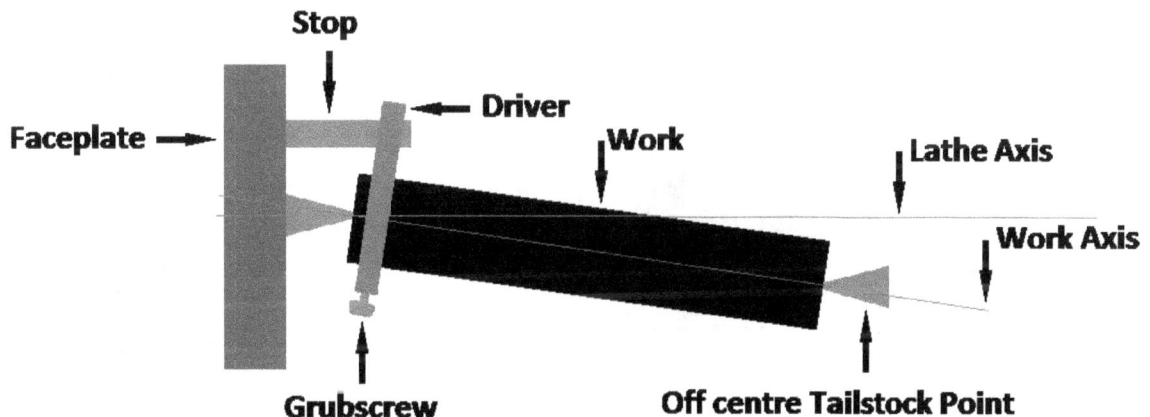

A diagram, looking down, of using a driver to rotate an off-set piece of work.

A close up of the Head Stock end, with the centre point, work with attached driver, and the stop bolted to the face plate.

'Off-setting' the tailstock to turn a taper.

The two (faint) vertical lines show the centre position for re-aligning the tailstock.

You can see the amount of offset from moving the tailstock looking towards the front of the lathe. This is limited to the amount of off-set available at the tailstock, and as with the Top-Slide tapers, is done a small cut at a time, with the tool **exactly at centre height**.

The same principle behind finding the diametric centre of a tube with the drill press is useful for determining the height of the cutting tool. Hold a piece of straight steel against the work, and see what the angle is. The tool in the next photo needs to be raised. When the steel is vertical, you're on the centre.

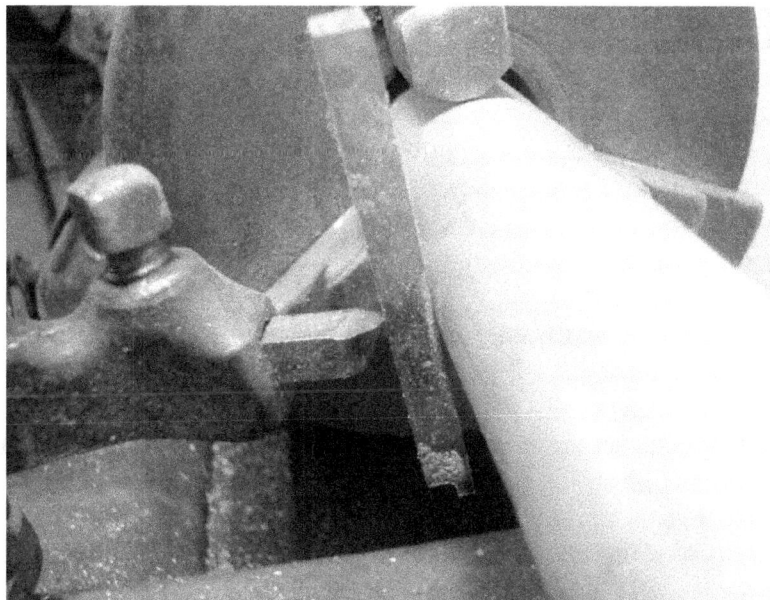

Form Tools

Form Tools are cutters which are shaped so that when they are pushed into the work they produce the required shape in one cut. They are very useful for making multiple pieces all exactly the same. The tools are effectively an HSS scraper, with the bevel facing down, held in the tool post. They are easy to make. These ones I made on the usual grinder, with the deep slot in the one on the left being made with a cut off wheel like the one being used on page 191.

The diagram shows the left one cutting a ferrule, and the right, making small 'feet '. Keep the cut at centre height, and work slowly. Form tools can be a great time saver on a wood lathe too, with the tool held in the hand, for shoulders, beads, stepped spigots etc.

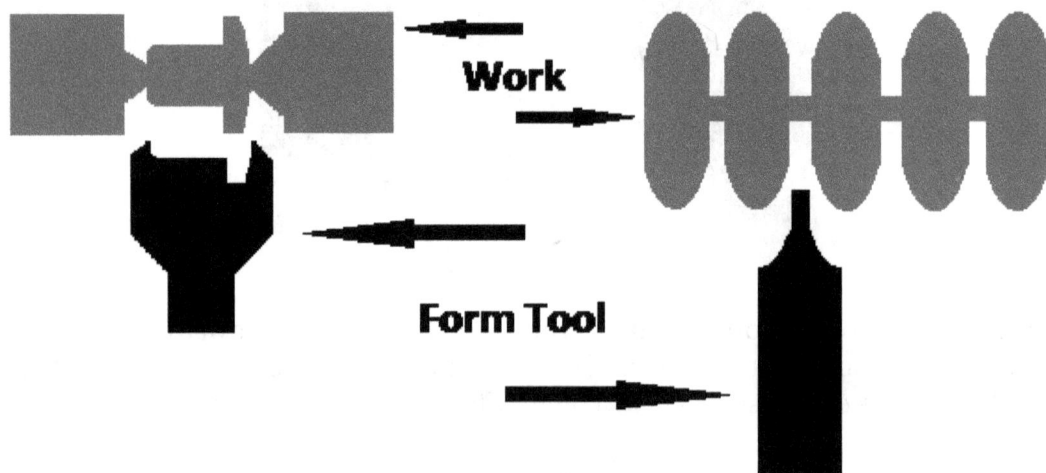

Work

Form Tool

Making Springs

These days springs are commonly available in a huge range of types and strengths. However, it is possible to wind them on a lathe. The set up is very simple. Hold a piece of metal in the tool post, with a small hole in it, through which you run the **spring wire**. You wind the springs on a shaft, which has a hole in it to accept one end of the wire. The spring, once wound, will expand when the tension comes off. Springs made from a small wire gauge expand the most often, to about twice the diameter of the shaft. Larger wire gauge springs expand less, so you will have to use a bit of trial and error to get it right.

Use the lowest spindle speed.

For tension springs, set the screw cutting gears to the diameter of the spring wire. So 12 gauge wire to 12 threads per inch, 16 gauge wire to 16 threads per inch and so on.

For compression springs, set the screw cutting gears to the required pitch (the distance between two points on the spring in a line) of the spring.

You can of course, run the springs in either a right or left hand direction, an important factor if they are to surround a revolving shaft; you don't want to have the spring unwind itself!

Winding a tension spring

Winding a compression spring

Metal Spinning

Professional Metal Spinning Lathes are very strong and solid affairs, with big heavy duty tool posts to stand the rigors of the work. As such, only relatively small and light gauge spinning is possible on a home workshop lathe, but with some practice, very satisfactory caps and such like can be made.

You need a **Form Chuck** which is mounted in the lathe chuck. It's essentially a metal (though wood will do for a short run) round section which you machine to be the exact size and shape of the inside of the desired piece. You also have a flat piece that is held by the Tail-stock centre, which squeezes the pre-cut disc to be spun between it and the form chuck. In the tool post, a bar is set up with a pivot, and the disc is physically forced, from the outer edge inwards, around and onto the form chuck by a smooth, preferably hardened, hand held 'spinning tool', really just a round bar. You can use soapy water or thin oil as a lubricant and plenty of it, never run dry, and use high rpm. Aluminium spins well, as do steel and brass but they may require annealing (making them red hot and then leaving them to cool slowly) to soften them as the action of spinning tends to harden the work, and it must be soft to spin well.

Once the shape has been achieved, trim the back edge off to a constant rim with a parting tool, usually held by hand.

Starting the metal spinning process

The finished cap, still on the form chuck, and a previously spun one.

Hand Turning

Brass (and alloys to some extent) can be turned in the lathe by using regular wood turning tools. This allows you to quickly form shapes that would, using the usual lathe tools in the tool post, be difficult or impossible. The brass is mounted in the lathe in the usual way, and a flat bar, with its top surface below the centre height, is held in the tool post to act as the tool rest. Keep the tools sharp. The skew chisel is very useful, especially using the sides, as are the very small bowl turning and finger nail gouges. Keep a very firm pressure down to the tool rest, and take small slow cuts and you can achieve a very good finish.

Care of the Lathe

Lubrication of the lathe is probably the most important thing to do. There are numerous oiling points on and around the lathe, and you should squirt some oil into these every day of use. Keeping the lathe bed clean and oiled makes the lathe operate more accurately and easily. There are a few different tools to use for lubrication.

From the top we can see, of course, the indispensible oil can. Perfect for oiling the ways (the lathe bed), the change wheels and all sorts of things!!

Below it is a 'Pom Pom' oil gun. This is able to deliver oil at a very much higher pressure than an oil can. The main body of the Pom Pom is filled, via the removable cap at the base, with oil, and the tip applied to an oil nipple. The gun is repeatedly pushed in and out to force oil into the oil nipple. It's wonderful for oiling carriage oil points.

Below that is the common grease gun.

The swarf and dust that is generated is a source of wear. They can get under slides and abrade the surfaces, settle onto the lead screw and, left uncleared, even form a packed lump that can get in the way of the carriage. Brass chips can be very fine, and find their way into the smallest of gaps, and cast iron chips are also very fine, and very hard. New cast iron may very well have grains of the casting sand embedded in it, which will ruin the edge on the tools. Using compressed air to clean down the lathe is not the best way to do it, the force of the air can force dirt into the very places you're trying to keep it out of. Better to use a brush.

The Cross-slide and the Top-slide will have screws that adjust pressure on metal strips which press on the inside of the slides. These strips are called gibs. Adjust the screws one at a time and after each adjustment, run the slide the whole length of its movement, to check there is no binding. Even then, you may have to slacken them a little once they are all adjusted, the collective tightness may make it hard to move the slide. A tight slide will add unwanted pressure on the slide screw. Don't forget to tighten the lock nuts.
The Top-slide is much more stable when it's fully supported by the slides underneath it, in the same way that the tail-stock is better when as much of the shaft as possible is contained within the tail-stock casting.

Some lathes have a gearbox which is used to select the drive speed for the lead-screw. The gearbox will have a site glass for checking the amount of oil in it, and the only maintenance of the gearbox is to keep the oil at the correct level.

Keep the chuck threads clear of swarf and chips, use the tool shown on page 106. It is bad practice to force a chuck onto the mandrel when it won't smoothly fit. Once again, compressed air is likely to force chips into the scroll gear area, and so make the working of the jaws difficult, and cause undue wear to the chuck mechanism. Chucks should be stored on their jaws so dust doesn't settle on the scroll gear.

Be cautious when using a used taper shank chuck, drive or drill. Check the taper carefully, and be sure to remove any burrs. Burrs will not only prevent the taper from fitting correctly, so compromising the accuracy of the alignment of the chuck or drill, they also prevent proper grip of the taper in its hole. If the taper has been seriously damaged, it may not tighten fully at all. Here, providing it is made smooth first, a small piece of paper can be wrapped around the taper ONCE, and not overlapping, before fitting to the shaft. The paper will give excellent grip, and prevent further damage to the shaft, should the taper slip.

And as with the wood lathe, in very cold conditions you may need to use low spindle speeds to warm up the headstock bearings.

THREAD TAPS and DIE NUTS

Cutting threads, or screws, both internal and external, is a very common requirement in the metal workshop. The most accurate way to do this is to cut the required threads using the metal lathe. However, while this gives the best results, there are times when it is simply not possible to use the lathe because, for example, the work piece is too large. Also, when a simple thread needs to be cut that only has to be accurate enough to have a nut or bolt fit it, it does not justify the time it takes to set up the lathe.

In these cases, the use of **Die Nuts and Thread Taps** is the method to use. The vast majority of threads are cut with them, either off the lathe completely, or by using the lathe simply as a guide. Both Die Nuts and Thread Taps fit into a wrench made for them.
In the case of using a **Thread Tap**, a pilot hole is first bored which is smaller in diameter than the outside diameter of the bolt. This allows the thread to be cut into the side wall of the hole. A list of drill sizes to use for common threads is given in the Appendix, page 208.

Thread Taps typically come in three shapes: Taper, Second Cut and Bottom.

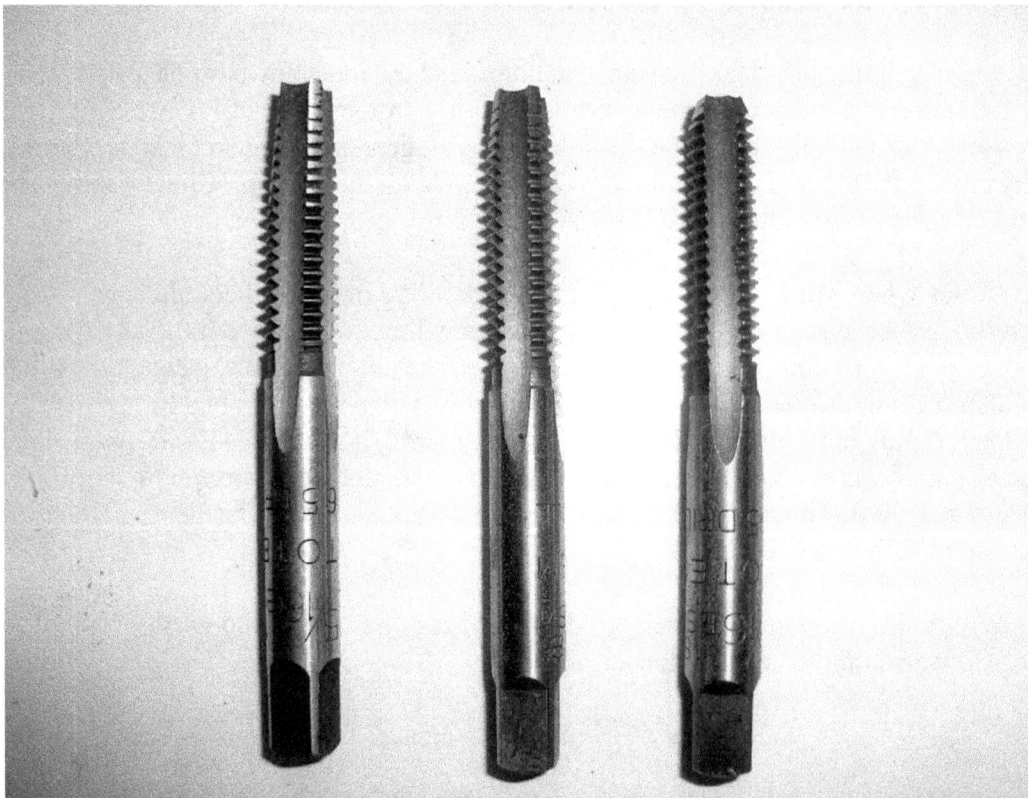

From left; Taper, Second Cut and Bottom

The taper tap has a long gentle taper which allows the tap to easily enter the hole, and to start the tapping process. Once it has reached the bottom limit, the second cut tap is used which has a very much reduced taper, and then finally the bottom tap which has almost no taper at all and will cut the thread very close to the bottom of the hole.

When using a tap, be very careful to keep the tap aligned exactly with the bored hole, or you risk snapping the tap. Taps are extremely hard, and brittle, and so are not only easy to break, but the broken piece stuck in the half formed thread is almost impossible to remove.

 It will be jammed tight, and being so hard, you can't drill it out.

Once the tap has started to bite, you must reverse the direction frequently, say at ¼ turns or so. This is to clear the swarf from the cutters on the tap. Every few full turns, remove the tap entirely and clear the hole and the cutters before resuming the work. If you have the room, make the hole deeper than you intend to cut the thread.

The tap is most likely to snap when it reaches the absolute bottom of the hole and comes to an abrupt stop.

Steel, cast iron and aluminium require lubrication, and be cautious when tapping plastics, as they will get hot, and may melt inside the hole and bind the tap, leading to breakage. You can lubricate the plastic too. Holding the work in the head stock chuck in the lathe, and the tap in the tailstock chuck is a great way to ensure the thread is cut exactly in line with the hole. Leave the tailstock unlocked from the bed, so it can slide in and out as you work. Don't turn the lathe on, just you your hand to rotate the headstock chuck in and out. Once again, only rotate a small amount, ¼ turn or so each way.

Taps are available with right and left hand threads.

There is a list of drill sizes to use for the various thread taps on page 208.

Die Nuts cut the thread on the outside of a piece.

A nice solid ½ inch BSW (British Standard Whitworth) Die Nut

Once again, the piece needs to be correctly sized before the thread is cut. The method is similar to that used with the thread tap, in that work slowly, by a small amount, ¼ turn forwards, and then back to clear the swarf. You can get cheap die nuts which are really much too small in their outside dimension. They are very prone to snapping when even a small amount of swarf is inside them, so be very careful to frequently remove swarf.
A small taper on the front of the work will make it a bit easier to start the thread. The die nut will cut the thread in one pass (unlike the tap which has various tapers), so it will generate more swarf. If you can hold the work in the headstock chuck, then you can use the lathe to ensure the thread is true to the axis of the work. Lock the headstock with the back gear, and lock the tailstock in position as well. If you use the jaws of the tailstock chuck to provide thrust to the outside of the die nut, the die nut will be kept square to the work and the thread will be more accurate. Expand the jaws so they press on the nut at as large a diameter as possible. Now use the tailstock to provide thrust with your right hand, and turn the die nut wrench with your left hand, as you can see in the next diagram. As the die nut begins to cut the thrust is diminished, so you will have to advance the tailstock shaft as you work, to maintain good thrust. You have to use both hands at once in both directions; to maintain thrust while cutting and also allow clearance for the die nut to be wound back to clear swarf. Once the thread has been cut right through the die nut, you can remove the tail stock as you no longer will need the thrust, the die nut will be true to the axis and you can continue to work with just the work piece held in the head stock chuck.
Die nuts also come in left and right hand threads.

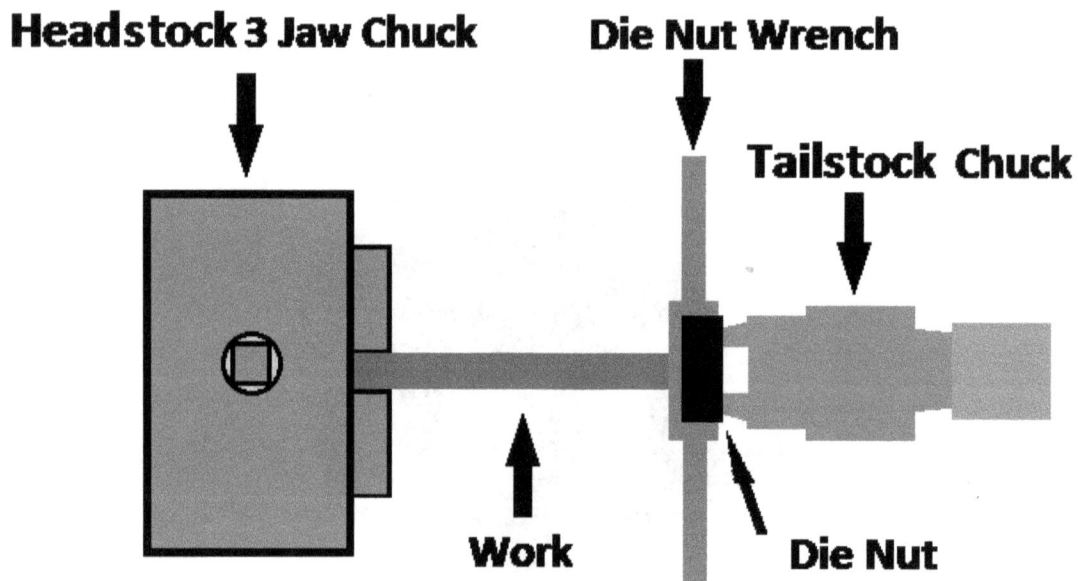

Using the Tailstock chuck to guide a Die Nut

VICES, CLAMPS and CRAMPS

A vice is an indispensible tool in a workshop, and there are a wide range to choose from. Here are some points of the common ones.

The measurement of the vice is how wide the jaws are, so a 5 inch vice will be 5 inches wide, but may open to 6 inches.

The **Wood Vice** has wide, flat and smooth jaws, and will typically be able to accommodate boards up to 12 inches wide. It should have a quick release action which releases the main screw from its nut, and allows the front jaw to quickly be slid in and out. Release the quick release lever, and tighten by the hand bar.

The vice should be set in the front of the bench, its top flush with the bench surface. Bolts hold the vice in place, going down through the vice mounting holes and the bench top. Be sure to set the bolt heads well below the bench top surface, if they stick up they will be forever a nuisance and a hazard for tools.

An un-mounted wood worker's vice

An **Engineer's Vice** is mounted on top of the bench surface. The jaws are grooved to give extra grip, so covers or smooth strips may be needed to prevent the pressure of the jaws marking soft materials. A quick release mechanism is sometimes an option.

These vices come in a variety of shapes, from a straight vice, to ones where the jaws are on an angle, to those that allow the jaws to pivot.

There are typically three bolts holding them to the bench, one either side, and one at the rear, accessible when the front jaw is removed.

Vices have to cope with all sorts of work and so must be firmly mounted. There's nothing worse than having the vice loose when you're trying to do some accurate work. Having large thick steel plates underneath the nuts helps to stop the bolts working loose on a wooden bench, and you should always use as large a bolt diameter as the vice mounting holes will allow. Make sure the front of the rear jaw is beyond the edge of the bench; the vice in this picture is badly mounted, and causes no end of frustration.

Wrong !!

Right !!

The **Flat Vice** has been mentioned in the drill section. They are vital for accuracy and safety with a drill dress, and are frequently clamped to the drill table, bearing in mind the safety issues involved with clamps and machines, mentioned below.

Often, it's tempting to hold a piece to be drilled on one side of the vice. This is hard work for the vice, as all the pressure is concentrated on just one side of the screw. It's better to have a similarly sized piece in the opposite side as well, to even up the pressure, and to make the vice jaws grip more squarely on the work.

G and F Clamps are very useful for all sorts of jobs.

A variety of hand clamps. From left, G and F, the locking plastic clamp and spring loaded plastic clamp. These last two are weak, and shouldn't be used with machinery.

Of the two, **G Clamps** are the more stable and will provide a tighter grip. **F Clamps** on the other hand, are very quick to use. Try to have the threaded section of the F clamp between the foot and the head itself quite short, they will grip better that way. Clamps are useful for holding temporary stops and guides on machines, like saw benches and moulders, and for holding guides for routers and drills. A G clamp is always the safer option when doing this sort of work. The F clamp can be prone to loosening itself via the vibration of the machine, with disaster a very real outcome. Some F clamps are more susceptible than others to working themselves loose, so do be careful when using them in these situations. Two clamps working together can double the distance they will cover, but once again, not on or with machinery.

Sash Cramps are the ones to use for long work. The strongest ones are the **T** sectioned ones, but of course the most expensive. Flat **Bar Cramps** are very good though. Either of these two kinds of cramps can have their tail piece removed, and their bars bolted together to form a much longer cramp, with a screw head at each end. Flat bars do this more agreeably because the flat bars fit together nicely, but if you want to bolt two T bar cramps together, a slice of plywood or scrap the thickness of the combined depth of the Ts in between the bars will keep them aligned. Usually though, a small misalignment doesn't matter. Two bolts will stop the bars acting like a giant pair of scissors, which can be dangerous to you and/or the work. Even with cramps of differing hole spacing, you can usually find two sets of holes that coincide.

A long water pipe cramp and two 'T' bar sash cramps bolted together for extra length.

Also available are the head and tail sections of a cramp that uses **steel water pipe** as its main bar. The head section screws onto a threaded portion (as it's a water pipe the thread is B.S.P or British Standard Pipe thread) and the tail section slides up and down on the pipe, locking in any position with an off-set foot. They are a very versatile cramp, because they are as long as you make the pipe, and the foot is able to swing around the pipe, so you can clamp with the foot at 90° (or even 180°) to the head.

The natural action of any of the cramps is to pull out of line with the bar, because the axis of the screw is set away from the axis of the bar, though the axes are parallel. Over time, and especially with enthusiastic tightening, the head and sometimes tail ends of the cramps become bent out of true alignment with the bar. So when cramping up, say, a cupboard door frame, the tendency is for the cramp to pull the door frame so that the edges of the frame where it touches the cramp are in full contact with the cramp, but the frame itself is pulled out of true. The remedy is to have a scrap of wood between the cramp and the door frame, but to lift the scrap up so the force of the cramp on the scrap transfers the force to the door frame exactly in the centre of the frame, so keeping the frame true, see below. Of course, it is often good practice to have a scrap between the cramp and the work anyway, to avoid pressure marks from the cramp jaws. (Next photo)

154

A **Hose Clamp** makes a quick and easy piston ring compressor, but use a thin strip of a soft material (drink can aluminium is ideal) between the hose clamp and the precious piston rings to avoid damaging them.

This piston was too large for even two hose clamps joined together, and I didn't have three, so a homemade one of a strip of aluminium and a gutter bolt did the job beautifully!!

LAMINATING, WOOD GLUES and COATINGS

Laminating Wood

Laminating wooden strips together gives great strength to a structure that otherwise might be fragile, or it can be done simply for decoration.

For example, if you were to just band saw an 'S' shape from a piece of 8 x 2, there will be areas where the grain is running through a very short section, and the wood is almost certain to fail along these points. However, if you laminate some 2 inch wide strips of 2 or 3mm thickness together, the resultant 'S' will be extraordinarily strong.

The thinner the strip the tighter the radius it will happily bend to. Veneer will bend to an amazingly tight bend. The strips should be of clear wood, so no knots. The strips are glued together and then they have to be held in a former until the glue sets.

For a simple arch, you can use just the inside former, and stretch the strips around it. You must bear in mind that the outer-most strip must be longer than the inner-most one because of the increased radius. Generally though, I always make sure I have plenty of spare length, at either end. Use a full former; if you just have one or two points the laminate will not be a smooth curve. The strips will tend to stay straight, in-between the points.

For a more complicated shape, like our 'S', you need a full form on both sides.

The easiest way to make one is to decide on the finished thickness of the laminate and cut the complete shape out from a block, so the 'waste' wood from the block becomes the 'laminate'. A sandwich built up to the required thickness, made from ply or particle board, makes a good block to cut the former from. Be sure not to have any nails or screws where you want to cut! Liberally coat the former's faces and edges with candle wax to prevent excess glue sticking to it, and a piece of newspaper between the laminate and the former also helps with removal.

For really tight bends, heating the strips and putting them into the former without glue until they are cold, then gluing them up helps stop them snapping.

If they will fit, wrap them in a damp towel and heat them for a short time in a microwave oven. You can heat them in hot water, but then you'll need to allow them time in the former to dry, and even then use a glue that will be O.K with damp surfaces.

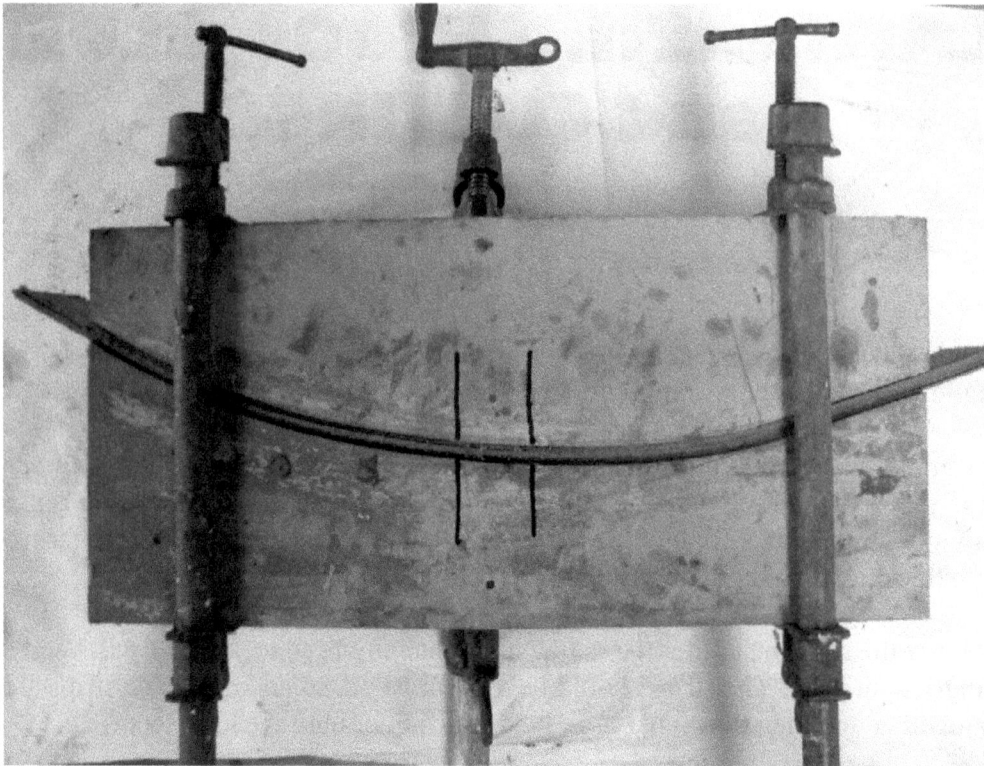

The two black lines help to align the former correctly. Having a cramp underneath stops the two on the top pulling the press out of 'square'.

An example of a cylinder laminated from pine and kauri to leave a 125mm diameter hole running the full length inside. The usual lathe centres are driving onto fixed plywood discs.

If you are laminating just for decoration, you can enhance the effects by using alternating kinds of wood, or add colour to the glue. Water based paint powder works well, just mix the powder straight into the glue. All the glues except the resorcinol-formaldehydes can be coloured. Adding sanding dust to the glue will make the glue darker than the original wood, and gives a nice effect.

Wood Glues

There are a few different kinds of wood glues, and quite a number of each kind.

You need to have decided on a range of criteria that will help you determine exactly which glue is the suitable one for the job at hand. For example, what timber is going to be glued, what conditions will the resultant join be subjected to, and how much you have to spend!!

Animal or Hot Glues were the industry standard in the past. They are still available but not very commonly used, although they are still used for musical instruments. They are applied hot (by melting the glue in a vat in a hot water bath) and adhere as they cool.

PVA (polyvinyl acetate) **Glues** were extremely popular when they were first introduced because of their ease of use (squirt it straight out of the bottle), fast drying times and low cost. They don't like dampness in the timber to be glued, or being subjected to damp conditions afterwards. They have only moderate strength and life. They are nicely summed up as a 'hobbyist' glue, I think, useful in the workshop for glue and paper chucking, and layering up sanding drums and the like, though there again, I would use it in conjunction with nails or screws. They dry clear.

Polyurethane Glues, like 'Gorilla' (TM) are quickly finding a following. They adhere to an astonishing range of materials, like leather, rubber, plastics, glass, ceramics, metal, and of course wood. They are easy to use, cheap to buy and better than PVA in damp areas, but you wouldn't build a boat with it. They are quite good for furniture and also dry clear.

Urea-Formaldehyde Glues are inexpensive (compared with epoxies), and are strong and easy to use. A powder is mixed with water to form a paste which is applied to one side of the join, the acid hardener is applied to the other. They cure overnight, are excellent glues for furniture, and will dry clear. They are not good in wet or very hot conditions.

Resorcinol-Formaldehyde Glues are very strong and resistant to boiling water and pretty much everything else. In past years they were considered the only way to go for wooden aircraft frames. The resin is mixed with a powder. The result is rather runny, so doesn't fill gaps like the epoxies do. Also it is poisonous, and has a deep purple colour.

Epoxy is a term which covers a whole bunch of different glues. Essentially a resin is mixed with a hardener in ratios determined by the manufacturer. They are resistant to water and heat, so great for boats. They can produce rashes, so avoid skin contact. Also they are rather expensive. They usually dry milky to clear. Some are in a gel formation, while others require the use of fillers to bring the consistency up to a gap filling level. Various hardeners are available for most of them for full curing at low or high temperatures.

With all the glues, for use with furniture and the like, some rules apply which are worth mentioning. The surface should be dry and dust free. Wood which is oily in nature will accept a glue more readily if the wood is de-greased first by swabbing it down with a clear solvent. Be careful with the solvent, of course, avoid skin contact, breathing vapours and sources of ignition.

When laminating boards, to make a table top for example, don't have the gap between the boards absolutely zero, or clamp them up too tightly. You will 'starve' the joint of glue, and it won't be as strong as it might have been. If the edges of the boards are very smooth, roughen slightly with fine sandpaper to allow the glue to 'key in'.

Cleaning away most of the excess glue while it is still soft will save time later, but keep a bit handy to check on the level of cure, it can be difficult to tell how cured a glue is if you can't touch it !

Mixed urea-formaldehyde glue resin will remain viable for weeks in an airtight container, and will then set when the hardener is applied, whereas glues with hardeners mixed in will simply set. The PVA and Polyurethane glues will patiently wait for years in their bottles, if they are airtight.

Epoxy glues are exothermic, which means they give off heat as they cure. So if you mix half a litre and have it sitting in a tin can, it can become so hot that the whole lot cures in just a few minutes, before you've had time to use it. So quickly mix it and then spread it out over a large area with a stick, to allow the heat to dissipate harmlessly.

Old telephone books provide endless pages of good paper for glue mixing. Just tear yesterdays one off and go again! Ice block sticks make great stirring sticks. They are cheap and free from dust and fibres.

Coatings

The issue of finish coating both metal and wood is an important consideration.

Surface coating of metal for the home workshop is generally confined to a variety of paints, and powder coating. The coatings not only enhance the look of the article, but prevent rusting and corrosion. Invariably, the surface to be coated must be clean. This means free from oils and waxes, rust and corrosion, and even moisture. Bead blasters, sand blasters and fine (1200 grit or so) 'wet and dry' paper can be used to prepare the surface, and the tiny scratches left give a good key to the coating.

I'm of the opinion that paint was really invented just to show up all the flaws in the surface which you think is ready for finishing!!! Paint will usually require a primer. The safest option is to discuss your needs with the paint supplier, and depending on the metal, (steel, brass, copper, alloy etc) different primers may be required for the different top coats.

Spray cans are a very convenient way to paint small jobs. They are pre-mixed to the correct viscosity, and don't require the unbelievably difficult task of completely cleaning out a compressed air spray gun. In fact, the cleaning of the spray gun is so difficult and time and solvent consuming that I have a gun that has only ever had clear lacquer in it. Spray cans are available with primers and even spray putty for getting a very smooth surface for the paint. Be sure to allow plenty of curing time between coats, and to clear the nozzle by holding the can upside down and letting some gas come through. Shake them VERY well, before use; the steel ball in them MUST rattle freely and leave lots of dents in the bottom of the can.

Powder Coating is very achievable and affordable for the home workshop. Very well priced units are available, and they work really well. They use exactly the same powder as the commercial units, so there's no compromising on the quality of the result, and a huge variety of colour, clear and texture is available. The clear is about the only thing I've ever found that will successfully coat polished brass.

The powder is held in a pottle, similar to a paint spray gun. Compressed air drives the powder through the gun, but where the paint sprayer uses lots of air, the powder coater is very gentle, and you can barely hear it. As the powder is forced through the nozzle, it passes electrodes which are at a very high voltage. The little guns are at about 50,000 volts the big ones over 100,000. This static charge on the very fine powder particles means that when they leave the gun, they are attracted to the work piece which is kept at 0 volts by an earth wire. This process means the powder coating is very even, and will even go round corners to a degree, but is only designed for electrically conductive pieces. The piece is then put in an oven and baked, at around 180C-210C for 10 minutes, so an old domestic oven is suitable though any heat source will do, I've even used a gas burner in a steel box.

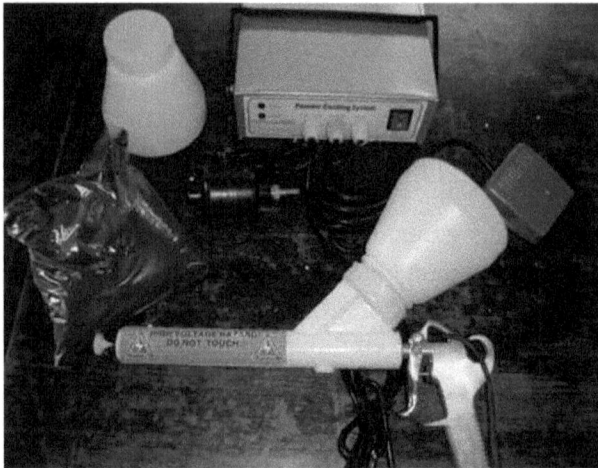

The complete small workshop Powder Coater seen on the left. Comprised of the power supply with foot switch, gun, water trap, two pottles and a bag of powder, they are very affordable.

The wire hooks the pieces are hanging from also provide a convenient way to attach the earth wire during the coating process, and a way to handle the piece without disturbing the powder, which is fragile till baked. Note the old oven !

Just never use the oven for food again, as the gases given off are toxic.

The powder melts, and after slow cooling, becomes the hard durable coating we know. You can coat non-conductive things, but as the powder is not attracted to the surface, you have to just let the powder settle onto the surface, so you can really only do flat pieces.

'Over spray' can be re-used if it's clean and dry, so spraying, (with a **dust mask**) in a small booth (I use a cardboard box on its side) is a good idea. Make a swivel, attach the earth wire to it and hang it from the roof of the booth. Hang the pieces to be coated on wire hooks, so you can handle them easily, and the hooks also act as a conductor, to achieve a good earth path from the piece to the earthed swivel. This way, you can turn the pieces round easily without disconnecting the earth wire every time, and quickly get an even coat. Don't use a fishing swivel as the coatings on them are insulating.

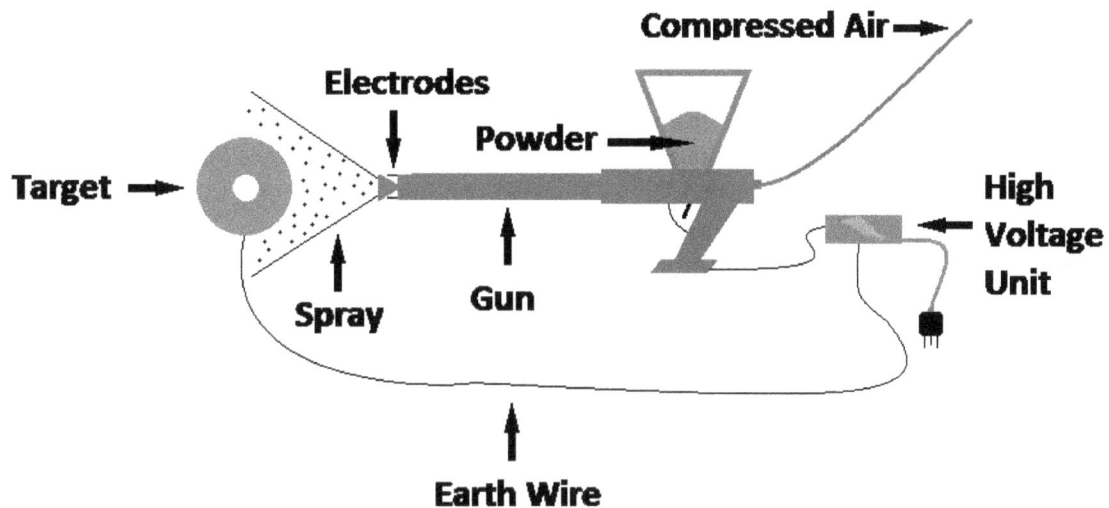

A diagram of a powder coating set up.

Wood Finishings are many, varied and likely to cause disagreements between their supporters!! I tend to be somewhat pragmatic with the coating of my work.

There are numerous oils available which can be slopped on to finished work. Among the most common are **Linseed**, **Tung** and **Danish Oils**. While Linseed is considered a drying oil, to my way of thinking it offers very little to the wood worker. It looks nice to begin with, and of course is cheap and easy to apply. However, it will soak into the wood, and needs constant re-application to retain that initial glow. This is part of the problem, it continues to soak into the wood, despite being a drying oil, and eventually the wood becomes soft and saturated. It can soak into and break down glued joins. It provides little protection against knocks and bumps, and none at all against water or water vapour. I will never forget my rain covered newly finished spinning wheel.... The rain marks never came out. Linseed may also go mouldy. Setting agents can be added, Tung oil being one, but do be careful, some of the setting agents still contain lead.

Tung oil will actually set, (and can be added to Linseed to set it). It is better than Linseed for water resistance, but is no better really than Linseed for scratches. It is easy to apply, and after successive coats, with a rub down with steel wool in between, will produce a nice satiny feel finish.

Danish oil is made from Tung or Linseed oil and is certainly better at protecting the wood. It is applied, like the other two, by brush, roller or cloth. Wipe off the excess, and once dry, give a rub down with steel wool before a second or third coat. Balled up cloths soaked in it can spontaneously ignite, so keep them flat till dry.

None of these oils are really suitable for kitchen ware because they are so pungent, but this is one area where I agree that oils do have a role to play. Even though linseed can be harmlessly ingested, stay with a nice olive oil!!

Synthetic coatings such as **Polyurethanes** and **Nitrocellulose Lacquers** have pretty much replaced oils, particularly from a commercial viewpoint. They offer very good scratch resistance, and can withstand boiling water. However, they are expensive compared to oils, are much more difficult to apply, and pose more of a threat to the applicator and arguably the environment.

I have used polyurethanes on furniture. I won't do it again!! Once I even used, at the customer's request, Moisture Curing Polyurethane. What a nightmare. It uses atmospheric moisture to cause a chemical reaction and sets extremely hard, well beyond the abrasive powers of my beloved steel wool. To smooth the first coat down was a herculean task with 'wet and dry' sandpaper. It will look as good today as it did 30 years ago I'm sure, because it was like coating the furniture in glass, but avoid it. Great on floors though and a good argument can be mounted for its use on kitchen benches, where the rub down is easier, and recoats not impossible.

A similar story, though not quite so dire, goes with simple polyurethane. It can be sprayed, brushed or wiped on. Not a great finish for furniture, and not hard wearing enough for floors or benches.

Nitrocellulose lacquers have become very popular with industry for finishing furniture. A sanding sealer can be used first, indeed, it, once dried, can be buffed to a reasonable sheen, recoated and left as the finish coat. However, the full system recommends the sealer, then the lacquer as the top coat. The lacquers are available in a wide range of gloss percentages, and if you care to, you can make your own gloss preference by mixing. I have found them to be reliable, long lasting and to offer good protection, though they really need to be sprayed on. Allow good drying between coats, steel wool before the next application, and allow a day or so to really cure. They require a very volatile thinner, so be safety conscious and wear a good respirator. There are 'universal' thinners available which are much cheaper than the recommended thing, and work just as well. Not that the manufacturer would agree!!!

Wood Stains come and go, in and out of fashion.

There are two broad categories; water based and spirit based. Both tend to be difficult to get an even colouring of the wood.

I found that applying with a cloth is the best way, and as the first point of contact would always result in a darker patch than the later bits, I thin the stain out to a huge degree, maybe 80% solvent to 20% stain, spirit or water based. This means that the surface of the wood can be made running wet, and so you have plenty of time to get it evenly applied over the whole work, and even time to rub the excess off with a dry cloth. Be sure to wear rubber gloves. Stains, even the NGR (non grain raising) ones raise the grain in the wood, making your nice smooth finish all rough and hairy. Don't panic, get the steel wool out. Be sure the stains, particularly the water based ones are dry before top coating. And finally, be aware that the stains will make it easier to get 'runs' in the top coats because the grain of the wood won't absorb the same amount of the first coat. Go lightly to start with, especially when spraying.

ACRYLIC

Acrylic is a wonderful material for making all sorts of things, and I have had extensive experience in machining and using acrylic during my 30+ years of making kaleidoscopes.

Acrylic is made by two different processes; casting where the liquid acrylic is cast in mould or formed into sheets between two sheets of glass, or extruded in its liquid form through dies to make the shapes. It is therefore available in a variety of sections (shapes) like rods, tubes and sheets. Coloured acrylic is available, but is more likely to be cast. Generally, cast is more expensive, so I usually use extruded!! It comes with a paper cover over each side of the sheets and clear film over the extrusions. The paper can be a challenge to remove. Avoid tearing it by keeping the pull angle low, and if you do tear it, stop and work somewhere else. Very old paper can be **very** difficult to remove.

Either cast or extruded acrylic can be cut on the table saw, drop saw or band saw. It is very brittle, so use fine teeth if you can and work slowly. Definitely wear eye and ear protection, but then you always do, don't you!! Acrylic can be filed, bored with twist bits, flat bits augers and forstener cutters, and tapped. The main danger is one of heat. So work slowly, clear the swarf often and when tapping or using die nuts I like to use a little thin oil. When cutting threads, frequently remove the cutter and clear all the swarf. If you don't, not only is there a risk of the tool binding, you can strip the thread you have made with the swarf build up, and ruin the job.
You can machine acrylic on the lathe as you would steel, with a small tip radius on the tool and slow feed, or just use hand held wood turning tools.

When you machine extruded acrylic in particular, stress is built up in the material close to the machined edge, in a greater degree than cast. You won't see the stress until you glue one piece to another, like when I machine a tube true on both ends and then glue a disc cover over it. Once the glue has cured, I'd find zillions of little cracks have appeared, totally ruining the appearance, never mind the structural integrity. The only way to rectify this is to anneal the acrylic **before** you glue it up. You need to put all the pieces, once they have been completely machined, into an oven set to around 80°C for a certain amount of time which varies according to thickness, and then turn the oven off and leave the pieces in there overnight to slowly cool. Once the stress has been removed by the annealing, you can successfully glue it up. Be warned though, at this temperature the acrylic is soft, and will change shape if you let it. There's a table of annealing times in the Appendix, page 208.

It also tends to shrink slightly when hot, so a disc with a 25 mm hole in the centre will be a slightly smaller disc with a 24 mm hole in the centre. No use if you're wanting to put a 25 mm shaft in there, though the shaft will shrink a little too. So I always make my discs too big (you can safely machine the glued up piece later), and put a metal keeper (spacer) in the hole, to prevent it shrinking. Keep everything on a good flat surface, for instance, a steel plate or sheet of glass. Your tube will go out of round too; if you care, put keepers inside.

For my kaleidoscope chambers, I didn't care so much if the tube shrank, as long as the sides fitted. The final shaping was always done after glue up.

Here is an example of an acrylic kaleidoscope chamber, in the next picture, with hand turned, and clear powder coated brass fittings.

The Chamber pieces were made as described, then one end glued on, cured, and the pieces added to the Chamber before the second side was fixed. The discs had shoulders cut into them that were a loose fit, because of the shrinkage, so the Chamber was pretty much true to the axles. A small screw with washer is just visible on the far side for filling with liquid, and full cure of the cement was achieved by inserting a small tube into the chamber through this hole and pumping, with an aquarium tank air pump, tiny amounts of air through for 12 hours to clear the vapour.

Once cured, I would put it back in the lathe for machining the outside edges. The first edge was easy to machine as the other side which was still square could easily be held in the three jaw chuck. The second one was a bit trickier because the large radius on the first side to be rounded gave poor grip to the chuck, and I needed to be careful not to damage the surface. I would hold the rounded end lightly in the chuck, and maintain position with the tail stock live centre running in the glued in axle on the other side.

 The basic cutting of the sides was done with the regular engineers lathe tool, the radius and finishing with a hand held skew chisel.
Acrylic will sand with a fine 'wet and dry' and steel wool gives a nice quick finish.

The final polish is achieved with a gas flame; any will do, played carefully on the edges you want to polish. This melts the acrylic surface until it's like the original surface was. It will bubble and catch fire if you are too enthusiastic, so be careful.

The photo above shows a collection of some of the pieces that make up a complicated kaleidoscope. Most of them are acrylic, machined on the engineers lathe after rough cutting on the band saw. They have all been flame polished after sanding and a steel wool, and then painted. Enamel paint will take to acrylic just by itself, though a primer is available. The finished kaleidoscope is seen below. The large ring has been glued to the Ball with epoxy. Acrylic doesn't take to epoxy very well. It works here simply because of the large surface area. The large aluminium disc has been powder coated black, the brass fittings powder coated clear.

The complete kaleidoscope.

Finally, acrylic sheet can be slumped into shapes. Almost any thickness can be used; I have slumped 1 inch thick sheet. You simply put the acrylic in an oven and gently heat it to around 80°C, for a few hours. Too much heat can cause bubbles. Have the mould you are going to use ready and close by, the sheet needs to be hot and will cool surprisingly quickly.

The acrylic doors and sides on this kaleidoscope cabinet have been slumped.

WELDERS, WELDING and SOLDERING

The field of professional welding is too enormous for any in depth discussion here, so some general points will suffice. Usually the choice is between electric welding and gas welding.

A gas welder allows you to weld, braze, solder, gas cut steel, heat bend steel, temper steel and flame polish acrylic. However, you often have to hire the bottles rather than own them outright, and you run the risk of an unused set losing its gas through slight leakage.

An electric welder will just weld, usually steel. You invariably own the machine though, and if the electrodes are kept dry, they will last for years, so the welder is always ready to go when you need it.

Electric (arc) **Welders** come in all sorts of kinds, but for infrequent amateur use, a simple AC or DC welder is quite adequate. They both use an electrode, which is a metal rod encased in a hard flux. The heat of the arc melts both the rod, and the flux. The flux prevents oxidation on the surfaces that you are welding. The electrodes come in various diameters, and the larger the electrode, the bigger the weld fillet, and the more current is required. The choice is largely determined by the job at hand. The process generates large amounts of nasty gases you don't want to breathe, and of course, an incredibly bright and retina destroying light. Early cinema projectors used exactly this process to generate the intense light for the projectors. As well as a blinding light, a large amount of Ultra-violet light is produced, so a full face mask with an approved eye shield is essential. The finished weld has a 'slag' covering it. This is the solidified residue of the flux, with any impurities it has absorbed from the metals. Just be careful when chipping the slag off the finished weld. It's often still hot, and is very hard and brittle. It's just the thing for serious damage to your eyes, so wear safety glasses.

Inert Gas electric **Welders** are fine though they are a lot more expensive. The inert gas in the MIG [metal inert gas] welders, for example, shields the work area from atmospheric oxygen and so you don't need a flux. Essential for full aluminium welding but great for steel, and stainless steel too.

Gas Welding uses a supply of flammable gas through a welding 'torch' to heat the parent metals so that they are melted and fused together, usually with a filler rod as well.

Brazing uses a filler rod which is melted into the weld area and bonds to the parent metals which are themselves not melted. Filler rods are varied; steel, stainless steel, brass and other alloys. Usually they use a flux, often in the form of a powder or paste into which the hot tip of the filler rod is dipped. The flammable gases used are commonly acetylene or propane, and they are usually mixed, in the torch itself, with oxygen to give a greater temperature.

A special tip is available which uses the venturi action of the flammable gas coming out of the torch to suck in air, and mix with it, to give a good flame. The temperature is less than that of the pure oxygen mix, but adequate for low temperature brazing.

Keep the cylinders upright and cool at all times, and be sure to have a reliable regulator to keep the pressure below 15psi. Above this acetylene is explosive.

When brazing tool-steels avoid overheating the work. Once brazed, allow the work to cool gradually, do not quench it. Stainless steel brazing needs special fluxes, and I like to put them on before you start, when the work is cold. Again, don't overheat the work, and don't quench.

Cutting torches are available which have an extra control valve. Once the steel is pre-heated you inject extra oxygen into the flame for fast and accurate cutting.

Soldering is similar to brazing, though not as strong. The metals are only heated to the melting point of the filler rod, solder, which is a much lower temperature than that used for brazing. Soldering can be done by heating the work with a gas torch (carefully), a soldering iron pre-heated in a fire or by a flame, or with an electric soldering iron. A flux is used, though with solder for electrical wires, the flux is embedded in the solder wire itself. Otherwise, the flux is in a liquid or paste form.

Avoid over heating the work. Soldering is best done just above the melting point of the solder.

Solder used to always be, and sometimes still is, a mix of tin and lead, in varying ratios depending on the task at hand. The gases generated by using these types of solder are very toxic, from the lead, so good ventilation is needed. Nowadays leadless solder is available and commonly used for plumbing and electronics, and lead lighting work.

Aluminium is a difficult metal to weld in the home workshop as it usually requires the use of inert gas welders. However, aluminium can be 'welded ' by use of a product which is sort of like a solder. A rod like solder is used, in that it melts below the melting point of the parent metal. However, the parent metal is melted too.

The method used is to bring the aluminium temperature up to the melting point of the rod. You can do this in any way you choose, LPG flame, oxy-acetylene flame or even by putting the piece on a hot plate or in an oven. When the work is hot enough to melt the rod, push the end of the rod into the work area, and it will melt and form a molten blob. However, the heating process will have formed an impenetrable oxide film over the surface of the aluminium, and the 'solder' is unable to bond. Now you use a stainless steel point to scrape away under the oxide layer **underneath the molten blob** where there is an oxygen free environment. Now the rod is able to chemically combine with the aluminium, and so will form a good bond. You can use the stainless scraper as a trowel, and manipulate the molten rod, once it has bonded with the work, so it will cover holes and cracks, and happily join a drink can to a thick block. It is remarkable stuff and can be used on any alloy with a melting point higher than the rod. The join is very strong, quite hard, and has more resistance, electrically, than aluminium.

ELECTRIC MOTORS

Electric Motors are the heart of the modern workshop. It's very easy to have several running at the same time. There was a time when I would have up to ten running at the same time. I was running some serious production equipment mind you. I had two motors running on an auto lathe, two on an auto sander with another one on the extractor, a disc sander with a dust collector, a saw-dust extractor for the lathe, and I would occasionally use the grinder and air compressor. All for one operator!!

There are a wide variety of electric motors available, all with their own niche. In a workshop, they tend to fall into just a few categories and so we'll only consider the ones you might be most likely to come across.
 There are many different electrical supply systems throughout the world, running different voltages and frequency. You will invariably simply buy motors in your local area which are suitable for your supply, so we don't need to concern ourselves with those details.
The basic principles behind the motors are the same.
Motors are measured in terms of their work output, usually watts or horsepower.
Electrically, 1 horsepower (HP) is the equivalent of 750 Watts, so a 2 HP motor is
 1500 W.

The Appendix on page 204 has a guide to approximate HP required for various machines.

A watt is a measurement of power, a combination of voltage and current : $W = V \times A$: Watts equals Volts x Amps (current). So with a 110 V supply the 2 HP motor draws 13.6 amps, with a 230 V supply 6.5 A. Cables and extension cords for a 110 volt supply have to be heavier because of they carry twice the current of the 230 volt cables.

Electricity is generated in three phases, thanks to Tesla, any one of which can be used as a single phase supply. Electric motors most commonly use either one phase or three phases. I strongly recommend a three phase supply to a workshop to run three phase motors, because they are so much better than single phase motors.

Three Phase Motors

 A motor which is using the same amount of electricity, but using all three phases can be expected to be more powerful than a single phase motor.
When all three phases come in together, their sine waves are 120 degrees apart. This means that as the alternating current is applied to the three windings on the motor, one winding for each phase, the magnetic field they produce rotates naturally around the windings, and so no starting winding is required; the rotating magnetic field pushes the motor one way or the other. Because they do not require a start winding, they don't require a starting switch either, making the motors cheaper to make.

The windings push the armature three times per revolution compared to a single phase motor, and the supply voltage never reaches zero in the three phase supply because the three phases, being out of step with one another by 120°, never reach the zero voltage point simultaneously, whereas it does three times in one cycle in the single phase system, when the single sinusoidal wave form crosses the zero voltage line. As such, the three phase supply delivers constant power to the load, so the motors also run more smoothly, increasing the life of the bearings. Three phase motors are also much more efficient than single phase motors, typically 150% more than a single phase motor in the same power range. Conductors (wires) in the motor can be 75% of the size of single phase motors of a similar power, so the 3 phase motor can be smaller and so cheaper.

3 phase motors are perfectly balanced loads, in that they draw the same current from each phase. Therefore, they don't need a neutral. Each phase takes it in turn to act as the neutral return path for the other phases.

To reverse a 3 phase motor, simply swap any two wires on the supply cable, at either, but only one, end.

Single Phase Motors

A single phase supply means that there is just one pair of wires, one phase wire supplying voltage to the motor and one neutral. A single phase motor reaches its output limit at around the 2 ½ to 3 HP range because by then the current is running at the maximum available in a single phase system without special wiring. When an AC voltage is applied to a motor, the armature begins to spin. However, there is only one phase, and so before it is running it receives a voltage coming the other way, if you like; in fact 50 or 60 times per second !! So without a starting mechanism, the motor just sits and hums, vibrating one way then the other at the supply frequency. The current runs wild, and before long fuses blow, thermal protectors trip, or the motor catches fire!! So a start winding has to be included in single phase motor designs. Once the motor is running, the sine wave supply will keep it running in the same direction.

Without delving too deeply into the theory behind electric motors, irrespective of which voltage you are using, 110V, 230V or whatever, there are four commonly found kinds of single phase motors found in the workshop.

There are **Induction Start**, **Cap** (short for capacitor) **Start**, **Cap Start/Cap Run**, and **Universal Motors**.

Universal Motors will in fact run on either AC or DC, hence the 'Universal' tag. They have a very high starting torque, (they deliver a lot of power at start up), a high running speed which is not linked to the supply frequency, a high power to weight ratio, and are light and relatively easy to speed control. Hence they are mainly found in power tools, and power tools invariably use them. But the downfall of the Universal Motor is their use of commutators and brushes, which have a relatively short life, and require relatively high maintenance. The commutator is the bit at the end of the armature which has copper segments where the brushes touch. A certain way to ruin the armature is to let the brushes wear down to the point of being so short that they don't bear on the commutator correctly, which causes sparking. Eventually an arc is formed going right round the commutator, quickly ruining it. New brushes are cheaper than new armatures!!

The chief practical difference with the **Induction** and **Cap Start Motors** is the method of starting the motor.

With an **Induction Start Motor**, the start winding is different from the run winding, which gives the motor a 'push' in the right direction, because the induced magnetism is different between the coils. When the motor has achieved nearly half of its full rpm, the start winding is switched off with a centrifugal switch.
Because the 'push' is quite small, these motors tend to be used where the start-up load is quite low like fans and small grinders for example. Start-up is also quite slow, taking a few seconds to reach full speed.

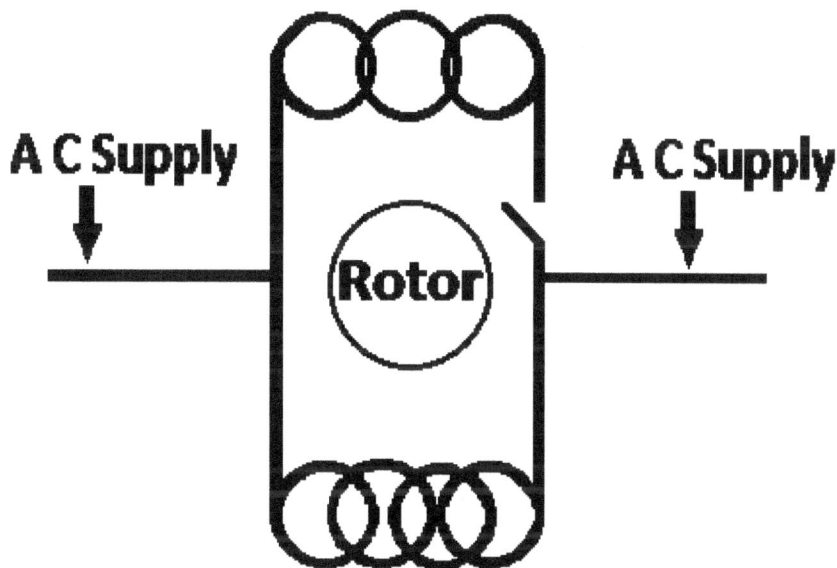

Induction Start Motor

A **Cap Start Motor** has a start winding too, also one that is switched out when the motor is almost at 50% of its full rpm. But here, the 2 windings are the same, with the start winding having a capacitor in series with it. . The capacitor effectively changes the sine wave in the start winding to being at 180 degrees from the run winding, and so 'pushes' the motor in one direction.

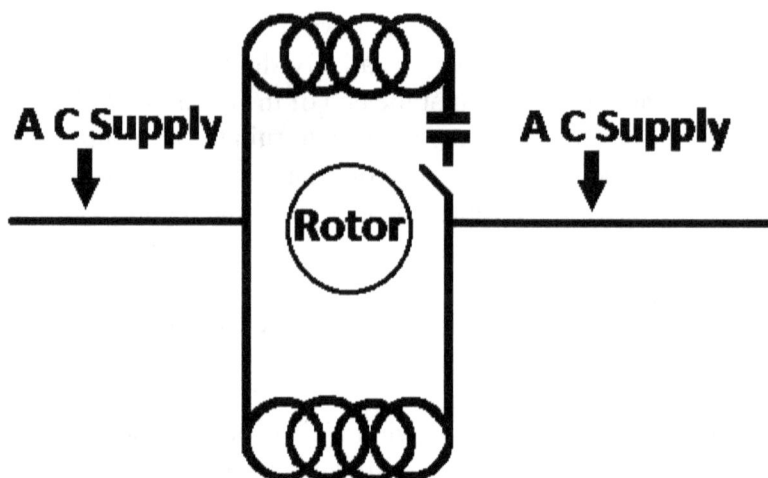

Cap Start Motor

The **Cap Start/Cap Run Motors** achieve the 'push' in much the same way as the cap start motors do but they do not switch the start windings out, just the starting capacitor. The much smaller (in capacitance) run cap is left in circuit, which improves efficiency.

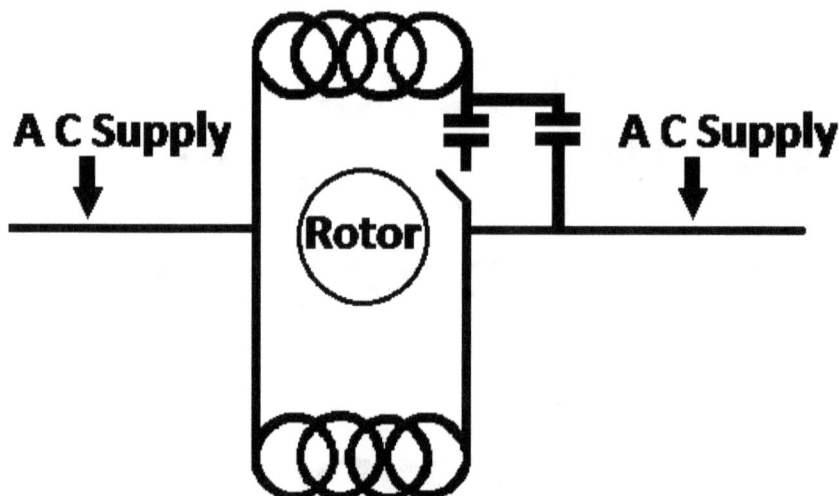

Cap Start/Cap Run

These two types of motors have a high starting torque many times that of the running torque, so are suitable for high torque starting loads, like compressors, lathes, thicknessers etc.

The identification of the wires on a single phase motor is usually clearly marked under the connection box lid, on the motor.

To **reverse the direction of rotation** of a single phase motor, you need to identify the end wires of the start (or run, but only one or the other) winding and swap them around. This reverses the magnetic field generated by that winding on start up, and so pushes the motor the other way.

POWER TOOLS

Power tools fill an increasingly important role in the home workshop, and are becoming more and more affordable, while becoming more accurate and versatile; there seems to be a power tool now for every job! They are ideal for occasional and short work times. For example, the modern mitre saws are wonderful for highly precise cutting in a home workshop environment making a set of windows, but won't replace a 3 phase cut off saw working all day in a sawmill, and a router will happily rout out recesses in a stringer for a flight of stairs, but a moulder would be happier running a house lot of skirting boards.

Little maintenance is required with power tools other than, of course, ensuring any slides and pivots are lubricated, and brushes regularly checked and replaced when necessary, as I mentioned on page 171. Replacement is usually easy, the brushes sit under removable screw caps at the commutator end of the motor.

Cordless tools are becoming more common as their batteries become more efficient and longer lived, and these, while not having the power of their wired cousins, do get away from the dangers and inconveniences of the power cord.

As a rule, I prefer to buy power tools, wired or battery, with as large a motor, in terms of its power, as I can afford. Buy a brand that has a good reputation, it will be much more reliable, and is more likely to supply replacement brushes!

Power tools are almost always noisy, from the high speed of the motors, and any gearboxes that are needed to bring speed down and the torque up. Ear protection is recommended!!

TOOL SHARPENING

Sharp tools are absolutely essential for ease of use, accuracy and safety. You are more likely to have an accident trying to force a piece of wood through a table saw which won't cut, than you are if the saw is easily able to do the work. And a blunt saw will cut **you** just as easily as a sharp one!!

Tools with carbide tips such as saw blades and router cutters are best sharpened by the professional, as are planer knives and complicated cutters for moulding heads which must be exactly the same, and are often dressed using a master pattern. Pretty much everything else you can sharpen yourself. As I have mentioned, I like to sharpen wood turning tools on the electric grinder, running a white wheel (see page 26). The angle of the tool is largely determined by trial and error and what you're turning; too steep and the tool can't cut, too shallow and the tool will grab. Treat the grindstone as you would the wood. HSS lathe tools can also be ground on the same grinder, but carbide tips are much better ground with a green wheel, and can be kept dressed with a diamond hone.

A **Honing Guide** really helps keep wood chisels and hand plane blades sharp.

The honing guide, plane iron and oil (slip) stone.

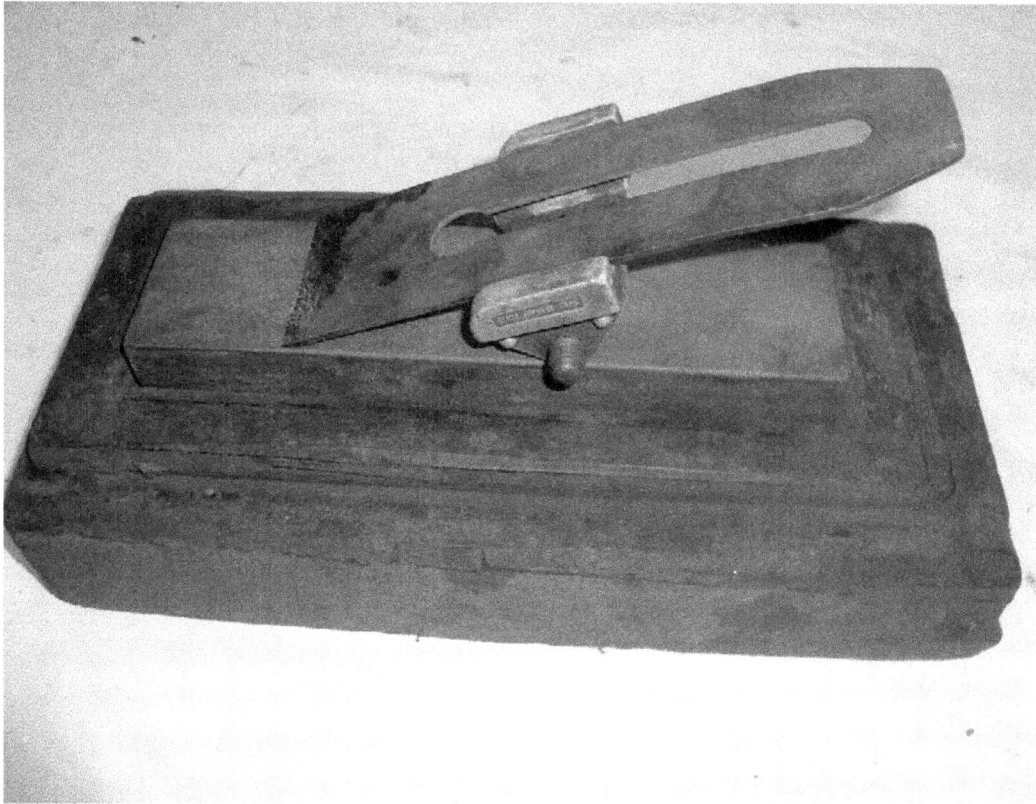

The Honing guide in use.

If you have a very bad blade, grind it first on the electric grinder, then mount it in the honing guide. Grind the blades back to about 25° and then hone to around 35°.

Most oil stones have a course side and a fine side. You can cut with the course side of the oil stone, then leave the tool in the guide, and use the fine side of the oil stone. Then hone the **back** (the underside) of the blade flat on the oilstone.

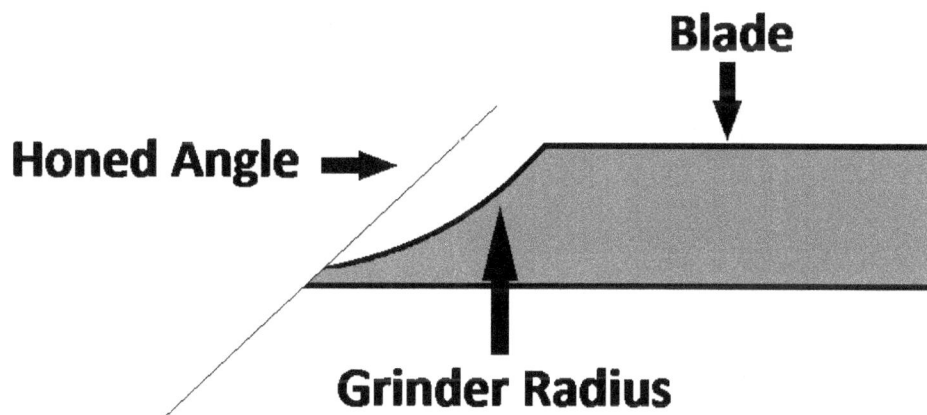

For a final sharpen, a **Strop** (a strip of leather rubbed with jeweller's rouge or a cutting compound) will hone it to a razor's edge.

If you want to use the strop with the honing guide, tightly stretch and glue the leather to a board to keep it very flat.

A band saw could be hand sharpened, but the saw doctor ha the equipment for it, and my blades have nearly 1200 teeth, so his fee is worth it!!

However, a **steel** toothed circular saw blade is easily sharpened, and in fact really only needs to visit the saw doctor for a full gulleting, when the gullets (the deep rounded areas between the teeth) need to be deepened.
 If the steel blade has been damaged, perhaps by striking a nail in pre-loved timber, then it may be worth **'dressing'** it; evening the height of teeth by running the cutting edge of the blade into the edge of an old file which you hold on a piece of scrap wood in order to see where the cut is. Just allow the file edge to remove the smallest amount, until the tips of each tooth have been cut to exactly the same height. It does sound scary, deliberately pushing a file into a working saw blade, but with the scrap wood there, it is surprisingly easy to control. Go **very** slowly and lightly, and make sure the table is clean, smooth and waxed.

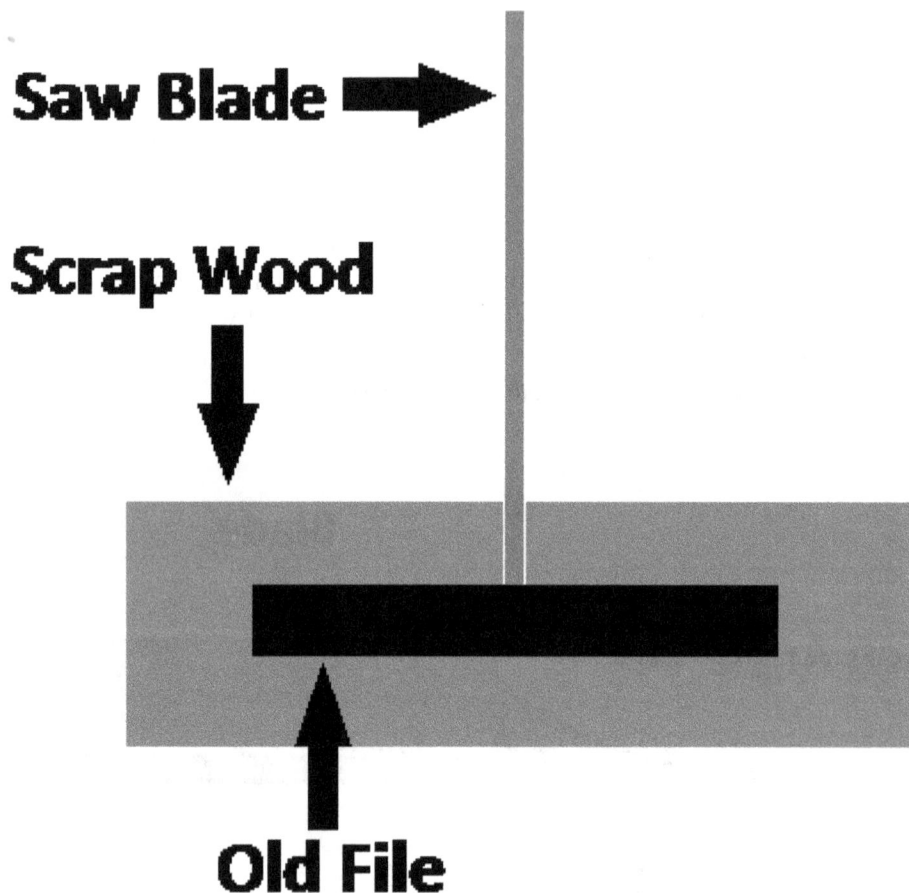

Saw Blade ➡

Scrap Wood

Old File

A diagram looking down at a steel blade being 'dressed' to even up the height of the teeth

Then stop the saw, and using a flat file with very fine teeth file the saw teeth, in the direction of their set, working from the back of the tooth to the front , just enough to remove any of the 'flats' left from the dressing.

Otherwise, with no 'dressing', just give each saw tooth the same number of strokes with the file, keeping as much as you can to the original angle.

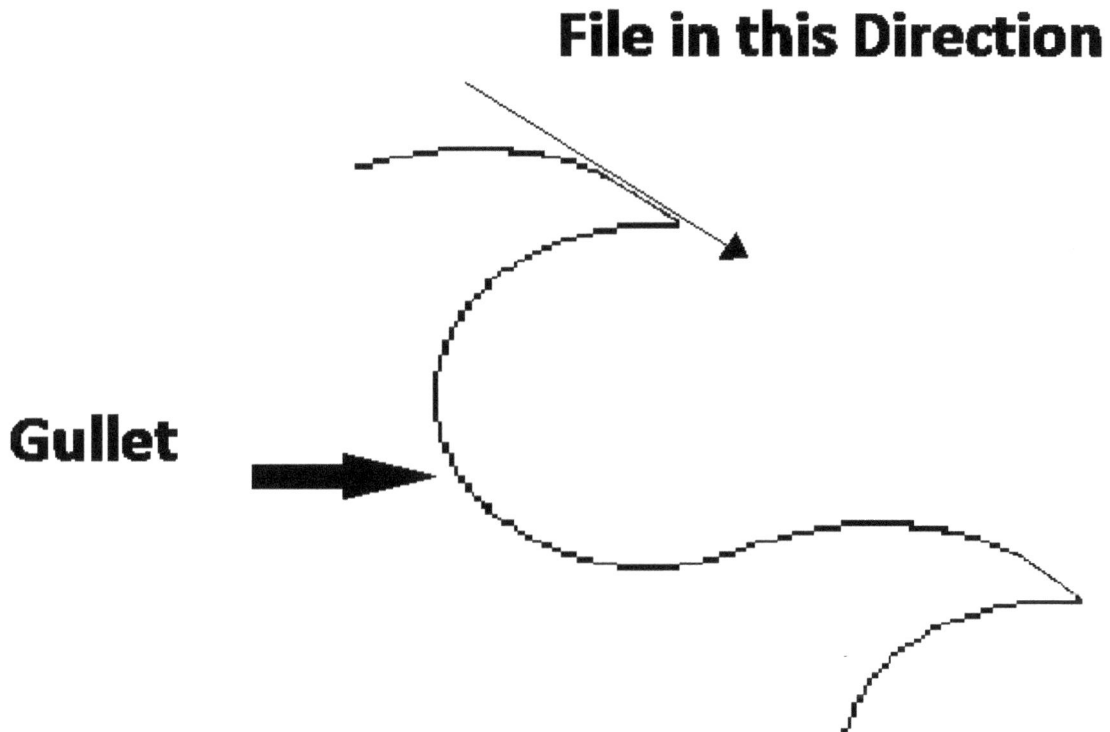

File in this Direction

Gullet

Under no circumstance should you ever 'dress' a carbide tipped blade.

Planer and thicknesser knives are best done by the saw doctor, who once again, has the necessary equipment. However, in an emergency, you can do a quite reasonable job by mounting as thick a grind stone as the spindle will take, in the saw bench.

You will have to remove the access panel from the bench top. Lay the blade on the bench bevel down, and adjust the height of the grindstone with the rise and fall adjustment until the bevel is held up just a fraction, maybe ¼ mm. Clamp a straight edge, I prefer a steel one, at right angles to the wheel across the bench. You now run the blade back and forth across the wheel until it isn't being cut anymore when flat on the bench. If you need to cut some more, you can raise the wheel a tiny bit, but should the damage to the knives (say from an unseen nail) be quite deep, moving the straight edge guide **in** is better, because the angle of the grinding wheel becomes steeper the more you raise it up, eventually making the angle too steep for proper cutting.

Make sure you do all the knives in the set at each setting of the grinding wheel or straight edge, so the set remains matched.

Grinding a damaged HSS thicknesser knife on a white grindstone mounted in the saw bench

The straight edge is clamped across the saw bench table, using the mitre guide to keep it square. The knife's bevel is **down**. The blade is moved across the grindstone until it isn't being cut anymore. Remove any burrs from the back of the blade with an oil stone.

Rotation

Saw Table

Straight Edge   **Knife**   **Grindstone**

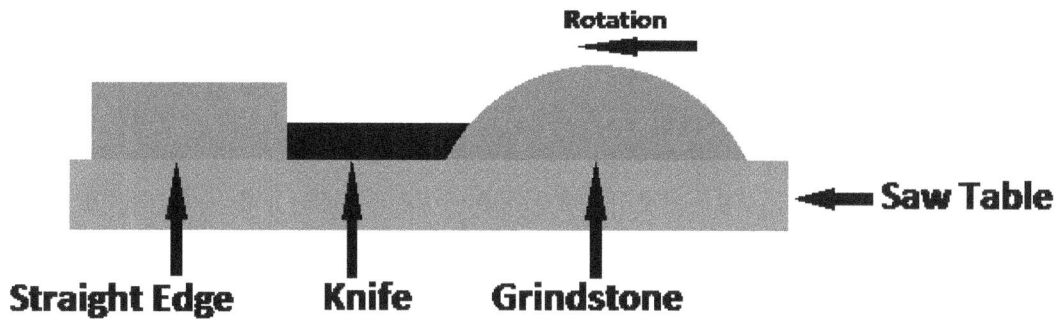

A diagram of the set up to grind HSS machine knives on the table saw

A **Diamond Embedded Hone** is a wonderful tool for keeping HHS and carbide tools sharp. They come with either a plastic or steel substrate (backing) of various sizes, and can be found in a variety of grits. They don't last forever, but will give great service quickly doing a job that is hard to do any other way. They are reasonably priced and a 'must have' for me.

I prefer, as I said earlier, to sharpen my **Wood Turning Tools** just on the grindstone. There is, in my opinion, no advantage in dressing the tool, as you do a plane iron (blade) or joinery chisel, with a wet stone or hone. The heat of the turning action on the tool, instantly ruins such an edge, so I find it a waste of time.

There is no exact angle for the bevel (the short radii) on turning tools. It really comes down to what attitude you adopt when standing at you machine, and what you've turning. Because the tool is held in your hands, we all tend to hold them a little differently. So, unlike an engineer's lathe where the tool is set to the correct height no matter who the machinist is, wood turners should hold the tool so it's comfortable. The same applies when sharpening the tool. In a way, the action of sharpening the tool is exactly the same as cutting with it. In both situations, you approach a revolving item and apply the tool to it. So grind the tool holding it as you do when cutting with it.

Wood turning tools fall into 4 loose categories: **Parting Tools, Skew Chisels, Gouges** and **Scrappers.** Parting tools, skew chisels and scrappers are easily made (see the section on tempering) and sharpened. In the diagram below, you can see that they are pretty much of the same section: i.e. flat bar. The sizes of the bar vary, but the parting tool is likely to be around ½ inch wide and ¼ thick, whereas the other two will be ¼ thick, but up to 1 ½ inches or so wide. Up to you though.

The wide side of the **Parting Tool** in 'A' is ground to a shape like that on the right. Exactly how far down the tool the radii come is up to you, but too short and it won't cut cleanly and easily, too long and the tip will heat up too readily and ruin the temper. It can be tempting to also radius the short sides, like the dotted lines in the left hand diagram. It

gives very good clearance, but is very wasteful of the tool itself; as you grind the tip down, you get to the point where the radii work against you. The tip becomes narrower than the steel behind
 it, and severe binding can result. For me, I leave the tool parallel.

'B' shows the two profiles of a **Skew Chisel**. The wide side is given a long angle which is then bevelled back either side of the centre axis. Too long a bevel will get into tighter corners, but will be more prone to 'digging in'. Too short will not turn tight radii on those lovely beads and vase shapes you want to make.

'C' shows a **Gouge**. Gouges are further divided into two groups. The ones shaped from a flat bar, and those ground from round stock. Gouges are ground to a wide radius looking down (top diagram) and bevelled back seen side on (bottom diagram) with the cutting bevel ground to give a leading edge. The amount of bevel is really just what suits you – I cannot use tools ground by someone else. I hate other people sharpening my tools, and feel embarrassed when asked to show someone what to do with **their** tools because I always want to grind them to suit me!!

Scrappers, D, should you **have** to have one, are ground to a profile on the wide surface and a single bevel ground from top to bottom, angled back. They can be ground on the wide surface to almost any shape.

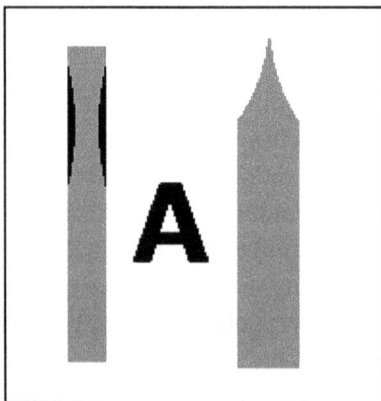

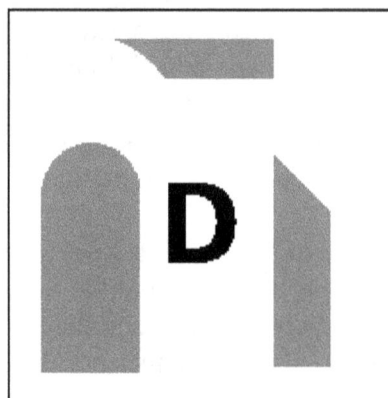

Engineer's Lathe Tools are more rigidly defined, because they are clamped into the tool post in a regulated manner. Don't worry though, there's still plenty of room for creativity!!!

These tools will work with a surprisingly large amount of tolerance. The crucial point is really one of clearance at the cutting point. Too little clearance and the main body of tool steel will prevent the tool tip from cutting effectively, and too much will encourage a too deep a cut, and excess heat. For small lathes, bring the tool to a point as you can see in the next diagram, and then very carefully remove the very sharp tip, to provide a small radius instead of a needle point. A point will just score a fine thread on the work, without removing all of the material. A radius which is greater than the forward movement will remove all of the material, and with good sharpening give a nice finish.

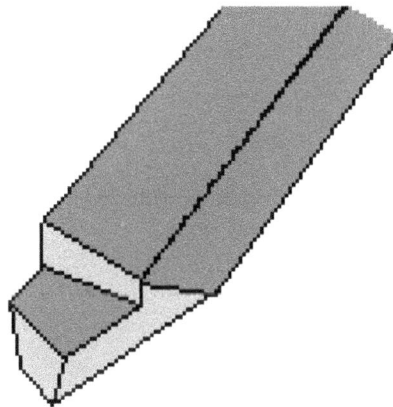

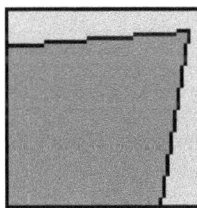
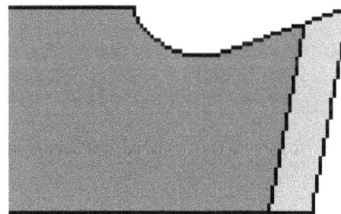

Front   Side

A small lathe tool, showing the rake (clearance) given to the end, face and top

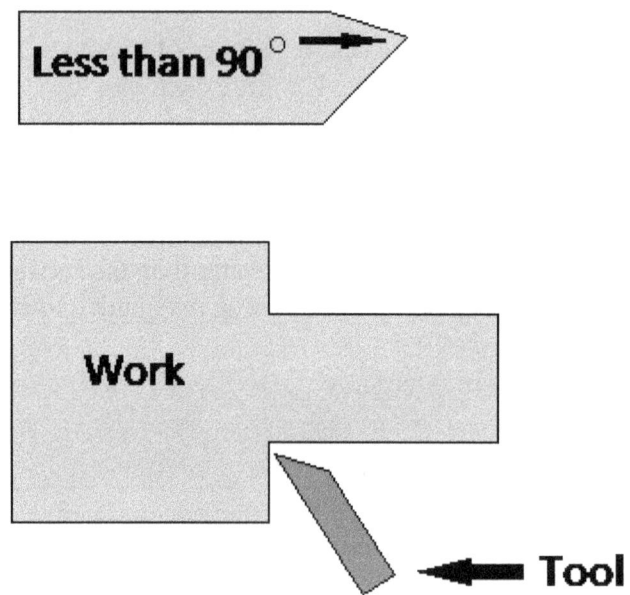

Looking down shows the angle of less than 90° gives good clearance when working up to a shoulder.

Three different views of a carbide cutter, braised to a mild steel bar.

A strange little tool to sharpen, but a real friend of the serious cabinet maker is the **Cabinet Scraper.** It is just a (usually) rectangular piece of good quality untempered 2mm thick steel. Any one of the edges can be sharpened, though because of the way you hold them, gripped between the hands with the thumbs pushing at the back to slightly bend the steel as you cut forward, having the side edges sharp can lead to cuts along your first fingers. So I tend to just sharpen the four long edges. For comfort during long sessions with a cabinet scraper, a pad under your thumbs will stop them burning, you generate heat working a cabinet scraper; like using a hand plane, it's a good workout!!

Firstly, hold the scraper in a vice, with some strips of wood along the sides to prevent jaw marks, with a long side up. Use a flat file with very fine teeth to file along the top edge. Go slowly and try to get the edge as straight, flat and square as possible. This removes any **burr** that is present on the top surface, and produces a small one down the side. You then, with a smooth round steel rod, work slowly along the edge, working from the side of the scraper up towards the top. The idea here is to force the newly formed burr up, parallel to the side and above the top edge. You then repeat the action, but working down, to force the burr to be proud of the side. It is this burr that does the cutting for you, and produces those wonderful, incredibly thin shavings and leaves behind it an almost polished surface.

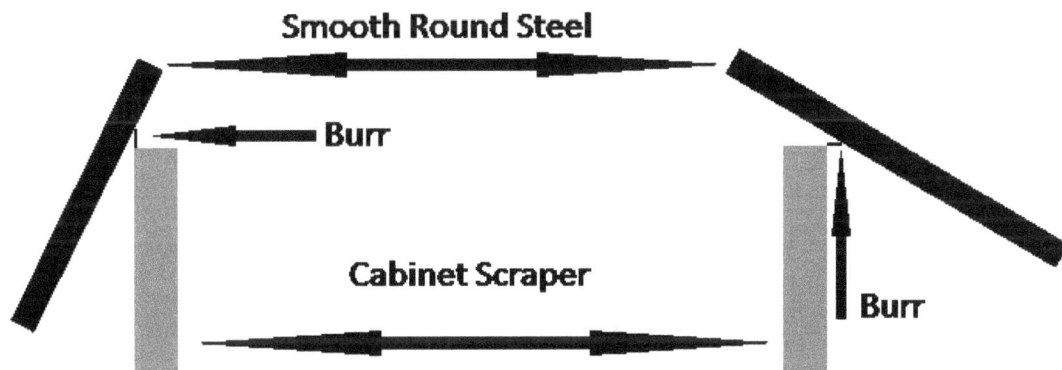

The diagram on the left shows the burr being forced upwards, and the one on the right shows the burr being forced down, into a cutting position.
As you work, the burr will lose its sharp edge, so you must repeat the rounding procedure to restore the cutting edge. Eventually this won't work anymore; in fact sometimes the burr will break off in a long sliver. Be careful when you handle it, it is still sharp enough to cut. So then you go back to step one and file the edge flat again.
 There's a real knack in sharpening a Cabinet Scraper, but persevere till you get it right; the rewards are many!!

HARDENING, TEMPERING and MAKING TOOLS

While the deep bowl turning gouges are ground from solid stock, wide roughing gouges can be made from flat bar. It's a fun thing to do, and very satisfying to use tools you've made yourself.

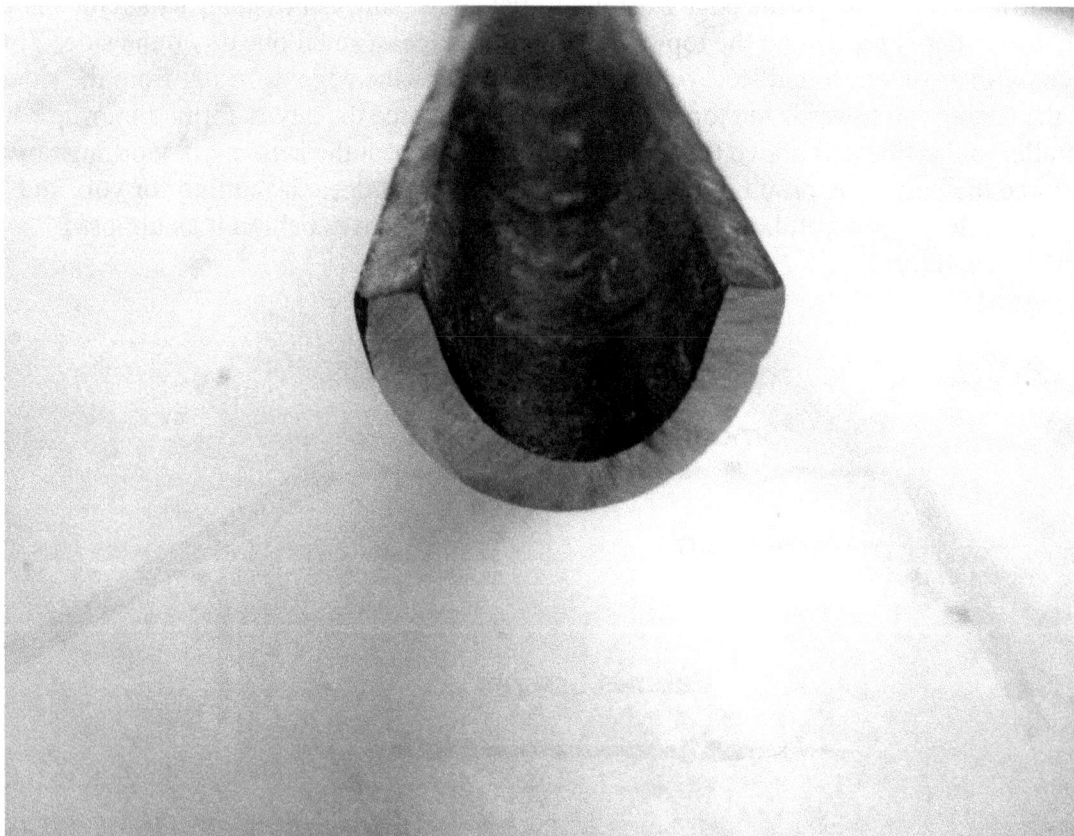

An old file can be used, the steel is of good quality, though the old file teeth can be a nuisance. Otherwise, use a good, high carbon steel. 'Gauge plate' is very suitable and comes in 500mm lengths which is enough for two gouges. The gouge shape can be formed by heating the steel to cherry red, and hammering a solid round piece into the hot steel which is held over a former, which is a piece of steel shaped to the outside shape of the gouge, as you can see in the next sketch. Keep returning the work to the fire to keep it hot, as it will quickly cool while you work it.

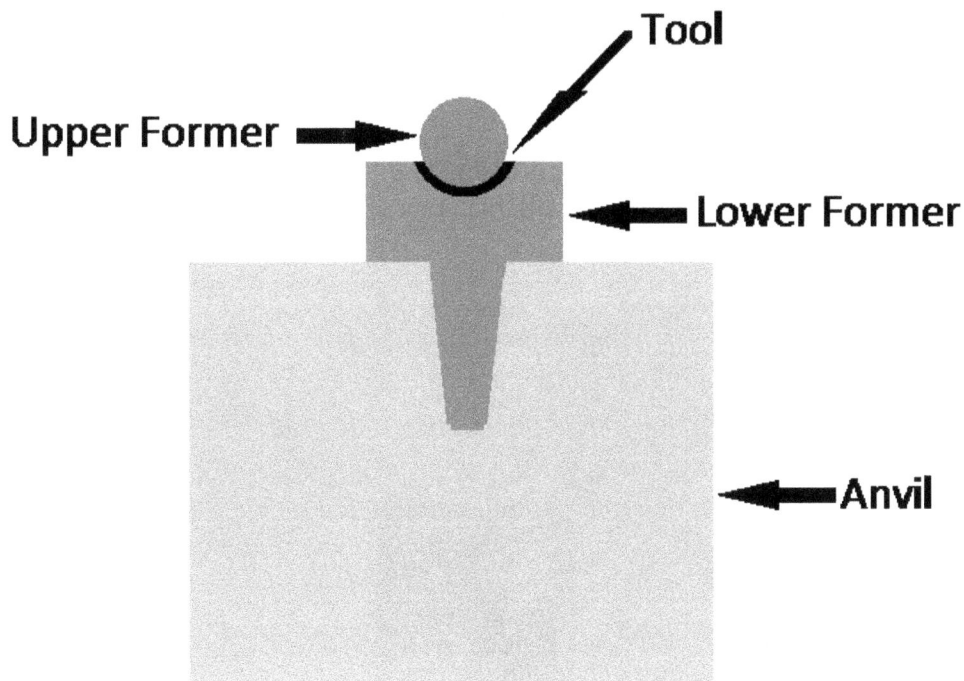

When you have the shape you want, you need to **harden** the tool. Re-heat to cherry, and plunge the steel into cold water. Of course, the 'water' will boil around the steel, and the bubbles of boiling air will provide an insulating barrier between the steel and the water. This will slow the rate of cooling, and also tend to form areas of differing hardness, where large bubbles formed. To avoid this, vigorously agitate the steel in the 'water' until the steel is quite cold. This gives the steel the maximum hardness, but the minimum durability. In other words, it's very hard, but brittle and prone to snapping. You now need to **temper** the steel. This will reduce the hardness of the tool a little, but gives a workable durability to it.

The method is to heat the steel to a particular temperature, and then quench again. Commercial works bring the steel to a very precise temperature in an oven and for a precise amount of time, but we can use the age old method of colour treatment.
The end of the tool should be ground (and you might as well grind it to a shape that you will use later) so that the end is clean and shiny. Now **slowly** heat the tool evenly over the whole of the length, watching carefully for changes in the colour of the ground end.
 It's important you don't just heat the end; you need the tempering to be along the length as far as the hardening process was, and for it to be as even as possible. If you are heating in a fire, use coal or charcoal if possible to increase the carbon content, and harden the outside surface. Keep the very end just out of the fire. If you are using a gas torch, don't play the torch on the end itself, and overheat it. Keep the end clean.
 As the temperature rises, you will see the colour of the clean silver of the freshly ground end change. When the colour reaches **light straw** (for a wood turning tool) remove the heat, or the steel from the fire, and quench to lock the temper at that hardness. The colour indicates the temperature of the temper. Light Straw (or yellow) is good for wood turning tools, twist bits need to be a reddish brown colour, screwdrivers, light blue.

Other temper colours are given in the appendix, page 207.

PURLS of WISDOM

A **De-Burring Tool** is irreplaceable for dressing and (slightly) enlarging holes in all sorts of materials. Replacement blades are available. You HAVE to have one of these tools!!

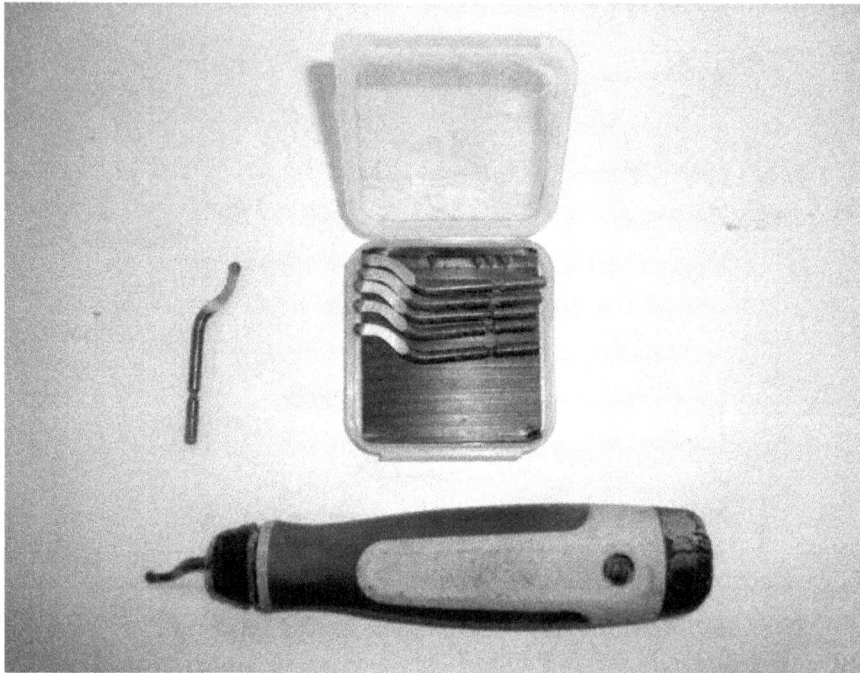

Carbide teeth from unusable saw blades can be brazed to a mild steel bar. They make a nice cutter for the metal working lathe.

The Fixed Jaw on an Adjustable Spanner, or slip joint pliers makes a great lever, for all sorts of jobs. The tools are designed for this kind of stress. The fulcrum is the rounded back, so the leverage is quite large. A large wrench will generate a lot of force!!

Here I am lifting a 1200Kg lathe with just a 16 inch adjustable spanner.

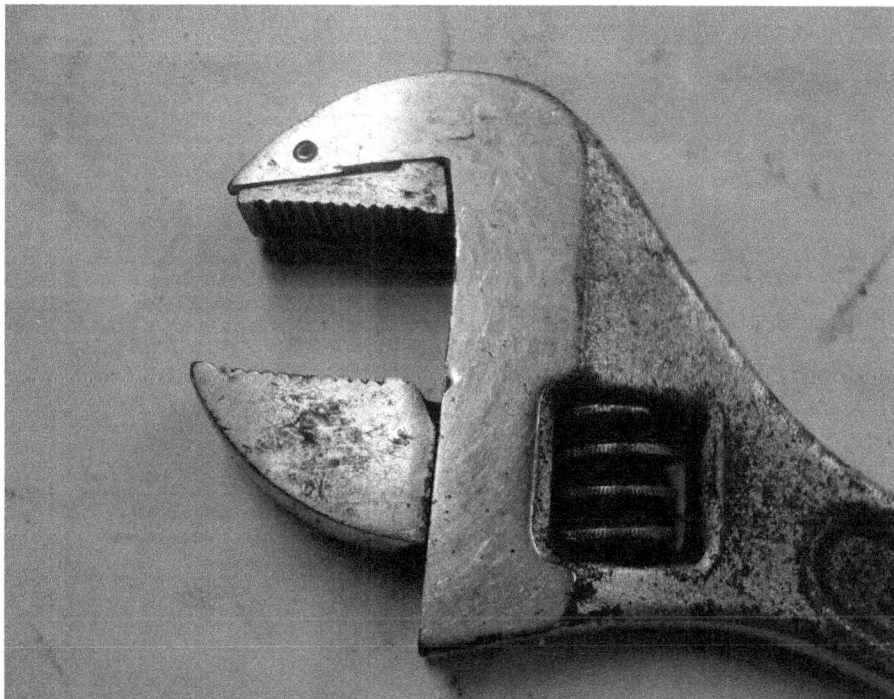

This **Adjustable Spanner** has a special addition to the top or fixed jaw, and can hold and turn pipes and tubes. It works really well, and is also great for removing a nut with a badly damaged outside.

A highly accurate Torque Wrench can be easily made from a socket set or spanner, and a spring balance.

Torque is a measure of force; foot-pounds or Newton-metres.
For example, a force of say 15 pounds with a lever 2 feet long gives 30 foot-pounds.

Measure the length of the bar or spanner and then calculate the force required on the spring balance to deliver the required torque. So for 30 foot-pounds, if my bar is 1 foot long, I must pull the balance till it reads 30 pounds.

 If my balance only reads to 10 pounds, then my lever must be 3 feet long to reach 30 foot-pounds.

V Belt Pulleys (sheaves) can be expensive, particularly the larger multi-belt ones, and sometimes difficult to find, if you want to have exactly the right size for a job where the rpm is critical. So make your own.

This wooden pulley has been driving my band saw with its 3.5 hp motor for 35 years using an old gear as the 'boss'.

Plywood is an excellent material to use for a wooden pulley. You need at least 10mm either side of the groove the belt runs in, and a similar amount between belts in a multi-belt setup. So for a **single** 'A section' belt (they come in a number of 'sections' or profile sizes), 3 pieces of 1/2inch ply sandwiched together is ideal. Glue them well, and run a few screws or nails through as well. The only difficulty you will have with a wooden pulley is fixing it sufficiently well to the shaft.

The simplest way to do this is to bolt the wooden blank to an existing pulley or cog that fits the shaft but is either the wrong diameter or unsuitable because it is a cog, has only a single belt and you want two, or some other defect. If you don't have something suitable, a metal boss (steel or aluminium will do) can be easily made.
The boss connects the wooden pulley to the steel shaft. It must have a hole the diameter of the shaft in the centre, one or two bolts or grub screws to lock it to the shaft, and 3 or 4 holes through which the wooden pulley can be bolted.
Now mount the boss on the shaft, bolt the wooden blank to the boss, and then turn the wooden blank true and machine in the V Belt grooves.

That way any inaccuracy is removed.

It is absolutely vital that the V Belts fit the angle of the grooves and that they can **never** touch the bottom of the groove, so make the grooves much deeper than the depth of the belt. An 'A' section belt is ½ inch across the top, and 5/16th inch in depth, so a groove **at least** ½ inch deep would be good. The belts grip only on the side of the groove, never the bottom, and as the torque increases they 'bite' harder into the groove walls. If they 'bottom out', they will slip, because they cannot grip the walls of the groove.

If you are adding a large wooden pulley to an existing pulley setup, as with the wooden lathe in the picture on page 79, you can turn the shaft with one of the other pulleys, and use a temporary tool rest to machine the new one, so it's exactly true.

Don't use **particle board** for a wooden pulley, it's not strong enough for the job. A single piece of, say, 12 x 2 pine will do nicely though. Be sure to have the boss bolts across the grain.

My 5.5 hp thicknesser has been quite content with its wooden pulley and homemade 'boss' for 20 years.

Two good examples of Number 8 Wire Technology!!

I was in a friend's workshop and needed two very accurate cuts, one on some PVC sheet and the other on a steel bar. He only had a hacksaw, which will give a very inaccurate cut. I mounted a thick (10mm) steel plate on, (above), or in, (below), the tool post with the tool post bolts. The work piece is firmly clamped with the G cramp/cramps. A small saw blade above is held in the chuck on a mandrel, the metal cut off wheel below on a centre sleeve, with thrust provided by the tail stock. Despite the exposed cutters, it was safely done as the work was progressed using the cross slide, and so my hands were kept well away. The result two **very** straight cuts!!

COMPRESSED AIR

Single Phase Air Compressors are now so readily available for a reasonable price that most home workshops can justify the expense. Apart from blowing down dusty machinery (with the cautions already mentioned in regard to forcing dust into cross-slides and chucks), compressed air allows spray painting, powder coating, tyres to be inflated and air cylinders or rams to be used.

Here is a photo of one of my lathes that has two rams mounted on it to remove the tedium of the work, and also speed it up hugely. This set up is for the boring of small kaleidoscope bodies, with the auger boring with the grain about 7 inches deep. To advance and retract the carriage by the hand wheel was hard work and by speeding the feed up, the auger was actually kept cooler, as it was always boring fresh, cool wood. By hand I could bore 50 per hour, with the air cylinder I could bore 150, and with no effort!! The small cylinder is operated by an air valve that triggers when the carriage begins to move forwards, and operates a clamp to hold the block in place.

Plastic water pipe is a very good and cheap way to run permanent pipes for compressed air around the workshop, with fittings around the machines and areas where you'll be likely to use it. An easy way to increase the air storage volume is to use a large pipe diameter. Use a pipe that will stand the pressure of the system of course.

Air tools, like screw drivers and wrenches are very powerful tools, but use a huge volume of air. Generally 'rattle guns' for vehicle wheel removal are the most common air tools in a home workshop.

For uninterrupted spray painting, 10-15 CFM (cubic feet per minute) is adequate, and available with a single phase machine. The more storage volume you have for the air the better, as this will tend to keep the pressure up as you spray.
With a spray gun, definitely have a water trap (and perhaps an oil trap as well) fixed in the line to remove water (and oil).

A compressed air water trap

Compressed air carries a lot of water with it, and traces of the compressor sump oil which can adversely affect the paint or lacquer.

An oiler, on the other hand, deliberately supplies small amounts of oil to the air, to lubricate cylinder walls and seals.

And if you want a challenge, a **Home-Built Compressor** is not too difficult to make from an old 4 stroke engine. A stationary engine will have a cooling fan incorporated into its design, to help keep the engine cool. Keep this cooling fan intact, compressing air causes the air to heat up.

The principal difference between an engine and a compressor is that the compressor has no expansion chamber. Remove the engine cylinder head, and replace it with a piece of steel, say 12mm thick. The piston must come right to the underside of the plate, so choose an engine with a flat topped piston. The valves are the only tricky bit to make, but you can just buy the valve discs (they are just hardened discs) and valve springs for a compressor, and fit them to the plate. They are very cheap.

A good project for the engineer's lathe!

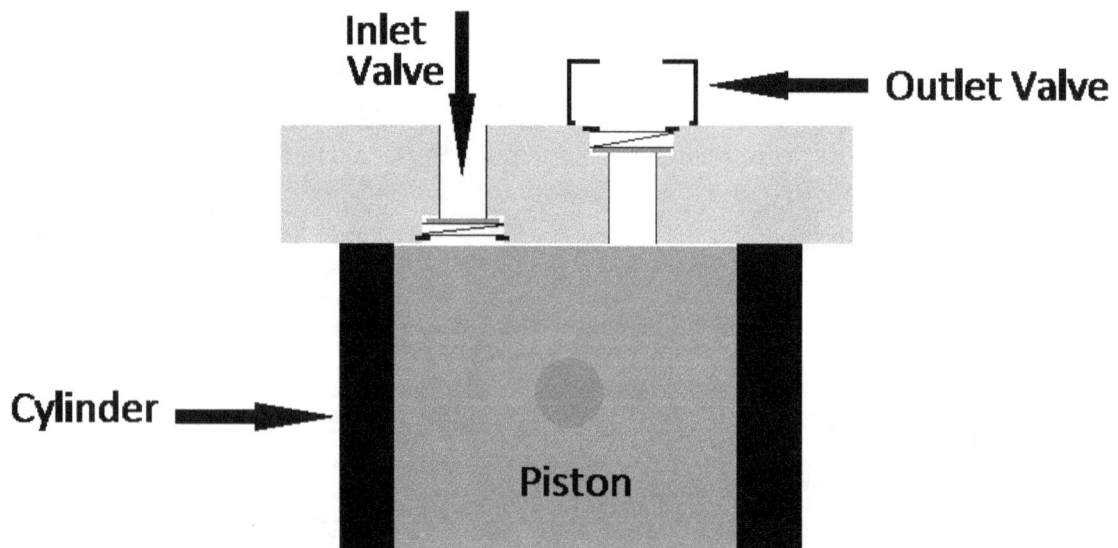

An Overall drawing of an engine to compressor conversion

A steel plate has replaced the original cylinder head. The outlet valve has a tube welded around it to accept a pipe fitting to channel the compressed air to a storage tank. The inlet valve should really have an air filter on the outside, to keep dust from entering the compressor.

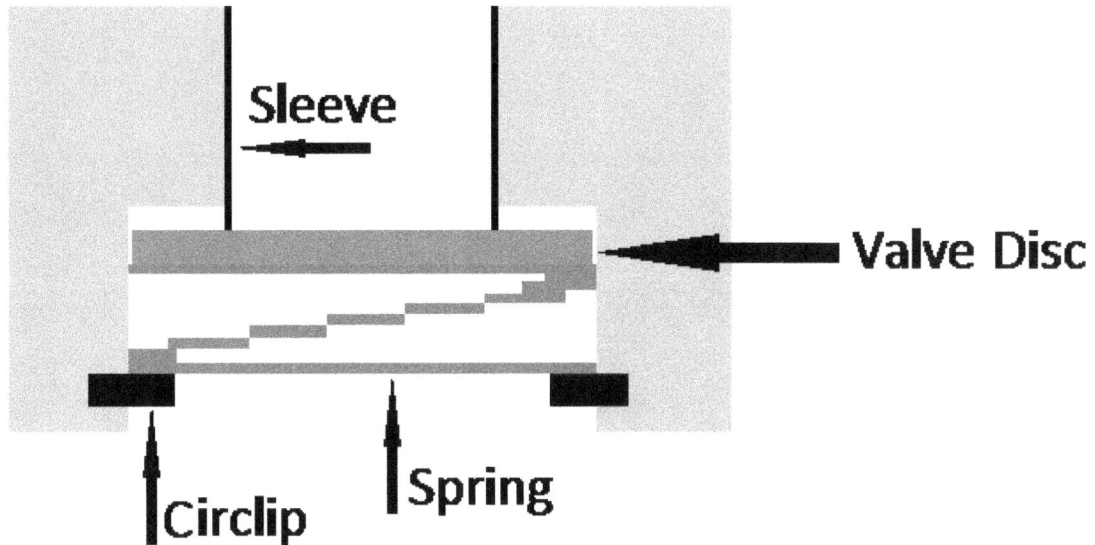

Details of the Valve Assembly

A steel sleeve is shown here passing through the new steel head. It makes the sealing of the hardened valve disc easier, and allows the air to pass by the valve more easily as it is proud of the surface.

Braise or solder the tube into place with a minimum of filler rod.

The valve disc is held in place while open by a small, light weight spring; both the valve and the spring are a little less in diameter than the large section of the stepped hole through the head. The spring is in turn, held in place by a circlip. The cutting of the circlip groove is the only tricky bit.

Hold the head onto the faceplate as described on pages 110 or 111, and machine the stepped hole and the circlip groove at the same time.

The spring helps control the valves, which are then kept closed by the pressure of the air being forced out on the upstroke, and by atmospheric pressure on the down stroke.

The compressor should be turned at a rate of around 1000 rpm (revolutions per minute). As it will pump once per revolution, the CFM (cubic feet per minute) delivered is simple. RPM x displacement (maximum volume of the cylinder).

Compressed Air Sand Blasters for home workshop use are available and surprisingly good! They have ceramic nozzles and can also pump water. Be warned though, they throw sand EVERYWHERE, so wear good safety clothes and a face mask and ear and eye protection!

If you use a booth, you can collect and re-use the sand.

A Small Sand Blasting Gun.

WARNING !!!

Be very careful with compressed air, it can quite literally be a killer. NEVER point a dusting gun at ANY body opening, thinking it will be a fun thing to do. Eyes and ears can be instantly destroyed and internal organs seriously damaged by compressed air forced into the mouth or lower regions, or air gun nozzles pointed into tight clothing, for example trouser legs and sleeves. I do use it to dust off my work clothes but I strictly keep it away from areas where it is astonishingly easy to cause harm. Please be very careful. Using compressed air can also cause hearing loss as it is very noisy. Wear protection.

DUST and SAWDUST EXTRACTION

An Extractor for Dust and Sawdust is a really nice thing to have in the wood workshop on several counts. Removing dust and sawdust away from machinery as it is formed reduces the irritation from having to breathe it, as well as greatly reducing the risk of a dust explosion.

A very good, and easily built system for a home workshop is the bag type extractor, which has a motor coupled to a blower unit which exhausts directly into a **cotton or canvas** bag.

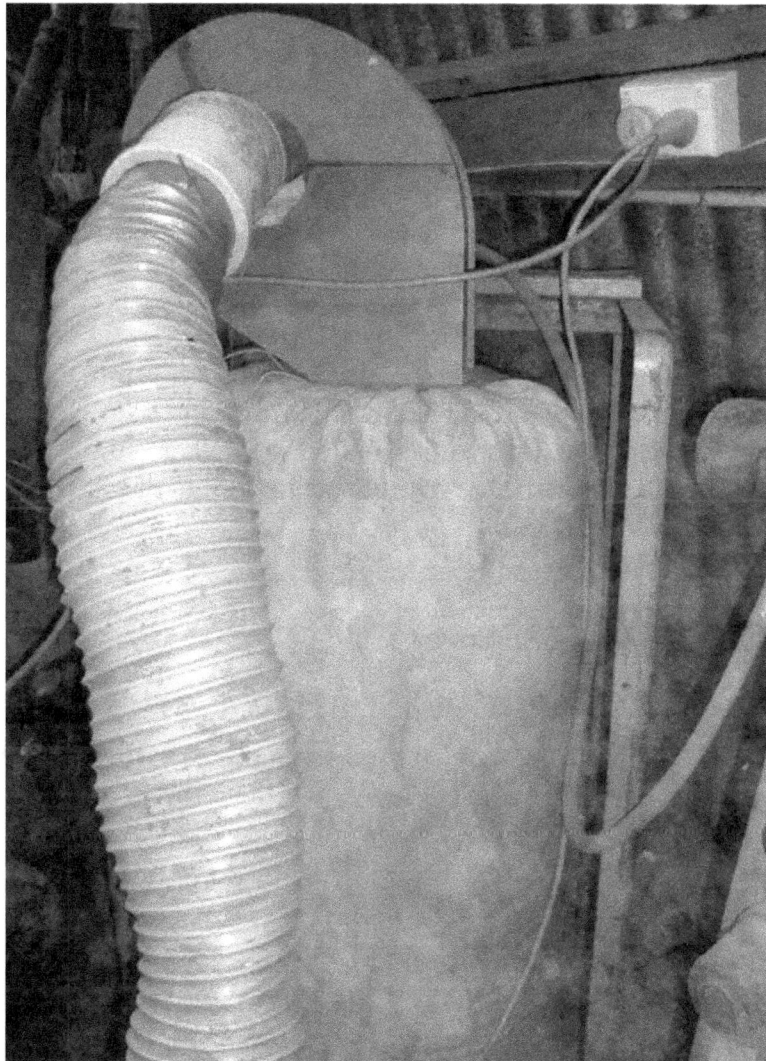

A single bag extractor

The suction end of the blower is attached to a flexible hose, often of 4 inch diameter, which can be fitted to exhaust vents on a saw bench or disc sander, or even taken down to the floor to pick up lathe shavings. The bag **must** be porous enough to allow the air to escape, but of a fine enough weave to keep the dust inside. A plastic bag, therefore, won't

work as the air can't escape, and a course hessian sack would let the dust out. I buy and use heavy duty commercial canvas bags two feet in diameter and four feet high.
These systems tend to lose efficiency as the bag becomes close to full because the surface area of the bag available to let the air out is reduced, slowing the air speed and thus its ability to move the dust. Sometimes though, a second bag is mounted above the first which is solely there to allow the air to escape, and not to act as a collector. Some systems have several collector bags.

The other most common type of extractor is where the suction side of a large blower is attached to a permanently fixed system of 6 or 8 inch diameter pipes which then have smaller diameter flexible 'droppers' to the various machines. The droppers which lead to machines that are not in use will have a method of sealing the end of the pipe, which helps to maintain the vacuum in the pipe system for machines which are in use. The exhaust side of the blower may go to bags similar to those in the smaller system described above, or to a collector or a cyclone, described later.

Any permanently fixed pipes in a system where large pipes are used should be of galvanised steel, not plastic. The reason is that the particles of dust move quickly in the pipes, and knock together and on the pipes, causing a static electrical build up. The steel pipes will dissipate this charge safely, whereas an insulating plastic pipe can allow the charge to increase enough so that eventually a spark is generated with the risk of a dust explosion.

I made a large plywood box to collect the extracted sawdust. It was mounted on wheels, with doors at the back for emptying, and a cotton fabric cover (under the weatherproof plywood roof), to let the air out. This worked extremely well, and the efficiency was always high, because the captured dust was not able to prevent the air from escaping as the fabric was in the roof.

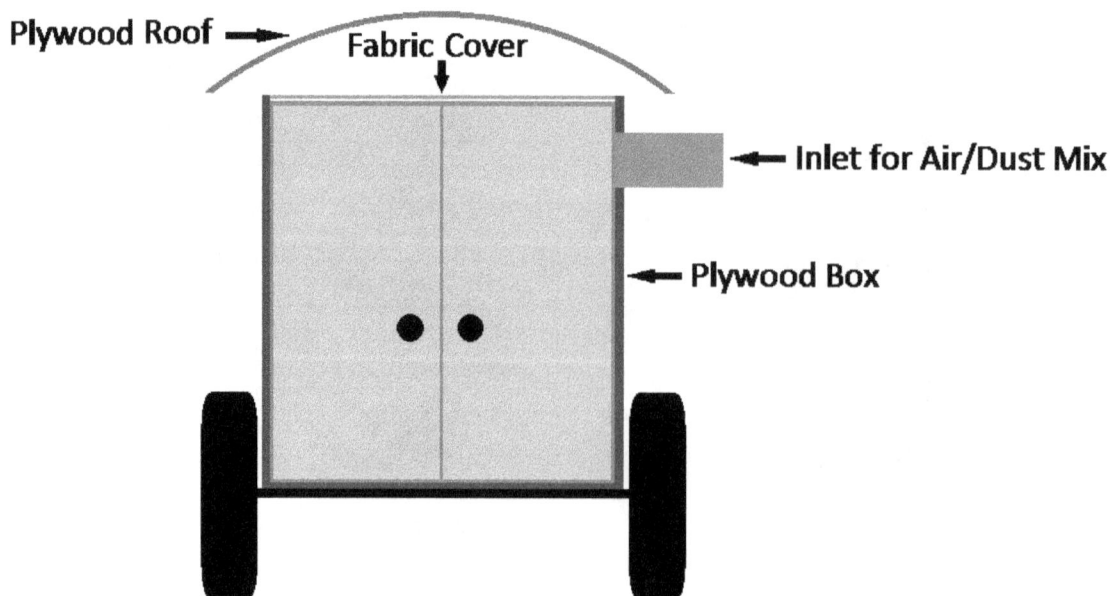

My Plywood Sawdust Collector

A steel **Cyclone Separator** system is often used in large operations. This is a large steel container and the air/dust mix is fed into the top. The shape of the separator causes the dust particles to lose their velocity, and so they simply fall down, through the bottom of the container and into a holding tank.

Usually too expensive a set up for the home workshop, (where either of the other two systems is quite adequate), though a small one could be made.

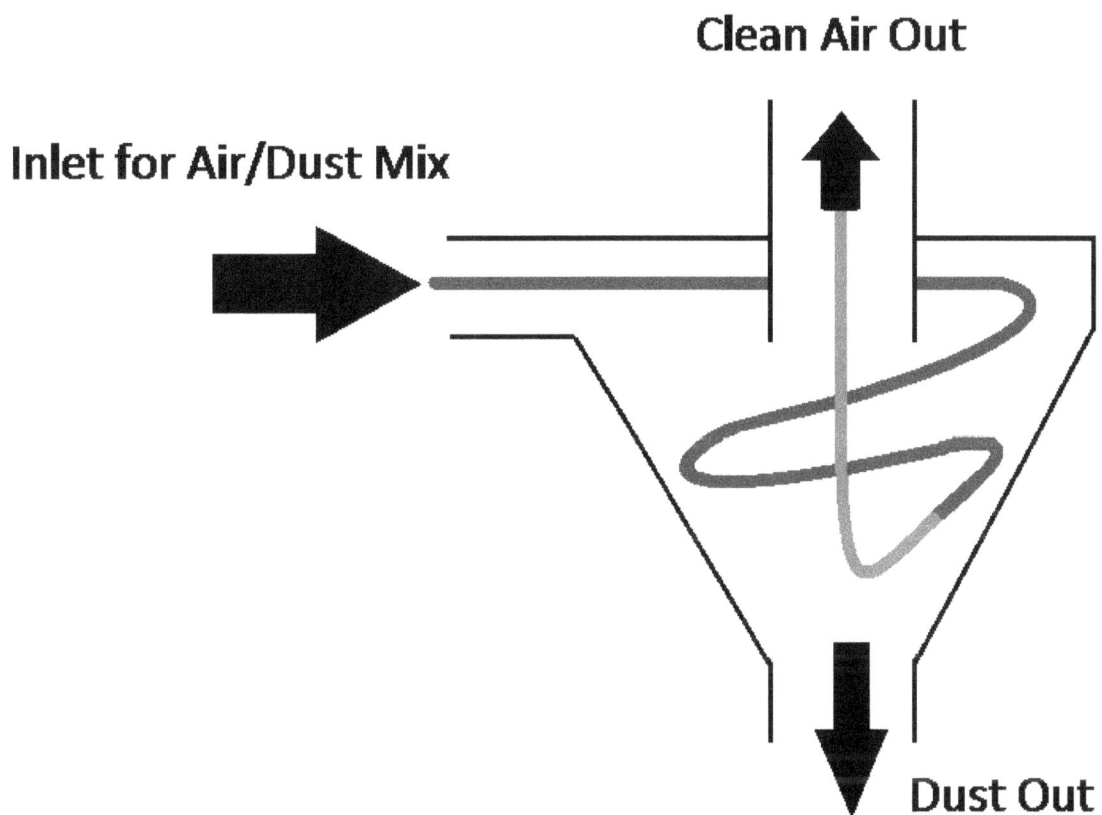

Clean Air Out

Inlet for Air/Dust Mix

Dust Out

A diagram of a Cyclone Separator

The air/dust mix is pumped into the top, and as it is forced by the shape of the separator into a decreasing downward spiral, the air loses its velocity. The dust drops out, as the now slow air cannot carry it, and falls to the bottom of the separator and out of the bottom chute. The now clean air is allowed to escape through the vent in the top.

WORKSHOP LAYOUT

Some serious thought needs to be given to the layout of the workshop. You need to decide which activities you will be doing, and what machines you have to do them. Some machines require only an East/West space, meaning they do not need to have much space behind them. Of course, there usually needs to be lots of room in front of the machine, because that's where you're standing, also so you can move out of the way if you need to!!

Lathes, bench grinders, and drill presses are good examples of these.

Band saws sit against a wall to the left, but need room to the right and in front and to the back.

Surface planers and moulders sit against the wall too, but the wall should be on the right of the machine.

Circular saws and planer/gauges need room front and back, but you need to be able walk around them, at least on one side.

The work bench can be up against a wall if you're tight for space, but it is really nice to have it as an island in the middle of the shop floor, and be able to walk around it.

If your workshop is in the garage, then machines like the circular saw can be just inside the main door so to allow you maximum room behind the machine. You can then open the door to have room in front of the machine. Not quite so nice if it's snowing .....

Organise the power supply to the machines so that you don't have cables lying around, waiting to trip you up. Machines against a wall are easy to power safely by clipping the cables to the wall, free standing machines can be fed with an overhead cable or, preferably, under the floor. If you have no choice but to run a cable over the floor, then consider covering it, at least with some duct tape.

Drawing a scale diagram of the workspace, with cut out scale shapes of the machines is also an easy way to quickly see how best to squeeze things in. Of course, you should also allow some room for shelves and storage, a fire extinguisher and first aid kit.

The rule of thumb is that the workshop is never big enough, and that the bigger the workshop, the bigger the mess!!!!

Lighting

Natural sunlight is really good for general work, but it can often be impractical. It might be a dull day, your roof doesn't have sky lights in it, or it may be night time! Also, especially with lathes, it's very important to have good lighting right there where you need it, at the work face.

 Above the lathe I recommend an adjustable lamp, one where you can point it in a particular angle, and it will stay put, over the work areas that need it. This is very useful for lighting inside a piece which you are boring out, for example, and for getting good light to the front of the lathe, where a shadow of the work piece itself would be cast onto the tool tip if the light was behind the machine.

Ideally, there should be general lighting as high as possible with individual lights over the machines as required. A circular saw doesn't really need a strong individual light, because you tend to set the fence and cut; the same goes with a thicknesser. A band saw might need a dedicated light, if you need to follow the shape that has been carefully traced onto the work. If this is the type of work that you are doing, an individual light is a great help. Lathes and grinders definitely do require their own light, drill presses maybe not so much.

A Word of Warning

Fluorescent lighting actually pulses in time with the AC current that feeds your workshop. While you generally don't notice this flickering, it can produce a stroboscopic effect on revolving things like saw blades, drills, and lathes. If the rpm of the machine happens to be at a factor of the AC rate (which is commonly 50 or 60 Hertz) the machine, though still making a noise, can appear to be stationary, and so can be dangerous. To avoid this have individual fluorescent lights running on different electrical phases from each other (if you have more than one phase available), and/or have some incandescent lights running as well. Incandescent lights don't have this problem, because the filament inside them doesn't flicker.

SAFETY

The issue of safety in the workshop cannot be overstressed. Very often it is simply a question of some very simple things, such as:

Wear eye protection when using machines where chips and swarf fly about.

Wear hearing protection when using noisy machines.

Wear footwear in the workshop. Metal swarf is razor sharp, and can be hot.

Keep your fingers away from cutters and blades. Always use a stick to push small work through a circular saw, for example.

Use the guards supplied with the machines.

Never wear loose or ragged clothing near turning machinery, bare skin is safest with lathes for example.

Keep long hair tied back, especially near turning machinery.

Keep tools sharp, and machine tables clean and smooth.

Avoid, as much as you possibly can, having electrical leads and air hoses lying about. An overhead or under floor supply can be a good idea for a permanent machine.

Dust and paint overspray explosions are easy to avoid if you make sure the air is clear when using welders and flames.

Always have a working fire extinguisher and a stocked first aid kit in the workshop.

Never leave the chuck key in a chuck.

APPENDICES

Table of Sine Values for Circumference Divisions:

Number of Holes	Angle/2	Sine A/2
3	60	0.866
4	45	0.7071
5	36	0.5878
6	30	0.5
7	51.43	0.4337
8	45	0.3827
9	40	0.342
10	36	0.309
11	33.73	0.2823
12	30	0.2588

(Note: These Sine values are for <u>half</u> the included angle.)

Weights of Various Materials:

Metals: Measured in pounds per cubic inch.

Lead : .41   Copper : .32   Brass : .31   Magnesium : .063

Silver : .36   Nickel : .31   Wrought Iron : .28   Steel : .28

Cast Iron : .26   Tin : .26   Zinc : .26   Aluminium : .097

Wood (approximate):   Measured in pounds per cubic foot, dry.

Alder : 33   Ash : 43   Balsa : 7/8   Bamboo : 25   Beech : 40   Cedar : 30   Cherry : 37

Chestnut : 37   Cork : 16   Cypress : 40   Ebony : 73   Elder : 40   Elm : 40   Fir : 64

Hazel : 39   Ironwood : 75   Jarrah : 57   Larch : 38   Mahogany : 48   Maple : 40

Oak : 48   Pine : 30   Poplar : 26   Rosewood : 55   Spruce : 30   Sycamore : 40

Teak : 50   Walnut : 31   Willow : 33

Melting points of Various Materials: Celsius

Wrought Iron : 1800 to 2400   Steel : 1800 to 2250   Nickel : 1450   Cast Iron : 1200 to 1500   Copper : 1000 to 1100   Gold : 1063   Brass : 1000   Silver : 1000   Aluminium : 650   Zinc : 420   Lead : 327   Tin : 232

Beeswax : 65   Tallow : 38

Temperature Produced By:

Electric Arc : 5500   Oxy-acetylene : 3500

Approximate Horsepower Required to Run Machinery:

Small Engineers Lathe : 0.5   Wood Lathe : 1   Small Drill Press : 0.5 to 1
Wood Thicknesser (600mm wide) : 5
Table Saw : 12 inch blade 3 to 5. 1HP per inch of cut   Large Grinder : 3
8 inch grinder : 0.75   Band saw (20inch Wheel, 8 inch swing) : 3
Compressor 15cfm : 1.5   Single Bag dust extractor : 1

Useful Formulae:

A & a = Area. B & b = Base. C & c = Circumference. D & d = Diameter. H & h = Height.
P & p = Perpendicular. R & r = Radius. S = Span or Chord. V = versed sine.
n° = number of degrees.

Square:

A = Side². Side = $\sqrt{A}$. Diagonal = Side x $\sqrt{2}$. Side x 1.4142 = Diameter of Circumscribing Circle. Side x 4.443 = Circumference of Circumscribing Circle. Side x 1.128 = Diameter of Circle of Equal Area.

Rectangle or Parallelogram:

A = BP

Trapezoid:

A = Mean length parallel sides x distance between them.

Cone or Pyramid:

Surface = Circ of Base x Slant length/2 + B

Contents = Area of Base x 1/3 Vertical Height.

A & a = Area. B & b = Base. C & c = Circumference. D & d = Diameter. H & h = Height.
P & p = Perpendicular. R & r = Radius. S = Span or Chord. V = versed sine.
n° = number of degrees.

Circle:

Area = πr^2 = πD = $D^2\pi/4$ = $.7854D^2$ = 0.5CR.   C = $2\pi R$.   C = πD

Segment of a Circle.   A = Area of Sector –Area of triangle = 4xV/3 x $\sqrt{(0.625v)^2 + (1/2s)^2}$

Length of Arc. = π x n°r/180

Length of Chord. = SinA x D. Where A equals 1/2 the included angle.

Sector of a Circle. A =0.5R x Length of Arc. = n° x area of circle / 360

Side of Equal Square = 0.8862D.   Side of Inscribed Square = 0.7071D

D=0.3183C.

To find Side of Inscribed Square. D x .7071. C x 0.2251. C/4.4428.

D = C x 0.3183.   D = C/3.1416

Sphere:

Surface = $D^2\pi$ = $4\pi R^2$ = D x C.

Contents = $d^3\pi/6$ = $4\pi R^3/3$

Parabola:

A = 2/3BH

Wedge:

Contents = 1/6 (length of edge + 2 x Length of Back) bh

Prism:

Contents = area of base x height

Cylinder:

Area of Surface = D x 3 times the length / 7

Capacity = 3 x R^2 x H / 7

Conversion Factors:

Inches to Metres : 0.0254   Metres to Inches : 39.37

Inches to Centimetres : 2.54   Centimetres to Inches : 0.3937

Feet to Metres : 0.9144   Metres to Feet : 3.2809

Metres to Yards : 1.0936   Yards to Metres : 0.9144

Miles to Kilometres : 1.6093   Kilometres to Miles : 0.6214

Sq Inches to Sq Centimetres : 6.4516   Sq Centimetres to Sq Inches : 0.155

Cu Inches to Cu Centimetres : 16.387   Cu Centimetres to Cu Inches : 0.061

Cu Feet to Cu Metres: 0 .028   Cu Metres to Cu Feet : 35.714

Cu Feet to Litres : 28.32   Litres to Cu Feet : 0.0353

Cu Centimetres to Pints : 0.00176   Pints to Cu Centimetres : 567.9

Gallons (English) to Litres : 4.4561   Litres to Gallons (English) : 0.22

1 Gallon (English) of water = 277.2 cu inches = 4.546 litres = 10 pounds =4.546 Kgs

1 litre of water weighs 1 kg

Ounces to Grams : 28.35   Grams to Ounces : 0.0353

Pounds to Kilograms : 0.45359   Kilograms to Pounds : 2.2046

Us Gallon (3.785 Litres) = 1.2 English Gallon (4.546 Litres)

Inches = Millimetres

1 = 25.4   2 = 50.8   3 =76.2   4 = 101.6   5 = 127.00   6 = 152.40   7 = 177.80

8 = 203.20   9 = 228.60   10 = 254.00   11 = 279.40   12 = 304.80   24 = 609.60

36 = 914.40   ½=12.70   ¼ = 6.35   ⅛ = 3.18

Temperature:

$°F = 9/5 \, °C + 32$

$°C = 5/9 \times (°F - 32)$

Tempering Colours with Approximate Temperatures in °F.

Pale Yellow: 430F: Lathe Tools.

Straw Yellow: 450F: Hammer Faces. Razors. Wood Engraving Tools.

Straw Brown: 470F: Screw Cutting Dies. Taps.

Red Brown: 510F: Hand Plane Irons. Twist Bits. Augers. Wood Chisels.

Light Purple: 530F: Cold Chisels for Steel. Axes. Hacksaw Blades.

Dark Purple or Blue: 550F: Planer Knives Circular saws. Screwdrivers.

Very Dark Blue: 570F: Springs. Handsaws.

Different materials require different spindle speeds, feed speeds, depths of cut and lubricants.

Mild Steel: Slow RPM. Slow Feed. Small Depth of Cut. Light Cutting oil, kerosene.

High Grade Steel: High RPM. Slow Feed. Small Depth of Cut. Light Cutting oil, kerosene.

Cast Steel: Low RPM. Slow Feed. Medium Depth of Cut. No Lubricant.

Brass: High RPM. Slow Feed. Small Depth of Cut. No Lubricant.

Alloys and Copper: High Speed. Slow Feed. Small Depth of Cut. Light Cutting Oil, kerosene.

As always, have the tools as sharp as possible.

Drill Sizes for various Taps:

Metric (in m/m)

M1 : 0.75   M1.5 : 1.2   M2 : 1.6   M2.5 : 2.1   M3 : 2.4   M3.5 : 2.9

M4 : 3.25   M4.5 : 3.75   M5 : 4.1   M5.5 : 4.6   M6 : 5   M7 : 6   M8 : 6.8

M9 : 7.8   M10 : 8.5   M12 : 10.2   M14 : 12   M16 : 14   M18 : 15.5

M20 : 17.5   M22 : 19.5   M24 : 21   M 27 : 24

Whitworth/Unf threads with metric Drill pilots.

W ¼ : 5.1   U ¼ : 5.2   W5/16 U 5/16 : 6.6   W 3/8 U 3/8 : 8

W7/16 : 9.4 U 7/16 : 9.3   W1/2: 10.7 U ½: 10.8   W 9/16 : 12.3 U 9/16 : 12.8

W 5/8 : 13.7 U 5/8 : 13.6   W3/4 : 16.7 U¾ : 16.5   W 7/8 U 7/8 : 19.5

W 1: 22.4 U 1 : 22.3

Annealing Times for Acrylic:

Temperature 80°C

Acrylic Thickness (mm)	Minimum Heating Time (hours and minutes)
1mm	3hrs 30 min
3mm	4hrs 30min
5mm	5hrs 15min
6mm	5hrs 45min
10mm	7hrs
15mm	9hrs
20mm	11hrs

GLOSSARY

Annealing: heating metal or glass and allowing it to cool slowly, to remove internal stresses

Arbor: an axle or spindle on which something revolves

Armature: the revolving part of an electric motor

Chuck: the device for holding work in a lathe, or a tool in a drill using moving jaws

Commutator: In a Universal Motor, the brass or copper strips at the end of the armature, that the ends of the windings are connected to, and the brushes rub on

Diametrical: where a straight line through the centre of a circle intercepts the diameter on opposing sides

Former: a device or mould to shape materials

Grain: the direction that the wood fibres run

Kerf: the gap left by the cut of a Saw Blade

Mandrel: a shaft or spindle in a lathe on which work is fixed for turning

Pitch: the distance between the teeth of a blade or gear

Quill: the shaft in the Drill Press on which the chuck is mounted

Set: the amount of left and right off-set of the teeth on a saw blade, resulting in a cut wider than the width of the blade itself

Shank: the long part of a tool between the handle and tool end, or the round end of a drill bit, that is held in a drill or drill press.

Spindle: the revolving rod in the headstock of the lathe that is driven by the motor, and usually has the chuck mounted on to it

Stock: the raw material being used, e.g. wood or steel

Swarf: fine chips or filings produced during machining

Swing: the maximum diameter able to be turned in a lathe, determined by the gap between the spindle and lathe bed

Temper: the degree of hardness of steel, for example

Ways: the lathe bed

INDEX

213

Andrew lives with his wife Robyn in Kerikeri, New Zealand. He is still involved in making kaleidoscopes. You can see some of his kaleidoscopes at www.kaleidoscopes.co.nz

www.ingramcontent.com/pod-product-compliance
Lightning Source LLC
Chambersburg PA
CBHW080501110426
42742CB00017B/2961